Alan A. Cavaiola, PhD, CADC
Charles Wuth, LCSW, CAC

Assessment and Treatment of the DWI Offender

Pre-publication
REVIEWS,
COMMENTARIES,
EVALUATIONS . . .

"In recent years, counselors have been called on more and more to deal with convicted drunk drivers. This trend is likely to continue in the future, as courts and lawmakers increasingly and correctly view education and treatment as important ways to reduce the toll of drunk driving on our roads. One challenge for counselors working with this population has been the lack of good sources of information designed specifically for those working with convicted drinking drivers. *Assessment and Treatment of the DWI Offender* is designed to meet those needs, and succeeds admirably in its goals.

The book begins by presenting background information on the drunk driving problem, including a history of research and prevention efforts. Later chapters deal with issues of more specific interest to the counselor, including psychological characteristics, assessment and diagnostic issues, resistance issues, and treatment strategies. The authors have drawn on the extensive research available to provide a solid set of guidelines and procedures for counselors to follow. This book provides a wealth of practical information for those working with DWI offenders, including summaries of the available research literature, presentations of model assessment strategies, and illustrations of treatment issues with case reports.

This book will be an important resource for any counselor working with DWI offenders. Those entering the field for the first time as well as those with many years of experience will benefit from the book's presentation of the broader picture within which the work with the DWI offenders occurs. This book will also be an important resource for any training programs that emphasize working with DWI offenders."

Robert Mann, PhD, MASc
Associate Professor and Senior Scientist,
University of Toronto,
Ontario, Canada

The Haworth Press®
New York • London • Oxford

Lisa M. Howard

Assessment and Treatment of the DWI Offender

HAWORTH Addictions Treatment
F. Bruce Carruth, PhD
Senior Editor

New, Recent, and Forthcoming Titles:

Shame, Guilt, and Alcoholism: Treatment Issues in Clinical Practice, Second Edition by Ronald T. Potter-Efron

Neuro-Linguistic Programming in Alcoholism Treatment edited by Chelly M. Sterman

Cocaine Solutions: Help for Cocaine Abusers and Their Families by Jennifer Rice-Licare and Katherine Delaney-McLoughlin

Preschoolers and Substance Abuse: Strategies for Prevention and Intervention by Pedro J. Lecca and Thomas D. Watts

Chemical Dependency and Antisocial Personality Disorder: Psychotherapy and Assessment Strategies by Gary G. Forrest

Substance Abuse and Physical Disability edited by Allen W. Heinemann

Addiction in Human Development: Developmental Perspectives on Addiction and Recovery by Jacqueline Wallen

Addictions Treatment for Older Adults: Evaluation of an Innovative Client-Centered Approach by Kathryn Graham, Sarah J. Saunders, Margaret C. Flower, Carol Birchmore Timney, Marilyn White-Campbell, and Anne Zeidman Pietropaolo

Group Psychotherapy with Addicted Populations: An Integration of Twelve-Step and Psychodynamic Theory, Second Edition by Philip J. Flores

Assessment and Treatment of the DWI Offender by Alan A. Cavaiola and Charles Wuth

Countertransference in Chemical Dependency Counseling by Gary G. Forrest

Solutions for the "Treatment Resistant" Addicted Client: Therapeutic Techniques for Engaging Challenging Clients by Nicholas A. Roes

Assessment and Treatment of the DWI Offender

Alan A. Cavaiola, PhD, CADC
Charles Wuth, LCSW, CAC

The Haworth Press®
New York • London • Oxford

The Haworth Press, Inc., 10 Alice Street, Binghamton, NY 13904-1580

Cover design by Jennifer M. Gaska.

Library of Congress Cataloging-in-Publication Data

Cavaiola, Alan A.
    Assessment and treatment of the DWI offender / Alan A. Cavaiola, Charles Wuth.
        p. cm.
    Includes bibliographical references and index.
    ISBN 0-7890-0870-X (alk. paper)—ISBN 0-7890-1498-X (pbk : alk. paper)
    1. Drinking and traffic accidents. 2. Drunk driving—Prevention. I. Wuth, Charles. II. Title.

HE5620.D7 C375 2001
363.12'57—dc21   00-066456

We respectfully dedicate this book
to all those family members who have lost
loved ones, as well as those who were injured
in alcohol-related driving accidents.
You are the true heroes of this field.

ABOUT THE AUTHORS

Alan A. Cavaiola, PhD, CADC, has more than a quarter century of experience working in the addictions treatment field. He is a Licensed Psychologist, a Certified Alcohol and Drug Counselor, and a Licensed Professional Counselor in New Jersey. Dr. Cavaiola is currently Assistant Professor and a member of the Graduate Faculty of Monmouth University in the psychology department. In addition to his clinical work with DWI offenders, Dr. Cavaiola has also published extensively in this area, as well as in the treatment of adolescent chemical dependency. After receiving his doctoral degree from Hofstra University, Dr. Cavaiola served as the Clinical Director of the Monmouth Chemical Dependency Treatment Center, an affiliate of Monmouth Medical Center, for fifteen years.

Charles W. Wuth, LCSW, CAC, has more than twenty-five years of experience in the addictions treatment field. Mr. Wuth has also published previously in the DWI offender treatment area. In addition, both he and Dr. Cavaiola have presented several training sessions and workshops on the topic of assessment and treatment of DWI offenders at locations including the Rutgers Summer School of Alcohol and Drug Studies. Mr. Wuth is currently working in the mental health field and has a private practice.

CONTENTS

Foreword

For the first seventy years of the past century, two major U.S. health problems were alcoholism and drunk driving. Although related, they proceeded on separate tracks. Alcoholism has been recognized as a social problem since the nation was founded, but only in the twentieth century did it begin to be acknowledged as a public health problem with both prevention and intervention components. Prevention attempted to control sales and distribution, culminating in a nationwide prohibition. At the end of that flawed experiment, efforts at prevention continued through state laws controlling sales and dram shop laws making distributors liable for injuries cased by drunken patrons.

During the twentieth century, alcoholism began to be understood as a medical rather than a moral problem; however, interventions by health professionals were inhibited by the social stigma surrounding drunkenness. Consequently, physicians avoided the alcoholism diagnosis and either failed to treat the disease or camouflaged treatment under another diagnosis. The limited understanding of addiction, patient denial or relapse prevention, and the absence of effective medications, all conspired to limit medical interventions for alcoholism problems. Left on their own, patients had to create their own intervention procedures, as is illustrated by the widespread success of Alcoholics Anonymous (AA).

Society's efforts to prevent drunken driving also had prevention and intervention phases, both of which were built on law enforcement. Legal penalties—fines and jail—were designed to produce "general" deterrence by persuading motorists from getting behind the wheel after drinking. The same laws were also to produce "specific" deterrence by punishing the drunk-driving offender so that he or she would avoid impaired driving in the future. The principal advancement in drunk-driving enforcement during the first seven decades of the twentieth century was the development of chemical tests for intoxication based on the seminal work of Widmark (1932) in Sweden, who developed the relationship between alcohol consumption and elimination of the body's blood alcohol concentration (BAC).

In the United States, the founding of the U.S. Department of Transportation (USDOT)—which brought into being the Highway Safety Bureau, later renamed the National Highway Traffic Safety Administration (NHTSA), an agency devoted to the highway safety problems—was a major turning point in the attention given to the impaired driving problem. The new agency was tasked by the U.S. Congress to provide a report on "Alcohol and Highway Safety." That report (USDOT, 1968) brought to official attention the research of investigators such as Julian Waller (Waller and Turkel, 1966) who indicated that, based on their high BACs at the time of the crash and a prior history of heavy drinking and alcohol-related offenses, many of the drivers involved in fatal and serious crashes were problem drinkers.

Based on NHTSA's report, the U.S. Congress funded an $88 million program of thirty-five community Alcohol Safety Action Projects (ASAPs). These monies were spent for police, court, public information, and treatment activities in communities that established ASAP project offices to coordinate safety efforts for reducing alcohol-related crashes. The ASAP focused on the problem drinker who drove. Considerable efforts were devoted to screening arrested drivers for alcohol use and establishing alcohol education and treatment programs for driving-while-impaired (DWI) offenders (Nichols et al., 1978; Levy et al. 1977). When, after three years, federal funding for the ASAP program was terminated, most of the special enforcement and judicial effort ended, but the screening and treatment of DWI offenders continued because offender payments provided a reliable source of funds for treatment services.

In the early 1970s, the publicity given to the problem drinker as the cause of a major portion of serious injury crashes and the success of the ASAP program in bringing screening methods and treatment programs into the criminal justice system brought together the alcoholism and drunk-driving fields. Consequently, alcohol treatment centers received a new set of clients, many with characteristics rarely seen in traditional treatment facilities. These new clients roughly fell into three groups:

the risky driver who drinks, the problem drinker who drives, and the traditional dependent alcoholic.

The "risky driver who drinks" was the misfit for the treatment community because alcohol consumption was peripheral to his or her main behavioral problem, which manifested itself through risk taking and acting out on the highway, behavior that attracts the attention of the police and increases the likelihood of DWI arrest if the individual is drinking. Screening tests such as that by Mortimer-Filkins (see Chapter 5) were developed to direct these DWI offenders into education programs rather than into the lengthy and intensive treatment programs (see Chapters 8 and 9).

The "problem drinker who drives" included those offenders who abused alcohol, as indicated by binge drinking (see Chapter 3) or by high BACs (.15 or higher), but did not demonstrate the tolerance and dependence features typical of the full-scale alcoholic who had been the typical client of traditional treatment programs or self-help efforts such as the AA.

Despite the clear differences between the majority of DWI offenders and alcoholics (see Chapter 3), these offenders were forced into treatment facilities that, up to that point, principally had treated the "traditional dependent alcoholics": those who had completely lost control over their drinking and, in many cases, had "hit bottom" with broken marriages and lost employment. Consequently, the treatment community needed to separate this heterogeneous group and devise therapies appropriate to their varying needs. This was a major problem because many of these new clients presented comorbid conditions including drug abuse and psychiatric disorders.

The new reliance of the criminal justice system on the treatment community raised three issues that remain to be resolved completely. The first of these was mandatory treatment. The traditional treatment community had always relied on voluntary participation in treatment programs (see Chapter 7). However, it was generally recognized that most who signed up for therapy programs had been persuaded into treatment by employers, spouses, or other family members. This was particularly true of AA, where the general belief was that the client needed to be in a desperate "hit-bottom" condition before he or she was a good candidate for rehabilitation. Court assignees were generally reluctant participants who frequently failed to report or dropped out of treatment and, consequently, were forced to reenter the program by threats from probation officers or judges to revoke probation and jail the reluctant offender. However, most unmotivated offenders did attend the assigned treatment programs with some evidence that participation was associated with reduced drinking and driving (see Chapter 8).

A second issue raised by the court assignment of DWI offenders to traditional treatment programs was the objective of the treatment. Alcohol treatment providers were dedicated to promoting the recovery of individuals who were alcohol dependent, whereas the courts were concerned with reducing impaired driving. It was possible, at least in theory, to train offenders to avoid driving after drinking, known at "harm reduction" (Single, 1996), without significantly reducing their alcohol consumption. This conflict in goals was reflected in program evaluations; treatment professionals focused on client reports and other evidence of reduced drinking, while traffic safety focused on the easily available, objective measure of DWI recidivism.

A final issue, related to the first two issues, was the screening of offenders to determine what type of program was most appropriate to their needs or, in operational terms, most likely to reduce future DWI offenses. Initially, in the ASAP program, a simple two-category screening system—social versus problem drinker—was used to direct offenders into either a ten- to twelve-hour educational program or a more intensive, general group therapy program. This initial triage was accomplished by several methods. In some cases, the judge undertook this function, basing decisions on the offender's record, the arrest BAC, and the personal view of the offender's needs and the value of treatment. In other cases, the ASAP projects funded "pre-sentence investigators" to assess DWI offenders and developed practical assessment measures such as the Mortimer-Filkins interview and inventory (see Chapter 4). These measures, designed for use by technicians with limited training in alcohol treatment issues, were used to assess DWI offenders. These technicians interviewed the offender before the trial or before the sentence hearing, and recommended placement of an offender to be used by the judge in establishing probation requirements for the offender.

This rudimentary system has been extended during the past two decades to include more sophisticated assessment programs. A source of some comparison is the differentiation of *screening* from *assessment.* Screening is a triage process, primarily directed at providing information to the court as a basis for determining the type of program (education versus treatment), whereas assessment is a more detailed and extensive procedure designed to determine individualized treatment needs. Assessment generally occurs after an offender has been assigned to a treatment program to determine the specific type of therapy and counseling support needed. As discussed in Chapter 8, the research community believes it is important to tailor the therapy program to the individual characteristics of the client. However, Project MATCH (1997), a large national research program, failed to find a difference in the effectiveness of a treatment program based on matching therapy to the assessed needs of the client. Nonetheless, all treatment programs tested showed beneficial effects. The most important issue therefore is to get and hold offenders in treatment. As diagnostic methods improve, it may be possible to improve treatment outcomes. Of principal importance however, is ensuring that treatment is one element of the sanctioning process.

Currently, that process consists of four major elements: jail and the "three Rs"—*Restriction, Recovery,* and *Restitution* (Voas, 1999b). Incarceration is the motivator, the engine that powers the court to enforce the other remedial actions that reduce recidivism. Although DWI offenders cannot reoffend while in jail, the periods of incarceration assessed by the courts for all but major multiple offenses are too short to have a significant influence on recidivism. Substantial popular belief indicates that the threat or experience of jail is an important deterrent to recidivism; however, the evidence for such an effect is limited (Voas and Williams, 1986; Simpson, Mayhew, and Beirness, 1996) (see Chapter 6). Nonetheless, jail is the threat behind probation, which is the basic system under which DWI offenders are required to attend treatment.

The "three Rs" encompass those activities specifically directed at reducing recidivism. The first R—*Restriction*—refers to the various methods of reducing the risk of an offender having the opportunity to drink and drive before completing an intervention program. Also described as incapacitation (Ross, 1981), it is the process of applying sanctions to prevent offenders from driving for a substantial period. Although the behavior leading to a DWI can be modified, this traditionally has been achieved by suspending the driver's license. However, it has been recognized that up to 75 percent of the suspended offenders do drive (Ross and Gozales, 1988). Despite this, license suspension retains some effectiveness because those who are suspended tend to drive less often and more carefully (Nichols and Ross, 1990) (see Chapter 6). Because of the limited effectiveness of license suspension, states are beginning to pass legislation that attacks the vehicle of the DWI offender (Voas and DeYoung, 2001, in press).

Recovery (from alcohol problem behavior) constitutes the second R of the sanctioning processes. This is the critical element of interest to the readers of this book. Currently, there has been little focus on the relationship of the restriction period to the rehabilitation process. In concept, the driving restriction, which protects the public from the offender while he or she is going through the process of behavioral change, should belong enough to ensure that the offender has had an opportunity to recover from the drinking problem that produced the DWI. In reality, most states provide for relatively short periods of suspension for first offenders (perhaps six months) and limited periods for second offenders (generally less than a year). These short periods are further shortened by providing an offender with a limited license for traveling to and from work, which often results in full-license suspensions as short as one month for the first offenders and three months for second offenders. As a result, the trial often does not occur until after the full-suspension period is completed.

Rehabilitation is focused on reducing problematic drinking. The therapist, nonetheless, should be mindful of the opportunity to reduce harm by assisting the offender to separate drinking from driving. In a research study by McKnight and colleagues (1995), DWI offenders were interviewed about the night of their arrest. They found that after offenders left home in their own vehicles, it was highly unlikely that any intervention by others would prevent them from driving their vehicles home, no matter how much they had been drinking. Therefore, the key to reducing impaired driving was to train the offender not to drive to the event, but to plan for transportation to the event by arranging for a designated driver or by using another means to travel to the location. Such planning has been part of the education program for first DWI offenders since the earliest days (see, for example, Stewart and Malfetti, 1970). It is, however, less frequently a part of treatment programs for first offenders with high BACs or for second offenders.

The third R of the DWI sanctioning system is *Restitution.* Fines and community service are the principal means of reimbursing society for the damage caused by impaired drivers. Offenders or their insurance companies may be forced to pay damages if the DWI offense results from a crash. Because most DWI offenders are arrested by officers on patrol or at sobriety checkpoints, they do not injure other motorists. However, the state still sees itself as "injured" because it must maintain a police force to monitor the highways and courts to enforce DWI laws. The NHTSA has encouraged states to set DWI fines and fees at levels that would support this enforcement activity (McKnight and Voas, 1982). As a rule, however, fines have been set too low to meet this goal. Further, courts frequently do not impose the full fine, believing that many offenders are either indigent or unable to pay.

Community service is another way offenders can recompense the community for the cost of the DWI criminal justice system. In practice, however, community service principally has been an alternative to incarceration because jails are expensive and overcrowded. Thus, most state and federal laws providing for "mandatory" jail sentences provide for community service as an alternative.

Personal restitution to the victims of drunk drivers generally has been left to the state insurance companies and the civil courts. The state's role principally has been to require proof of insurance as a prerequisite for a driver's license and the vehicle registration. One theory holds that restitution play a role in rehabilitating offenders by reconciling them with the victim and the community (USDOJ, 1984), yet attempts at direct restitution to victims generally have not succeeded. A recent important development has been the Victim Impact Panels (VIPs) where offenders must attend a one- to two-hour presentation by victims of drunk-driving crashes on how their injuries have affected their lives. The theory behind these sessions is that many DWI offenders fail to recognize the extent of the injury that they inflict or can inflict upon others. The graphic, personal presentations by the victims are designed to make offenders aware of the potential costs of their impaired driving behavior. Although the effectiveness of the VIP programs remains to be fully demonstrated (Shinar and Compton,

1995), many courts have adopted the VIP program as a standard probation requirement of DWI offenders.

Currently, a significant national effort is underway to strengthen sanctions for DWI offenders built around the concern over the "hard-core drunk driver" (Simpson, Mayhew, and Beirness, 1996). "Hard-core drunk drivers" are defined as first offenders with arrest BACS of .15 or higher and all multiple offenders, which includes approximately two-thirds of the 1.5 million drivers arrested for DWI each year (Voas, 2001, in press). The primary government and private agencies concerned with drinking and driving—NHTSA, National Transportation Safety Board, National Commission Against Drunk Driving, The Century Council, and Mothers Against Drunk Driving (MADD)—have all adopted this definition of the hard-core drunk driver and promoted increases in sanction severity, particularly for second DWI offenders.

The passage of federal legislation (TEA 21, NHTSA & FHWA, 1998) has been influential, requiring states to enact laws that provide for a full year of "hard" suspension for second DWI offenders and the impoundment of their vehicles or the installation of alcohol safety interlocks. Finally, the Transportation Equity Act for the twenty-first century (TEA-21) law requires states to provide for mandatory five-day jail sentences and the screening of all second offenders for alcohol problems. Electronically monitored house arrest can be substituted for the jail sentence (Voas, 1999a). This trend toward toughening the sanctions for second offenders should provide the therapists with more control over the DWI offenders' attendance at treatment programs as courts will be given more sanction alternatives with which to motivate offenders' adherence to the probation requirements for attendance at treatment programs.

This strengthening of the sanctions (e.g., the provision of alcohol safety interlocks and house arrest keeps offenders from nighttime driving and controls the driving of high-risk offenders) may provide special opportunities for therapists in the future. Vehicle interlocks force offenders to plan for a drinking event before leaving home because it will prevent them from driving home if they drink. Using the interlock helps mold the offender's driving behavior into the safe nondrinking use of the vehicle desired by safety advocates. This behavior by participants is reflected in the significant reduction in recidivism while the interlock device is installed on their vehicles. After the interlock is removed, however, drinking-and-driving behavior returns to the pre-interlock levels (Voas et al., 1999).

The failure to retain a nondrinking driving habit after the interlock is removed, even when it has been in place for a year or more, is surprising and offers a special opportunity for the behavioral therapist. The interlock device provides a record of very breath test, and a breath test must be given each time the vehicle is driven. This can be an invaluable tool to the therapist in working with the offender to strengthen the habit of avoiding drinking and driving and can provide a measure of progress toward that goal as well as toward the goal of achieving abstinence. Special intervention programs for interlock participants, which integrate psychotherapy with the interlock program, are currently being tested (Marques, Voas, 1999; Marques, Tippetts et al., 2001).

For the trained therapist who is not familiar with the DWI client, this book provides an excellent background on the drinking-driving problem (see Chapter 1); the countermeasures to drinking and driving (see Chapter 6); and, more directly relevant to intervention with such offenders, the characteristics that differentiate them from the clients normally entering alcohol treatment (see Chapter 5). Those who are new to the field of substance abuse prevention and are preparing themselves for employment with a treatment provider will find this book an invaluable introduction to the field and to the extensive literature available on the rehabilitation of the drinking driver. Court officials and probation officers will also find this book useful to understanding the problems involved in treating DWI offenders and in promoting recovery from their drinking problems.

Robert B. Voas, PhD
Pacific Institute for Research and Evaluation

Acknowledgments

There are many people we wish to thank for their help in bringing this book to completion. We are especially appreciative of the assistance of Dr. Jim Frank of the National Highway Traffic Safety Administration. He was most patient in responding to our many questions and had offered many useful suggestions on how to track down much-needed information. We are also thankful to Dr. Tom Nochajski of the Research Institute on Addictions in Buffalo, New York, for his help on the assessment chapters. Tom has been a leader in the field of DWI assessment research and he directed us to some very useful information in this area. More locally, we would like to thank Rae D'Averso of the New Jersey Intoxicated Drivers Resource Program, who was helpful in sharing information on drugs and driving with us. Also, thanks to Donald Feeney of the Monmouth County Intoxicated Driver Resource Center. In the way of historical background, it was Don who suggested that we start a DWI treatment group in Southern Monmouth County back in 1983, which became the foundation for much of the DWI group work that we have done over the past twenty years or so.

We are also very much appreciative of the editorial assistance provided to us by the wonderful staff at The Haworth Press, especially to Dr. Bruce Carruth, our Developmental Editor, who helped to guide this project in its early infancy, and to Peg Marr, Senior Production Editor, and all of her staff for their help in bringing this project to fruition.

Last but not least, we could not have completed this work without the support and encouragement of our families. Our heartfelt thanks to Carolann and Cara, and to Alison, Jay, Chris, Jordan, and Jacqueline for their patience and understanding.

Chapter 1

Drinking and Driving in the United States: The Scope of the Problem

INTRODUCTION

Driving under the influence of alcohol has been a major social problem ever since the automobile came into popular use. It has been of worldwide concern for almost 100 years. The contribution of alcohol to increased risk of traffic accidents has been well established. Experimental studies and epidemiological surveys, conducted in a number of industrialized countries since the early part of this century, have documented consistent and reliable evidence of the correlation between alcohol consumption, increasing blood alcohol concentrations (BACs), and the increasing risk of involvement in an alcohol-related road accident. The recognition of the importance of alcohol-related road traffic accidents as a significant cause of mortality, disability, and economic loss has focused international efforts on the development of policies and strategies for the prevention of injuries and fatalities. Public concern in the United States has increased dramatically since the 1980s, resulting in a concerted attention at national and local levels to reduce the rates of drunk driving in our society. With the "get tough" attitude prevalent since the 1980s, great strides have been made in reducing the incidence of drunk driving. However, the rates are still unacceptably high. The National Highway Traffic Safety Administration (NHTSA), the agency responsible for overseeing highway safety issues in the United States, has set a goal of reducing annual DWI fatalities to 11,000 by the year 2005. However, the problem of drunk driving has proven to be a stubborn one that does not easily give way to solutions. The number of DWI fatalities for 2000 was 16,068. Recognition is growing worldwide for the need to address the issue of those drinking drivers who do not respond to sanctions and treatment, but continue to drink and drive even when facing severe consequences. This population causes a disproportionately large percentage of alcohol-related injuries, property damage, and fatalities compared to other drivers. More emphasis is being placed on the development of improved intervention strategies aimed at the drinking driver who is a high-risk problem drinker, a high alcohol consumer, and a chronic multiple DWI recidivist. Researchers and treatment experts in the alcohol and drunk driving field recognize that current intervention policies need to be modified in order to better address this "hard-core" population.

Deaths caused by drunk drivers are the most tragic aspect of this problem. Drunk driving threatens the lives and well-being of drivers, passengers, and pedestrians, whether they have been drinking or not. The drunk driver is most commonly portrayed in the media as a seriously alcohol-impaired individual driving out of control and causing fatal car crashes. This image misrepresents the true extent of the problem. The reality is that people of all types and of all backgrounds drink and drive for a variety of reasons. A growing body of research indicates that even low amounts of alcohol contribute to highway fatalities. From a sociological perspective, many of the ceremonial and institutional functions in our culture influence decisions to drink and drive. Examples of these activities are weddings, sports events, certain holidays, bar mitzvahs, bachelor parties, celebrations, and ceremonies. Other situations can be special events, such as family reunions, birthdays, farewells, and work-related social events. These types of drinking situations most frequently take place in the community, where the use of an automobile and driving after consuming some amount of alcohol is often involved.

When defining the impaired driver, we tend to identify those who drive above the legal threshold as the problem driver. It has been assumed that that those who are driving above the legal threshold are intoxicated, and those who are driving below that threshold are not impaired. This dichotomy oversimplifies the DWI population. It is more useful to view the drinking driver along a continuum that extends from the low-risk to the high-risk driver.*

Through worldwide efforts and experiences, much has been learned about this complex problem. Improved research techniques provide us with newer and better understandings so that more effective, efficient, and comprehensive strategies can be developed. More is known about the relationship between alcohol intoxication and driving than about any other drug. We have learned much about drinking and driving, but we still have much more to learn.

HISTORY OF THE DWI
COUNTERMEASURES MOVEMENT

The relationship between automobile crashes and excessive alcohol consumption has been long recognized as a problem. A classic editorial concerning "motor wagons" appeared in the *Quarterly Journal of Inebriety* in 1904. Initially, when this problem became evident, it was only vaguely understood. Lawmakers attempted to control drinking and driving solely by legal means. Legal punishment is a cornerstone of social control policy. The main tenet of this policy holds that punishment will deter citizens from engaging in an illegal act. In the early part of the century, the "Punishment-Response Model" was the primary deterrent action used to control the problem of drunk driving. Law enforcement was utilized as the primary mode of countermeasure for this problem. Penalties for this act were based on criminal law (see Figure 1.1). The focus of the law, referred to as "classical" (Ross, 1982a), had been on the grossly intoxicated driver. Laws prohibiting driving "while under the influence of intoxicating liquor," driving in an "intoxicated condition," or "drunk driving" targeted the unacceptable act of being intoxicated and driving an auto-

---

*An example of assuming impairment only above the 0.1 percent, reflecting the thinking of the time, is found in the June 1974 issue of Alcohol and Health, U.S. Department of Health, Education, and Welfare, *2nd Special Report to the U.S. Congress,* which states "A BAC up to 0.05 percent (50 milligrams of alcohol per 100 milliliters of blood) is usually considered safe; the person is presumed to be unimpaired in his ability to drive. . . . Between 0.05 and 0.10 percent (50 to 100 mg of alcohol per 100 ml of blood) usually no presumption of impairment is made."

FIGURE 1.1. The Punishment Response Model

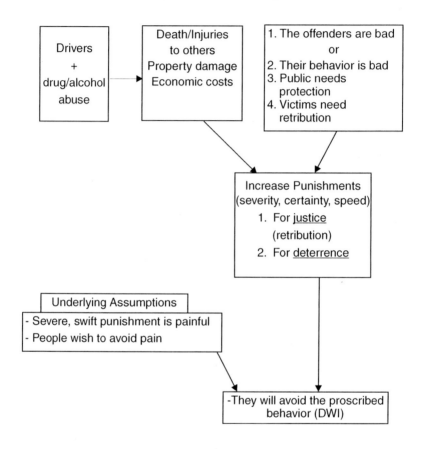

Source: Adapted from Robbins, L., National Commission on Drunk Driving, 1986.

mobile (Fischer and Reeder, 1974, p. 173). During this classical period, obtaining a conviction when the impairment did not result in a crash was difficult. Plea-bargaining and settling out of court were often-used strategies to delay, reduce, or avoid legal consequences.

Social science theory holds that the "efficacy of the legal threat is a function of the perceived certainty, severity, and celerity of punishment in the event of a law violation" (Ross, 1982a, p. 27). Early experience has shown that significantly increasing the threat of punishment for drinking and driving did reduce alcohol-related crashes. However, over time, drinking-driving problems would return to previous levels. The reasons for this phenomenon were not clearly understood. This was a universal experience in countries adopting anti-drunk-driving laws. It appeared that legal interventions were not achieving their expected outcome. Deterrence-model researchers attempted to better understand this phenomenon by studying variables impacting the efficacy of the model. Classical laws were not established with the intent of providing "certainty, severity, and celerity of punishment" as is necessary for deterrence to be effective. Based on these experiences, and the conclusions of research, it was apparent that changes needed to be made in the way the law was written. As a result, in 1936, the Norwegian Parliament established new types of drinking and driving laws, in an attempt to improve the effectiveness of deterrence measures. These laws appear to follow the principles of deterrence theory more closely. Provisions were made in the law to increase the likelihood of apprehension, conviction, and punishment. These laws, almost unchanged, are still in effect today. One significant change in the Norwegian laws centered on redefining the rules of proof of intoxication. Intoxication was now based on a scientific legal standard through the use of a fixed measurement of the quantity of alcohol in the bloodstream. Laws were written to include a presumption that all drivers above this level are intoxicated (per se is the legal term used to designate this presumption). A conviction could now be obtained per se, regardless of the drivers' performance at the time. A blood alcohol level of 50 milligrams per 100 milliliters of blood (.05g/dl) was considered proof of intoxication. As a result of establishing a scientific legal standard of intoxication, convictions were easier to obtain. Conviction rates increased, thereby increasing the certainty of punishment. With this change, the emphasis shifted from having to prove intoxication to determining whether a driver has a certain amount of alcohol in the bloodstream.

Sweden followed Norway's example in 1941 with the establishment of blood alcohol levels as proof of intoxication. They created a two-tier system of punishment based on two different blood alcohol levels. These changes in law formed the basis for what is known as the "Scandinavian Model." Norway and Sweden also developed serious punishments, which included imprisonment for severe cases, heavy fines for the less severe, and immediate license suspension pending trial. Norway and Sweden, which had already established roadblocks as a usual means to check on licenses and registrations, now included blood alcohol levels as part of these checks. World War II interrupted this momentum, and it was not until the 1960s that the movement regained its momentum and spread to other countries. Recognizing the effectiveness of these measures, other Western countries rapidly began to adopt the Scandinavian model. By 1970, Great Britain (1967), New Zealand (1967), Australia (1968), Canada (1967), and the United States (1966) had adopted the Scandinavian model. In the 1970s, the Netherlands (1974), France (1978), Denmark (1976), and Finland (1977) also adopted variations of the Scandinavian model.

Though punishment is seen as an important aspect of the criminal law system, rehabilitation is also a primary goal. As classic laws gave way to more modern intervention techniques, treatment became an important component in the attempt to control drunk driving. Germany has a long history of requiring DWI offenders with BACs of .13g/dl and higher to be evaluated for fitness to drive by medical/psychological experts before being relicensed. First offenders are generally referred to a driver improvement program. Sweden requires a medical certificate before license reinstatement. Any driver with a BAC of .15g/dl or higher is considered to be a problem drinker. After a twelve-month revocation period, a driver must continue to report for regular examinations for another eighteen months. Although it was generally viewed that mandating someone into treatment does not as a rule achieve the results intended, many theorists felt that the drunk driver would be highly motivated to rehabilitate in order to maintain driving privileges.

The treatment of the drunk driver has gone through a number of changes over time. Initially, in the Scandinavian model, treatment consisted of educational programs. As the treatment field became more experienced with this population, it underwent many modifications. Today, the European approach being adopted in many countries includes thorough medical/psychological assessment, selection and matching of offender to treatment, license reinstatement as an incentive to treatment, and follow-up provision after program completion.

Changes in the way the United States addressed the problem of drunk driving began in the 1960s. A number of developments occurred that resulted in modifications in the way the DWI problem was addressed in the United States. In 1964, Borkenstein and colleagues established the relationship between increasing alcohol levels and the likelihood of a car crash. The conclusions drawn from this research opened the way for classifications of drunk drivers who were problem drinkers, non-problem drinkers, and heavy social drinkers, as well as alcoholics. Psychometric test results were studies with the goal of being able to differentiate problem drinkers and alcoholics. This led to the later development of the Mortimer-Filkins Test at the University of Michigan in 1973. At the University of Vermont, studies were conducted on information gathered from convicted DWI offenders. Increasing efforts were made to identify the high-risk driver prior to the occurrence of a fatal crash by studying the population and developing drunken driver typologies.

Due to these efforts, increasing governmental concern led President Johnson to sign the Highway Safety Act of 1966. This act established the National Highway Safety Bureau, which is now the National Highway Safety Administration (NHTSA), under the Department of Transportation. The Secretary of Transportation was empowered to direct, assist, and cooperate with other Federal Agencies, state and local governments, and private industry to increase highway safety. Each state was to establish and develop a highway safety program designed to reduce traffic accidents, deaths, injuries, and property damage. The Secretary of Transportation was mandated to study the relationship between alcohol and accidents. Federal penalties were applied to states that did not comply. Laws, enforcement methods, treatment of alcoholism, and other policies were to be reviewed and studied in order to improve highway safety.

The roots of the DWI treatment field in the United States began as an outgrowth of this action. In 1966, the Phoenix Program was established. These programs were based on those developed as part of the Scandinavian model. These programs provided education and referral to treatment for DWI offenders. They consisted of four two-and-a-half-hour weekly sessions. Included in the content of these programs were informal structured discussions, films, readings, and oral and written exercises. An instructor conducted the sessions with a probation officer in attendance. A municipal judge would attend the initial session, and would describe the court's role in this program. Counselors were present to make referrals for treatment if necessary. These were considered diversionary programs, so that those attending would not be charged with the offense if they successfully completed the program.

In 1970, the National Institute on Alcoholism and Alcohol Abuse (NIAAA) was established with the enactment of the Alcohol Abuse and Alcoholism Prevention, Treatment, and Rehabilitation Act. The Department of Transportation, as a follow up to the Phoenix Program, funded the Alcohol Safety Action Program (ASAP) in 1971. ASAP goals were aimed at expanding the use of alcoholism treatment programs for people with alcohol problems, increasing public awareness through education, and evaluating, diagnosing, and referring for treatment. They established thirty-five pilot programs in designated states throughout the country. Approximately a quarter of a million drivers were referred to ASAP during its time of operation. The National Highway and Traffic Safety Administration (NHTSA) concluded at the end of this pilot program that the Alcohol Safety Action Program driver education schools had produced increased knowledge and positive changes. However, there was not much convincing evidence to indicate that these schools decreased subsequent arrests or crash involvement (Jones and Joscelyn, 1978). Many evaluations of the ASAP programs were conducted in the 1970s. The majority of these evaluations suggested positive results with first-time offenders, but did not impact the second offenders with more serious problems (Ellingstad and Springer, 1976).

A popular view at the time of the ASAP programs held that anyone who had a problem with alcohol was an alcoholic or drug addict. Implicit in DWI referrals to treatment was the view that people were either alcoholics or drug addicts or they were not. Estimates indicated that approximately 62 percent of first-time offenders were alcoholics, while approximately 84 percent of second offenders were alcoholics (Wieczorek, Miller, and Nochajski, 1990). Vingilis (1983) estimated that about 50 percent of DWI offenders were alcoholics. These estimates would vary somewhat depending on the diagnostic criteria employed to make this determination. With this underlying assumption, it was natural to turn to the only field successfully treating people who abused alcohol. The alcoholism rehabilitation field, therefore, provided the primary treatment for this group. What was more noteworthy was that, up to that point, many alcoholism treatment programs would not accept court-mandated clients. The prevailing view was that "alcoholics had to hit bottom" before they could be treated. The majority of DWI offenders (even those with multiple offenses) did not feel that they were alcoholics and the DWI incident did not represent a "bottom" for them. Therefore, the alcoholism treatment field was rather perplexed about what to do with these new, rather hostile and resistant clients. As these education programs began to mandate that DWI offenders attend open AA meetings in the local community, there was even more resistance. In New Jersey, for example, there were open meetings in which "countermeasures cards" were given out, which served as verification that the DWI offender had attended the meeting as stipulated.

There were two problems, however. First, many AA groups resisted giving out the countermeasures cards based on AA traditions pertaining to autonomy and the preservation of the anonymity of AA members in attendance at those open meetings. Many AA groups felt strongly that they ought not to have opinions on outside matters, but always remain neutral. AA members often thought that by forcing people to attend AA who had not "hit bottom," the unity required for common welfare would be disrupted and jeopardize the personal recovery of voluntary members. Second, DWI offenders soon realized that by bringing a few friends or family members with them to the AA meeting, they could collect many cards by attending just one meeting and never have to return. (The State Division of Motor Vehicles issued these countermeasures cards to designated AA meetings. An AA member was then responsible for obtaining these cards from the DMV and handing them to the DWI offenders after the meeting was over. The offender was required to attend a certain number of AA meetings per month, and then send the cards to the DMV Countermeasures Division as proof that they had attended.) Funding for the ASAP programs ended in 1976. Each state was then responsible for maintaining and/or developing its own system.

According to the NHTSA at that time, "the basic strategy of the program was to combine the functions by which agencies of state and local government identify and apprehend drunk drivers, process them through the courts, obtain a diagnosis of their alcohol dependency, and arrange for their treatment, education and penalties" (NHTSA, 1974). This program, by creating a mechanism for providing DWI offenders with information and treatment, caused major changes in the adjudication of cases. Courts greatly increased the number of referrals for presentence investigations, to probation, and to treatment and rehabilitation. Several states passed legislation requiring a diagnostic assessment of a person convicted of a DWI offense, and a provision for mandating treatment as a result of these efforts. This early legislation stipulated that persons convicted of a DWI offense could attend either an education or treatment program in lieu of sanctions, thereby avoiding conviction on an alcohol-related charge. Programs established based on these laws were called diversionary programs. An offender, unfortunately, could have multiple convictions but appear to be a first offender. Based on the recommendations made later by the Presidential Commission, this type of legislation was repealed. It was during this time that the role of treatment for the DWI offender was established, utilizing the mandate of legal sanctions.

In the early 1980s, as this effort was being made at governmental levels, other events were unfolding. Public pressure began to rise, demanding that more aggressive action be taken to reduce alcohol-related driving fatalities. The perception of the public was that nothing had really changed, and that the laws, enforcement, and punishment of the offender were not accomplishing their purpose. In 1982, the problem received the highest level of recognition, when President Ronald Reagan appointed a thirty-member Presidential Commission on Drunk Driving to conduct a national study of the problem. President Reagan called the problem an "epidemic" of drunk driving on the nation's roads. He stated, "Americans are outraged that such a slaughter of the innocent can take place on our highways. Our anger and frustration are matched only by the grief of those who have lost loved ones in such accidents" (Johnson, 1982, p. 2). John A. Volpe, a former governor of Massachusetts and Secretary of Transportation during the Nixon administration, was appointed to head the commission. Noting the need for a comprehensive approach, Mr. Volpe said, "By coordination and improving the ways in which the police, prosecutors, judges, and treatment personnel deal with the drunk driver, we have learned how to build on our own experience. . . . Americans everywhere are fed up with the toll the drunk driver exacts from us every year. Billions of dollars and almost countless human tragedies occur each year in an out, and it is time to begin to bring this under control" (Johnson, 1982, p. 2). The Commission was charged with promoting a six-point program that emphasized:

1. Conduct programs to deter the majority of drunk drivers who are never arrested, and to continue emphasizing treatment for DWI offenders
2. Emphasizing program development at the local level
3. Integration and coordination of enforcement, prosecution, adjudication, education, treatment, public information, and licensing functions at the local and state level
4. Generating community and citizen support for comprehensive community programs
5. Changing societal attitudes toward drinking and driving
6. Assessing fines, court costs, and treatment tuition fees to defray the costs of local and community programs

At the end of its term, the Commission made thirty-nine recommendations as a result of its study. Those recommendations included stricter laws, mandatory sentencing, improved criminal justice support, increased enforcement, administrative license revocations, encouraging citizen advocacy groups, general outreach, increased informational advertising about alcohol use and abuse and highway safety, national and state tracking and reporting systems, and requiring that courts or administrative licensing agencies enforce compliance with treatment prior to restoration of licenses. The commission was expected to serve a leadership role in the campaign to reduce driving while intoxicated that was initiated by the National Highway Traffic Safety Administration. Under the Department of Transportation, the NHTSA is responsible for developing programs and supporting initiatives aimed at reducing deaths, injuries, and economic losses from motor vehicle crashes. The Commission's recommendations serve as the foundation for many of the countermeasure initiatives that have been implemented.

NHTSA concluded at the end of the ASAP pilot program in 1976 that there were positive changes in clients' knowledge of alcohol abuse and drinking and driving. Evaluation of these programs concluded that "social drinkers" who attended this program had fewer repeat offenses. There was not much convincing evidence that these schools decreased subsequent arrests or crash involvement (Jones and Joscelyn, 1978).

Other than pilot programs such as ASAP, there were no established DWI treatment programs for the DWI offender. Therefore, those DWI offenders diagnosed as having a potential alcohol problem were referred to the local alcoholism treatment program. Little was known about the treatment needs of this population. Eventually, from some of these education programs had evolved more specialized DWI treatment programs. However, with the rare exception of DWI offenders who did benefit from more traditional alcoholism treatment programs, the treatment needs of the DWI offender were unique and treatment programs had to be designed to more specifically meet those needs. This approach coincided with the movement in the alcoholism treatment field toward more individualized treatment planning, rather than the "cookie-cutter" approach. This influence seemed to come about as more inpatient (and some outpatient) alcoholism treatment programs were vying for JCAHO accreditation. The Joint Commission of Accreditation for Healthcare Organizations began accrediting alcohol and drug treatment programs in the early 1980s. Programs that were accredited had a greater chance of obtaining third-party insurance reimbursement from the major insurance companies. Anyone who has ever been through a JCAHO review knows how strict they are in ensuring that treatment programs provide individualized treatment. Each patient or client must have an individualized treatment plan, and each group or individual session the client participates in must pertain in some way to that treatment plan. So too, therefore, was individualized treatment planning eventually brought to DWI offender treatment, although probably to a lesser extent than clients in other types of programs.

In the 1990s we have seen the continuation of a worldwide effort to do more toward reducing the rates of drunk driving and the injuries, deaths, and damage caused by this major problem. Improved research methods have provided a better understanding of this complicated issue.

OVERVIEW OF THE SCOPE OF THE PROBLEM

Before we explore the data, it would be useful to review how the information is collected and the agencies responsible for collecting it, as well as definitions of the terms used (see Glossary for more definitions of terms). The NHTSA defines a fatal crash as any motor vehicle accident that results in a death to a vehicle occupant or nonmotorist (e.g., pedestrian) within 30 days of the event. The fatal crash is considered alcohol-related if either a driver or a nonoccupant had a blood alcohol concentration (BAC) of 0.01 grams per deciliter (g/dl), or greater in a police-reported traffic accident. Persons with a BAC of 0.10 g/dl or greater involved in fatal crashes are considered to be intoxicated. Blood alcohol levels are usually measured as the number of grams (g) or milligrams (mg) of alcohol in 100 milliliters of blood. (One hundred milliliters is called a deciliter or dl.) BAC levels are also written in decimals as a percentage (percent).

The NHTSA employs a statistical model to estimate the likelihood that a fatal crash-involved driver or nonoccupant was alcohol impaired. Fatality estimates are based on data collected by the NHTSA's Fatality Analysis Reporting System (FARS). This system is responsible for collecting highway fatality data from each state. Estimates are required because many states do not test BAC levels consistently, and data can be missing. FARS applies a statistical model to crash characteristics such as time of crash, sex of driver, type of vehicle, previous driving violations, and day of week to the data collected from each state. By examining these characteristics, FARS is able to present figures that include a mixture of both known and estimated BACs.

Measuring fatalities does not provide information on the full impact of drunk driving. As a result, in 1988, the General Estimates System (GES) was established. The GES developed a method for collecting information from across the United States to determine the extent of alcohol-related property damage, injuries, and medical and economic costs. These three systems of data collection provide the primary way in which the NHTSA keeps track of the impact of the DWI problem and the effectiveness of initiatives.

Gathering data on the impact of drunk driving in our society has been more thorough since the 1980s. Many systems have been improved or put into place to keep count of the extent and severity of this problem. Numbers provide rates and percentages, but do not describe the personal tragedies that this problem causes in families, communities, and schools. The economic and emotional costs of this problem are far more devastating than the numbers could ever portray.

Fatalities

Traffic accidents are the leading cause of death in the United States for people six to thirty-four years of age. According to National Highway Traffic Safety Administration reports (NHTSA, 1999), alcohol still remains the major contributing factor to those traffic fatalities. According to the annual traffic safety report, alcohol-related fatalities dropped to 15,786 in 1999. Estimates are that one alcohol-related traffic fatality occurs every thirty-three minutes. This amount is the lowest number of alcohol-related traffic fatalities ever recorded in the United States. In 1982, when NHTSA began collecting data nationally on alcohol-related crashes, the numbers of fatalities estimated were 25,165 people annually (57.2 percent of all fatal crashes). The most dramatic declines are seen beginning in 1986, with rates going down steadily since that time (see Appendix A for comparison data between 1988 and 1999). A downward trend occurred from 1982 to 1999, which according to NHTSA, is independent of other highway traffic safety initiatives such as mandatory seat belt use and the use of child restraints (see Table 1.1).

It is generally believed that as alcohol levels increase, so does the risk of an automobile crash resulting in injury, property damage, or death. However, more attention is being given to the low-BAC driver and the impact made in highway safety. A 1992 study conducted in Texas found a significant risk of alcohol-involved fatal crashes in the

TABLE 1.1. Declines in Fatalities

Year	Alcohol-Related Fatalities	% of Total Highway Deaths
1982	25,165	57.2
1986	24,045	52.2
1991	19,900	48.0
1995	17,126	40.9
1998	15,935	38.4

0.02 percent to 0.05 percent range (Mounce and Pendleton, 1992). NHTSA (1996) data shows that alcohol was involved in approximately 2,570,000 crashes. Drivers with a BAC .10g/dl killed approximately 13,466 people. The same report demonstrates that drivers with a BAC below .10g/dl caused 130,000 crashes that killed 3,660. Young people, people with a previous DWI conviction, and white males are disproportionately involved in alcohol-related fatalities.

Injuries

Alcohol-related crashes not only result in fatalities, but many people of all ages are injured as well. It is estimated that three out of ten Americans will be involved in an alcohol-related crash at some time in their lives. Calculations are that one person is injured every two minutes in an alcohol-related crash. In 1996, NHTSA recorded that drivers with a BAC of .10g/dl injured 762,000 people. Drivers with BAC levels below .10g/dl injured 108,000 people. (The 1998 data are not yet available.)

Economic and Medical Costs

Alcohol is a factor in 35 percent of traffic crash costs. These types of crashes are deadlier and more serious than other types of crashes. The alcohol-related crash bill paid by people other than the drinking driver is $51 billion. The resultant costs due to property damage, hospital emergency room visits, physician services, rehabilitation, prescriptions, lost productivity, public services (such as helicopters, rescue teams, police, fire and ambulances), and quality-of-life services added up to more than $110 billion in 1998 (NHTSA, 1999). The cost of injuries is estimated to be $3.2 million annually, with the average cost of each injury estimated at $79,000. Auto insurance companies estimate that 16 percent of the $127 billion of total payouts is the result of alcohol-related crashes.

CHARACTERISTICS OF THE PROBLEM

Epidemiological data is gathered mostly from FARS, from roadside survey checkpoints, research studies, and arrest and conviction rates from various states. This data are gathered by NHTSA in order to identify the characteristics of the DWI population in an effort to intervene with high-risk populations. The data concerning drinking drivers not involved in alcohol crashes come mostly from roadside survey checkpoints. The most recent information gathered from FARS' 1997 data estimate that there were about 811 million to 1 billion drinking-driving trips in that year. Drivers aged thirty to forty-five account for about four out of ten drinking-driving trips. For every 100 drivers on the road, approximately three are driving with a BAC greater than .10g/dl. The sheer volume of these numbers underscores the necessity of a comprehensive strategy involving all levels of governmental and community organizations. Due to the extent of this problem in our society, NHTSA collects data to identify the characteristics of the drinking driver and factors that identify the high-risk drunk driver. From these characteristics, strategies are developed to target these groups for countermeasures. A relatively large number of characteristics have been researched, but it appears that only driver sex and age, and to some extent race, indicate a relationship with drinking and driving and fatalities, with males being the best differentiators of drinking drivers. The data indicate that male drivers of the Caucasian race, ages twenty-one to thirty-four, constitute the largest percentage of drivers involved in alcohol-related fatal crashes. It is estimated in the most recent NHTSA reports (1997), that in 1996, 86 percent of fatal crashes with a BAC of .10 percent or greater were male. It is not clearly understood why this is so, except to say that it may be that males do most of the drinking. However, research shows that the point of origin of drinking-driving situations takes place in bars, taverns, and friends' homes, where males are perhaps more comfortable drinking heavily.

There are certain patterns to the occurrence of drinking and driving. A greater frequency of alcohol-impaired driving occurs on weekends (52 percent) in the evenings (60 percent). FARS data show that the time of greatest risk for a single-vehicle alcohol-related fatal crash was between 5:00 p.m. and 8:00 p.m., and that the highest percentage of impaired drivers are on the road between the hours of 2:00 a.m. and 3:00 a.m. (see Figure 1.2).

Again, male drivers are over-represented in this population. According to data collected from the 1986 National Roadside Survey,

FIGURE 1.2. Alcohol Involvement for Drivers Killed in Fatal Crashes, 1988 and 1998

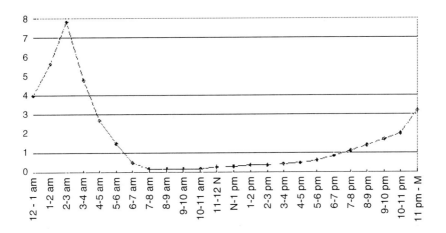

Source: Stoi, 1989.

these male drivers tend to be unemployed, without a college diploma, and moderate to heavy drinkers who are visiting friends. Drivers who appear in greater frequency on the weekends are impaired drivers who are employed, married, do not have a college diploma, and have a record of numerous traffic violations and prior DWI convictions. Some recent data indicate that the rates of female-involved alcohol-related fatalities are rising (NHTSA, 1998). Table 1.2 shows the overall rates in fatalities by gender and BAC levels. Data collected by FARS show that although the number of male fatalities has steadily decreased, female fatalities are increasing. Female impaired drivers were more likely to be older than their male counterparts, white, divorced or unmarried, with no prior DWI arrests. Females are less likely to repeat the offense than males (the gender issue will be explored in Chapter 3). In 1982, the total number of female fatalities was 10,675. In 1999 it rose to 14,792.

BAC levels are also associated with risk characteristics of this group. In regard to age, the highest intoxication rates in fatal crashes occurred in the age group twenty-one to twenty-four-years old (26.3 percent). The next highest age range was twenty-five to thirty-four at 23.8 percent.

TABLE 1.2. 1996 Motor Vehicle Crash Data from FARS and GES: Drivers in Fatal Crashes by Blood Alcohol Concentration (BAC) and Sex, 1982-1996

| | | Male | | | Female | |
| | | Percent | | | Percent | |
Year	Total	BAC = 0.01+	BAC = 0.10+	Total	BAC = 0.01+	BAC = 0.10+
1982	44,370	41.8	32.4	10,675	25.7	18.9
1983	42,812	40.5	31.4	10,958	24.8	18.5
1984	44,723	38.8	29.6	11,907	23.6	17.1
1985	44,846	36.7	28.2	12,142	21.8	15.5
1986	46,653	37.6	28.5	12,744	20.9	14.8
1987	46,884	36.4	27.6	13,614	21.0	15.0
1988	47,402	36.2	27.7	13,951	20.3	14.6
1989	45,448	35.0	27.0	14,054	19.8	14.4
1990	44,281	35.7	27.7	13,726	19.2	13.8
1991	40,731	34.5	26.8	12,825	19.0	13.6
1992	38,598	32.2	24.9	12,596	17.8	12.8
1993	39,556	30.5	23.7	13,082	16.5	12.0
1994	40,233	28.5	22.0	13,567	15.2	11.0
1995	41,235	28.5	21.7	14,184	15.5	11.1
1996	41,223	28.1	21.4	14,798	15.5	11.1

Source: National Highway Traffic Safety Facts—1998.

Note: BAC values have been assigned by NHTSA when alcohol test results are unknown. For more information, see NHTSA Traffic Safety Facts 1998, p. 7

The next highest age range was twenty-five to thirty-four at 23.8 percent and thirty-five to forty-four at 22.1 percent). BAC levels are highly correlated to risk of a fatal crash. Simpson and Mayhew (1992) studied the distribution of fatally injured drivers and concluded that at least 80 percent of fatally injured drivers had a measurable BAC greater than .10g/dl, 64g/dl had a BAC of .15g/dl or more, and 40 percent had a BAC of .20g/dl or higher (see Table 1.3). This situation has not changed very much, indicating the large role these drivers continue to play in the fatality rates. As noted earlier in this chapter, lower BAC levels are also associated with risk factors in the fatality data. Indications are that the chance of crash responsibility increases with low rates of alcohol consumption—between .00g/dl and .10g/dl.

Some evidence indicates that the accident risk is higher for females. Estimates based on FARS data and the 1986 National Roadside Breathtesting Survey (Lund and Wolfe, 1991) suggest that a female

TABLE 1.3. Fatalities by Highest Blood Alcohol Concentration (BAC) in the Crash

	1985	1990	1991	1992	1993	1994	1995	1996
Fatalities, total	**43,825**	**44,599**	**41,508**	**39,250**	**40,150**	**40,716**	**41,817**	**41,907**
Fatalities in alcohol-related crashes, total	**22,716**	**22,084**	**19,887**	**17,858**	**17,473**	**16,580**	**17,247**	**17,126**
Percent	51.8	49.5	47.9	45.5	43.5	40.7	41.2	40.9
BAC = 0.00								
Number	21,109	22,515	21,621	21,392	22,677	24,136	24,570	24,781
Percent	48.2	50.5	52.1	54.5	56.5	59.3	58.8	59.1
BAC = 0.01-0.98								
Number	4,604	4,434	3,957	3,625	3,496	3,480	3,746	3,732
Percent	10.5	9.9	9.5	9.2	8.7	8.5	9.0	8.9
BAC 0 = 0.10+								
Number	18,111	17,650	15,930	14,234	13,977	13,100	13,501	13,395
Percent	41.3	39.6	38.4	36.3	34.8	32.2	32.3	32.0

Source: NHTSA, 1998.

Note: BAC values have been assigned by U.S. DOT/NHTSA when alcohol test results are unknown. For some years rows do not add to total in source table.

driver with a BAC of .10g/dl percent or greater may be 50 percent more likely to be involved in a fatal crash than a male impaired driver. Although it is the high-level BAC driver that causes a disproportionate percentage of highway fatalities, highway risk factors and economic costs appear to involve crashes caused by the low-level BAC driver. Due to this evidence, there is an increased concern about the effect of the low-level BAC driver. National efforts are being made toward lowering BAC levels. Many studies are being conducted in cooperation with states that have lowered the legal BAC levels to below the current .10g/dl.

Overall, evidence is beginning to show that the characteristics of the DWI group may be changing. Besides the rising rates of females in this group, nonwhites, including blacks, Hispanics, and Native Americans, are overrepresented in alcohol-related fatal crashes, though lower in number than white males. NHTSA reported in a 1990-1991 study of 1,882 fatally injured drivers from seven states, drugs were found in 17.8 percent of the drivers.

Recidivism is a chronic problem related to the DWI population. Repeat DWI offenders constitute a relatively small percentage of the driving population, yet cause a substantial percentage of the traffic fatalities. It is estimated that 35 to 40 percent of fatally injured drivers had a prior DWI arrest (Simpson, 1995). Thirty-one percent of the 1.5 million drivers arrested in 1994 for DWI were repeat offenders. Fell (1993) found that 10 percent of drivers involved in alcohol-related crash fatalities had a prior DWI arrest within the previous three years. Nichols and Ross (1989) estimate that 35 percent of drinking drivers involved in an alcohol-related fatal crash have prior convictions. Estimates vary from one in three to one in five convicted DWI offenders will be rearrested. Rearrest increases with the number of prior arrests (Argeriou, McCarty, and Blacker, 1985; Maisto, Sobell, and Zellhart, 1979). Other data show that individuals with DWI occurring with convictions in the last three years were over four times more likely to be involved in a fatal crash than first-time DWI offenders (Fell, 1993). In New Jersey, prior to the inception of assessment and education countermeasure programs, there was an approximate 33 percent recidivism rate. Once first-time DWI offenders were mandated to treatment, the rate dropped to approximately 9 percent (Greene, 1985). These results, however, were confounded by tougher DWI legislation that was passed at the same time as these countermeasures programs were initiated. Therefore, it is difficult to discern whether these reductions in recidivism were related to treatment outcomes or punitive sanctions.

This information provides the most common characteristics of the drunk driver and when the most serious risk of offenses are likely to occur. Generally speaking, drunk driving is most likely to be committed at specific times on specific days, and involves a driver who has had a previous conviction. Although the term used to define this problem is "drunk driver," we see an increasing role of the drugged and the drunk and drugged drivers as a risk to highway safety. This additional characteristic of the DWI population is important to understand when determining which countermeasure strategies will be used. These changing characteristics are important to understand, since they determine which populations are targeted for countermeasures. It is the targeted group that will enter treatment, thereby requiring programs to adapt their content and methodologies to address the characteristics of these clients. FARS data reflects a trend toward a more diverse population, as females and minority cultures are represented in larger percentages. Treatment issues will be explored more fully in Chapter 8.

NHTSA, in attempting to identify an appropriate target group for its traffic safety programs, initially found that the national databases do not provide the information required to define a high-priority target population. They used a model that included four components: crash involvement, crash risk, contribution to the overall problem, and countermeasure effectiveness. However, they were able to identify two alcohol-related-crash target groups that showed up as high-risk and high impact on national alcohol-related-crash rates, and high risk and low impact on national alcohol-related crash rates. Priority targets in high-impact groups were young, beginner male drivers fifteen to twenty-five-years old, who had repeated moving violations, risky lifestyles, and did not wear seat belts. Priority targets in the low-impact, high-risk drunk drivers were:

1. Male Hispanics, twenty-one to thirty-five years old
2. Blacks, males, thirty to forty years old, of lower socioeconomic status
3. Native Americans of low socioeconomic status in rural areas
4. Male motorcyclists

THE COUNTERMEASURE INITIATIVES AND THEIR IMPACT

The term "countermeasure" is used to describe "measures" (i.e., strategies, programs, methods) that are implemented in order to "counter" or reduce, prevent, or intervene with an identified target problem. Deterrence is the cornerstone of countermeasures when dealing with the drunk-driving problem. Countermeasures to the drunk-driving problem have gone through many changes over the past 100 years, expanding from the reliance on stringent laws and scare slogans to the development of public health and nonlegal alternatives. There are two types of deterrence approaches. *Specific deterrence* methods try to change the drinking-driving behavior of the offender. *General deterrence* tries to change the behavior of the entire population—whether one drinks and drives or not.

Specific deterrence methods include legal sanctions such as arrest, fines, jail, and loss of license through conviction or administrative suspensions. A significant result of the Alcohol Safety Project was the combining of legal sanctions against DWI offenders, with treatment as a specific deterrent strategy. Controversy continues over the role treatment plays in reducing DWI rates. (This issue will be explored in Chapter 8.) The belief that if you drink and drive there is a high probability of being arrested and convicted has been demonstrated to be essential to the success of specific deterrence strategies. When the public perceives that police enforcement is not as great as it initially believed, rates go back up to previous levels (Ross, 1982a). It is well documented that DWI offenders commit many offenses without apprehension. This fact can severely limit the impact of deterrence measures. However, apprehending every drunk driver is not the goal of law enforcement. The estimated number of DWI arrests in 1997 was 1.5 million drivers, the most common reason for arrest in the United States. Approximately 20 percent of the licensed drivers drive while intoxicated. Of that 20 percent, the Federal Bureau of Investigation (1988) estimates that only 5 percent of the entire DWI population is apprehended within a one-year period. Estimates indicate one arrest for every 122 drivers on the highway.

The *Final Report of the Presidential Commission on Drunken Driving* (Volpe, 1983) estimated the probability of arrest to be between 1 in 500 to 1 in 2,000. Voas (1982) stated that one arrest occurred for every 5,000 miles driven while under the influence of alcohol. Theorists note that highly visible enforcement combined with timely, swift, and certain sanctions should have both specific and general deterrent effects (Nichols, 1990). Therefore, enhanced enforcement programs such as roadside breath test programs (RBT), are highly visible general deterrence strategies that can maintain the public perception of the likelihood of apprehension. Literature reviews of the effectiveness of deterrence in reducing alcohol-related fatalities demonstrate that highly visible enforcement efforts frequently, but not always, have resulted in declines in crashes (Voas and Lacey, 1989; Nichols and Dickman, 1989). "Visibility" is often an ellusive commodity that is difficult to measure. Enhanced enforcement of deterrence programs such as roadside checkpoints have been demonstrated to produce a 15 to 30 percent reduction in alcohol-related crashes.

These rates appear to be temporary, because the programs are short term. Programs that operate over a longer time can produce 20 to 35 percent reductions in alcohol-related crashes (Homel, Carseldine, and Kearns, 1988). Although these results are impressive, they have been criticized because they only reduce alcohol-related crashes while in operation and are expensive to maintain. However, the number of lives saved is significant, and few other approaches are able to achieve these percentages of reductions.

Just as the public belief that a risk of apprehension affects DWI rates, arrest without the certainty of swift conviction undermines the effectiveness of specific deterrence. Conviction requires that due process be followed in court proceedings. The length of time involved in this process can be substantial, and thereby dilutes the deterrent effect. In order to counteract this, many states have implemented administrative actions, which allow for the immediate suspension of licenses or impounding of vehicles.

Experts point out that the majority of the gains made in reducing the incidence of drinking and driving has been with the nonproblem and low-risk drinker (Andenaes, 1988; Laurell, 1991). Punishment seems to have the least impact on those who are most likely to cause a serious alcohol-related crash. Since drivers who have never been arrested for a DWI offense cause most of the alcohol-related car crashes, deterrence strategies other than apprehension needed to be developed. The assumptions made in the punishment-response model may be too simplistic for the complex issues surrounding drinking and driving behavior. This is evidenced by the percentage of people who continue to drive after drinking even when subjected to harsh penalties (see Appendix A). Many believed that Sweden was successful in reducing the DWI problem because of that country's universal social disapproval of drinking and driving, widespread publicity, and transportation alternatives to the car. The belief is that, when combined, general deterrence and social pressure could reduce the risk that people will drink and drive. The roles of public opinion, informal pressure, and public perception of enforcement were studied in an effort to determine the general deterrence potential of these approaches in the United States. As a result, public education about enforcement, increasing awareness of the dangers of drunk driving, and developing informal systems of social pressures not to drink and drive have been established as an integral part of general deterrence methods (see Figure 1.3).

The DWI problem is viewed as a national problem, requiring state and local solutions. In the 1980s, combinations of legislative actions, citizens' lobbies, public policy changes, and media attention were considered to have contributed to the decline in alcohol-related fatal crashes. There were approximately 1,200 anti-drunk driving laws passed during this time. In order to achieve these dramatic declines, many other strategies had to be developed, which now form the elements of a comprehensive approach. Many of these strategies were developed or supported through the surgeon general of the United States. In the continuing effort to develop more effective strategies, former Surgeon General Dr. C. Everett Koop convened a Workshop on Drunk Driving in 1988 in Washington, DC. Its purpose was to develop a coordinated campaign to save the approximately 25,000 lives that are lost annually to drunk driving. The workshop was planned by five cabinet-level agencies within the federal government: transportation, justice, education, defense, and health and human services. One-hundred and twenty experts and specialists in this area were invited to assist in developing strategies for resolving the problem of

FIGURE 1.3. Deterrence Components

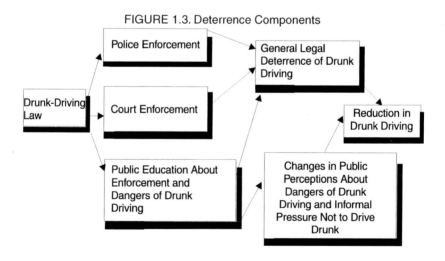

Source: Adapted from *Alcohol and Health Research World,* Volume 14, Number 1, 1990.

drunk driving. In his opening remarks, Dr. Koop outlined the challenge for this group with the following statement:

> First, let's consider the research agenda required for this issue of drunk and drugged driving. . . . Next, look at—or anticipate, if possible—the many policy implications of that research. . . . Third—also on the strength of an ongoing research program and its policy implications . . . lay out a plan with near-term and long-term public health objectives . . . and finally, devise an overall strategy for carrying out such a national plan. (See *Alcohol Health and Research World* Volume 14, Number 1 1990 for highlights of the proceedings and a more complete description of recommendations.)

As a result of this workshop, many recommendations were made and are listed below:

Pricing and Availability of Alcohol

- Increase excise taxes on ethanol
- Encourage responsible serving and selling by strengthening server liability statutes and policies
- Prohibit "Happy Hours"
- Restrict alcohol sales by time and place at sporting, music and other public events
- Adopt open-container laws that prohibit drinking while driving

Advertising and Marketing

- Counter alcohol advertising with pro-health and safety messages
- Eliminate alcohol advertising and promotion on college campuses
- Eliminate the use of celebrities in advertising
- Eliminate tax breaks on alcohol advertising and promotional activities
- Require ads to have warning labels
- Fund research to study advertising and promotional issues

Epidemiological and Data Management

- Require State and local police to obtain the BACs of all drivers involved in fatal crashes

- Develop a research agenda to identify the range of factors that inhibit the uniform collection of BAC data
- Create voluntary standards for research
- Facilitate periodic roadside surveys to collect valid data on BAC levels of all drivers
- Determine more accurately the characteristics of drunk drivers, and identify the contribution of those characteristics to the risk of crashes
- Improve data collection to determine the nature and magnitude of the drugged-driving problem

Judicial and Administrative Processes

- Require proof of compliance with an alcohol assessment or court order before reinstating a license
- Discourage plea bargains
- Make available to the judge, prior to sentencing of all defendants in alcohol-related offenses, an alcohol assessment by a competent certified person
- Increase emphasis on reducing driving without a valid driver's license due to driving while under the influence or other alcohol-related charges
- Complement license revocation with other mandatory sanctions, such as fines and jail

Law Enforcement

- Develop comprehensive DUI training program for chief executives of law enforcement agencies
- Apply innovative techniques of DUI enforcement such as passive sensors, preliminary breath testing (PBT) devices, mobile breath-alcohol testing units and other devices
- Implement DUI checkpoints in those jurisdictions not currently using this technique
- Make BAC testing mandatory for all drivers involved in accidents resulting in fatal and serious injuries
- Adopt administrative license suspensions and revocation procedures
- Maximize public perceptions of risk of arrest and punishment

Transportation and Alcohol Service Policies

- Form community task forces to review policies and priorities as to alcohol service and alternative transportation
- Develop community-wide designated driver programs
- Provide information to all individuals obtaining a new or renewed license about the relationship between alcohol consumption and the risk of injury or death
- Improve the effectiveness of alternative forms of transportation such as taxicabs
- Establishments who sell alcohol should have a plan to provide transportation to a patron who is impaired as well as training of managers and servers
- Modify dram shop liability laws to encourage responsible serving practices

Injury Control

- Foster technology that reduces risk of injuries
- Develop programs to use interlock mechanisms for DUI offenders
- Establish guidelines requiring BAC testing for all traffic-related injuries and train health care providers about alcohol abuse and injury control
- State trauma centers should track alcohol-related deaths, disabilities, and costs

Youth and Other Special Populations

- Comprehensive, school-based K-12 alcohol and other drug abuse education
- Encourage civil liability for intentionally providing alcohol to minors
- Limit or discourage beverage advertising and promotion directed at youth and minorities
- Increase enforcement of DWI laws relative to youth
- Increase public information and education to youth, Indian tribal leaders and members, Hispanics, and black community leaders

- Determine the extent of drinking and driving among ethnic groups and major demographic characteristics; investigate attitudes and patterns
- Assess the effectiveness of first- and multiple-offender rehabilitation programs for youth and ethnic minorities

Panel on Treatment

- Consider prevention measures aimed at elimination of drinking and driving
- Develop precise data on the incidence and prevalence of drunk driving
- Investigate the neuro-scientific basis of high-risk, impulsive behavior and recidivism
- Develop scientific evaluation of treatment modalities and the combination of various treatment options for the heterogeneous group that make up the drunk-driving populations
- Develop and evaluate newer treatment modalities in high-risk populations
- Assign the cost of treatment as much as possible to the offender
- Evaluate the effectiveness of new, short-term, low-intensity programs that have an impact on behavior from both an outcome and a process perspective

Panel on Citizen Advocacy

- Develop a coalition of national and local advocacy groups for the purpose of coordination exchange of information and strategic planning
- Establish a national clearinghouse of information about DWI issues and advocacy activities as resource for advocates and the general public
- Direct major advocacy efforts in court monitoring, victim assistance, influencing public policy and legislation, and increasing awareness and public information
- Significantly lower the per se BAC of .01 percent and apply this lowered standard to the general public
- Adopt uniform graduated penalties for DWI in the United States with special focus on multiple offenders
- Establish a national computer registry of DWI offenders

Many of the recommendations made by this workshop are in operation today. What is interesting to note about these recommendations is the combination of social, informal, grass-roots, and legal methods that were identified as possible strategies. Comprehensive approaches are inherent in modern countermeasure theory. As noted in the Final Report of the National Commission Against Drunk Driving to President Reagan in 1983 because drunk driving involves so many state and federal agencies as well as private groups, a systems approach must be used in order to coordinate the activities of these groups in order to be more effective.

Impact

Information gathered through FARS compares data over time, thereby providing trend data, which allows for analysis of the countermeasure's effectiveness. Overall, significant declines have occurred, indicating that countermeasures are having an effect. The key numbers demonstrating that these strategies work are as follows:

- Since 1982, alcohol-related traffic fatalities have been reduced by 37 percent.
- The rates of young people who died in an alcohol-related crash fatality declined by over 62 percent.
- Between ages fifteen and twenty, alcohol-related traffic deaths declined by 59 percent, from 5,380 to 2,201. This represented the largest decline in any age group. The next age group experiencing declines were drivers over sixty-four.
- Intoxication rates decreased for all drivers of all age groups involved in fatal crashes.
- The number of drivers with BAC levels of 0.10 percent or greater decreased from 25 percent in 1988 to 18 percent in 1998.
- It is estimated that anywhere from 90,307 to 128,520 lives have been saved since 1983 (NHTSA, 1998).

Though these reductions are dramatic, analysis of data indicates a slowing-down trend. DWI arrest rates declined almost 25 percent between 1990 and 1996. Since 1996, arrest rates have gradually increased to the most recent rate of 1.5 million arrests, still below the 1990 number of 1.8 million.

Meeting the goal of "11,000 by 2005" will require not only doing more, but also doing things differently. The new goal will require a 31 percent decline in the number of alcohol-related fatalities from the 1998 level.

Survey information also provides ways to evaluate the impact of countermeasures and track trends. Since 1991, the National Highway Traffic Safety Administration has conducted a telephone survey every two years to measure the status of attitudes, knowledge, and general drinking driver behavior (The National Survey of Drinking and Driving, NHTSA, 1997). The data represented in this survey were collected from October 12 through December 12, 1997, and summarized to show changes from previous surveys. Respondents were persons sixteen years old and older. This survey provides information on changes that are taking place in public attitudes, as well as collecting information from the driving population about drinking and driving practices.

Since the early 1980s, attitudes toward drinking and driving, as well as alcohol abuse in general, began to change as a result of the new anti-drunk-driving initiatives. Individuals became more aware of their own drinking and driving practices. The sales of alcohol in local taverns and bars saw a decline, as customers curtailed the amount they drank. Annual per capita alcohol consumption dropped in the United States from the 1980s level of 21.1 gallons to 19.2 in 1990. The "designated driver" became a new term incorporated into popular use. Taverns began to sell bottled water and other nonalcoholic beverages as a way to hold on to their customers. Bartenders and servers no longer looked at tavern patrons quizzically when ordering "seltzer and lemon," as they would have prior to these attitude changes. Corporations began to curtail holiday parties that provided "open bars," in reaction to host liability laws.

Below are listed changes reported in public attitudes and perceptions that are generally attributed to these expanded countermeasure efforts:

- Current laws and penalties are effective: 11 percent.
- Persons reporting that countermeasures are somewhat effective increased from 48 percent in 1993 to 53 percent in 1997.

- Proportion of population driving within two hours after drinking declined from 28 percent in 1991 to 24 percent in 1993, and currently remains at this rate.
- Riding with an intoxicated person declined a bit between 1993-1995, and remained at 11 percent up to 1997.
- 79 percent viewed drunk driving as threat to personal safety.
- 86 percent of those surveyed feel it is very important to reduce the problem.
- A larger percentage of people were aware of the BAC levels in 1997 (84 percent) than in 1995 (79 percent), although they may not necessarily know the correct legal limit.
- About 40 percent of drivers who drink report at least one time when they did not drive when they thought they were impaired.
- Three in ten drivers have acted as a designated driver in the past year.
- One-third of those too impaired to drive rode with a designated driver.

Unprecedented public attention was drawn to the problem of drunk driving during the 1980s, which produced major changes in the way communities, families, and drivers viewed drinking and driving. More systematic research is needed to better understand the social processes that produce social change expressed in attitudes, political pressure for legal reforms, and community programs.

The drop in the number of alcohol-involved fatal crashes is generally assumed to be the result of a number of factors:

- Heightened public awareness of the dangers of drinking and driving
- Efforts by many states to implement procedures to deter drinking and driving
- Raising the legal drinking age to twenty-one
- Prevention and intervention concepts and programs that emphasize alternatives to legal deterrents
- A declining population of young drivers
- A decrease in per capita alcohol consumption in the United States

Stricter enforcement, controls over alcoholic beverage advertisement, and sale and pricing regulations also are considered to have played an important role in achieving these reductions. No clear and conclusive data demonstrate the relationship between these interventions and the reductions. However, little doubt exists that these efforts contributed to the declines experienced (for a complete list of strategies, see NHTSA Impaired Driving Program at http:www.nhtsa.dot. gov).

SUMMARY

The problem of drinking and driving is pervasive in many societies throughout the world. Its causes are both numerous and complex. It is a stubborn problem that has not been simple to eradicate. Driving under the influence of alcohol and/or drugs has been a major social problem for decades. Both federal and governmental policies seem to shift from a strict punitive approach, which is evident in the recent upsurge in the building of prisons, and the humanistic approach of providing treatment for addicts. In the present times, our country appears to be in the throes of another strict, punitive approach to dealing with the problem of addiction, and this is also reflected in some of the current DWI legislation.

This book attempts to put under one cover the most current and up-to-date information on this problem. It is not all-inclusive, but rather reflects the major trends and conclusions currently permeating the field of DWI research and treatment. The information about this field seems to be scattered throughout journals and research articles. This book will provide treatment practitioners with relevant information in one easily accessible place. It is our goal to take this information and place it here, so that any practitioner treating an offender will be able to base their treatment on a greater understanding of th issues and problems of this population. Assessment, treatment planning, and treatment of the DWI offender is our primary focus, since it is effective treatment that plays an important role in working with the hard-core drinking-driving offender. A tremendous amount of research has been compiled contributing to an improved knowledge of the DWI offender within our field. The chapters in this book are designed to provide information based on this accumulation of knowledge, in the key areas vital to the assessment, treatment planning, and treatment of this group. The challenges ahead are going to require more innovative efforts by both the treatment community and the legal and grass-roots community in order to continue to reduce the tragic consequences of this crime.

Chapter 2

Psychological Characteristics of DWI Offenders

The purpose of this chapter is to provide the reader with an overview of research that attempts to capture the personality and psychological make-up of those individuals who commit DWI offenses and repeat offenses. For counselors, this information is valuable for two reasons. First, in performing assessments on DWI offenders, (as will be discussed in greater detail in Chapters 4 and 5), we know from clinical experience, as well as empirically, that the majority of DWI offenders are usually not willing participants in any assessment endeavor. Therefore, it is common to note a lack of self-disclosure on standard agency intake forms, databases, and standardized measures. With this in mind, having a profile of those characteristics that are common to the DWI offender may help to provide the counselor with some additional information by which to make a determination, whether the person being assessed fits the profile of the typical DWI offender, a DWI offender who may be in the early stages of alcoholism, or a DWI offender who may be more likely to become a recidivist. The research on psychological characteristics may also be useful to the counselor with regard to treatment matching or treatment planning. Being knowledgeable about what types of psychological profiles respond to specific types of treatment may be helpful in matching certain clients to certain types of treatment.

Another section of this chapter deals with psychiatric correlates of DWI offenders. As most counselors are aware from working with Mentally Ill Chemical Abusers (MICA) or dual-diagnosis clients, it is imperative to take psychiatric symptomatology into account when working with any client in order to provide more effective treatment. The premise of this line of research rests on the assumption that there is a correlation between personality characteristics and psychiatric symptomatology, which may contribute to or influence drinking and driving behavior. For example, Miller and Windle (1990) cite four ways in which this may occur. First, certain personality characteristics such as sensation seeking, poor inhibitory control, or deviance proneness may influence unsafe driving whether the driver has been drinking or not. Second, various personality characteristics such as risk-taking or sensation seeking may influence drinking location and time of day of drinking. Third, personality characteristics such as impulsivity or low frustration tolerance may influence drinking behavior (e.g., knowing when to stop), which in turn influences driving (e.g., knowing when to ask for a ride). Fourth, certain personality characteristics such as hostility or aggressiveness may result in stressful events such as arguments with family members, which then may result in excessive drinking and irresponsible or reckless driving. (This notion is similar to Problem Behavior Theory [Jessor, 1987], which theorizes that many problem behaviors are interrelated in such a way that both personal and situational factors that influence one behavior [e.g., drinking and driving] may also influence another behavior.) Another example in which personality factors may influence driving behavior is when the individual manifests traits that reflect a disdain for authority or rules. This may result in a belief that DWI laws are superfluous or that these laws do not apply to him or her.

Prior research has suggested, therefore, that certain personality characteristics (e.g., hostility, sensation-seeking, antiauthority attitudes) will contribute to being a high-risk driver, and no one would dispute the fact that drinking while driving also will place an individual at high risk for crashes, fatalities, and so on. The premise of this line of research goes one step further, however, in suggesting that there may be a synergistic effect when alcohol is combined with certain personality characteristics which may place one at even higher risk (Clay, 1972; Pelz and Schuman, 1974; Donovan, Marlatt, and Salzburg, 1983; Donovan et al., 1985).

Chapter 3 discusses the demographic, familial, and social correlates of DWI offenders as well as an exploration of how DWI offenders compare with alcoholics, which will shed more light on the profiles of DWI offenders, repeat offenders, and multiple offenders.

WHO ARE DWI OFFENDERS?

Although this may seem like a simple question, it is really quite complex when several factors are taken into consideration. As Miller and Windle (1990) point out, the population of drinking drivers is a very dynamic one, due to the fact that new DWI offenders are constantly being added; "old members" drop out because of changed drinking patterns, changes in drinking-driving behavior, injury, or death; and obviously a number of drinking drivers never get caught. Miller and Windle also point out that the dynamics of the DWI population are also subject to changes in the law, federal funding policy, and social factors. Therefore, any "social-legal-political change" can influence both the size and characteristics of the DWI population. An example of this was found in New Jersey back in 1976, when tougher DWI laws were enacted which, in addition to stiff fines and license suspensions, also included screening of DWI offenders and mandated education and treatment programs. There was concern expressed by the Bureau of Alcohol Countermeasures, which is a department within the New Jersey Division of Motor Vehicles, that both state and municipal police would consider these laws too tough and too time consuming to process an arrest properly. Therefore, funding was provided to police departments in order to enact DWI Enforcement Task Forces, which included roadside checkpoints and additional officers on patrol during peak drinking-driving hours. In shedding further light on the complexity of defining this population, Perrine (1990) makes a distinction between "the Quick" (i.e., those drinking drivers who have escaped arrest), "the Caught" (i.e., those drinking drivers who are apprehended and convicted of DWI offenses), and "the Dead," who are the fatally injured drivers who have positive blood-alcohol levels at the time of their fatal crashes. In the following sections we will be attempting to provide more definition to the question of just who the DWI offenders are. Surprisingly, however, little empirical rigorous research has been undertaken with offenders when compared to the vast literature on problems drinkers or alcoholics. Perrine (1990) also questions whether the research that has been done with DWI offenders ("the Caught") is truly representative of the drinking-driver population, as it is estimated that they represent only a small portion of impaired drivers. This notion will be discussed in more detail at the conclusion of this chapter.

PERSONALITY CHARACTERISTICS

A number of studies have attempted to identify psychological characteristics of DWI offenders, repeat offenders, and multiple offenders, some with the goal of trying to differentiate factors that might distinguish these subgroups of DWI offenders (see Table 2.1). For example, Selzer, Vinokur, and Wilson (1977) found in comparing groups of alcoholics, DWI offenders, and nonoffenders that the alcoholic group had scored as being the most aggressive on aggressive-hostility scales, followed by the DWI offender group, who differed significantly from the nonoffender group. Donovan (1980), in comparing a group of DWI offenders with high-risk drivers and nonoffenders, found that the two offender groups differed significantly from the nonoffender group in levels of assaultiveness, overt and covert hostility, and verbal hostility.

In a later study, Donovan and Marlatt (1982) studied 172 male first offenders and found five basic personality subtypes. Two of these subtypes had tested as having high levels of "risk-enhancing traits." The first group was comprised of individuals who exhibited high levels of driving-related aggression, competitive speed, sensation seeking, assaultiveness, irritability, and indirect and verbal hostility. The second group was comprised of individuals who were characterized by high levels of depression and resentment, but were also found to have the lowest levels of assertiveness, emotional adjustment, and internal locus of control.

Donovan, Marlatt, and Salzburg (1983) later summarized several personality variables associated with increased risk for DWI and other driving risks, which included irritability, impulsiveness, thrill-seeking, overt hostility, resentment, low frustration tolerance, low levels of assertiveness, an external locus of control, oversensitivity to criticism, feelings of inadequacy and helplessness, and overall emotional instability. In a similar study, Donovan and colleagues (1985) compared a group of DWI offenders with a group of high-risk drivers and a comparison group of nonoffenders on measures of drinking, driving attitudes, personality, and hostility. Both the DWI and high-risk driver

TABLE 2.1. Summary of Personality and Psychiatric Characteristics

Trait	DWI Offenders Studied	Authors
Hostility	First offenders, high-risk drivers	Donovan, 1980
	First offenders, high-risk drivers	Donovan and Marlatt, 1982
	First offenders, high-risk drivers	Donovan, Marlatt, and Salzburg, 1983
	First offenders, high-risk drivers	Donovan et al., 1985
	First offenders, high-risk drivers	Donovan, Umlauf, Salzburg, 1990
	First and repeat offenders	Jonah and Wilson, 1986
	First and repeat offenders	McMillen et al., 1992
	First and repeat offenders	Murty and Roebuck, 1991
	First and repeat offenders	Nolan, Johnson, and Pincus, 1994
	First offenders	Selzer, Vinokur, and Wilson, 1977
	First offenders	Wilson, 1991
Resentment	First and repeat offenders	Jonah and Wilson, 1986
	First and repeat offenders	Vingilis et al., 1994
Overcontrolled hostility	First and repeat offenders	Cavaiola, Wolf, and Lavender, 1999
Aggressiveness/ assaultiveness	First offenders, high risk	Donovan, 1980
	First offenders, high risk	Donovan and Marlatt, 1982
	First offenders, high risk	Donovan et al., 1985
	First offenders	McCord, 1984
	First and repeat offenders	Nolan, Johnson, and Pincus, 1994
	First offenders	Selzer and Barton, 1977
	First offenders	Selzer, Vinokur, and Wilson, 1977
	First offenders	Wilson and Jonah, 1985
Sensation-seeking/ risk-enhancing traits	First offenders, high risk	Donovan and Marlatt, 1982
	First offenders, high risk	Donovan, Marlatt and Salzburg, 1983
	First offenders, high risk	Donovan et al., 1985
	First offenders, high risk	Donovan, Umlauf and Salzburg, 1990
	First and repeat offenders	McMillen et al., 1992
	First and repeat offenders	Murty and Roebuck, 1991
	Repeat offenders	Nochajski, Miller, and Parks, 1994
	First and repeat offenders	Nolan, Johnson, and Pincus, 1994
	First offenders	Wilson and Jonah, 1985
	First and repeat offenders	Vingilis et al., 1994

TABLE 2.1 *(continued)*

Trait	DWI Offenders Studied	Authors
External locus of control	First offenders	Cavaiola and Desordi, 1999
	First offenders, high risk	Donovan, Marlatt, and Salzburg, 1983
	First offenders, repeat offenders	Jonah and Wilson, 1986
	First offenders, repeat offenders	Wilson, 1991
Irresponsible	First and repeat offenders	Wilson, 1991
Impulsivity	First offenders, high risk	Donovan, Marlatt, and Salzburg, 1983
	First offenders	Jonah and Wilson, 1986
	First offenders	Vingilis et al., 1994
Low frustration tolerance	First offenders, high risk	Donovan, Marlatt, and Salzburg, 1983
Low assertiveness	First and repeat offenders	Reynolds, Kunce, and Cope, 1991
Introverted	First and repeat offenders	Reynolds, 1988
Depression	First and repeat offenders	Cavaiola, 1999
	First offenders, high risk	Donovan et al., 1985
	Repeat offenders	Nochajski, Miller, and Parks, 1994
	First offenders	Selzer and Barton, 1977
	First offenders	Selzer, Vinokur, and Wilson, 1977
	First offenders	Sutker, Brantley, and Allain, 1980
	First offenders	Windle and Miller, 1990
Psychopathic/ social deviance	First and repeat offenders	Cavaiola, Wolf, and Lavender, 1999
	First offenders	Finch and Smith, 1970
	First and repeat offenders	Nochajski et al., 1991
	First offenders	Sutker, Brantley, and Allain, 1980
Obsessive-compulsive	First and repeat offenders	Pristach et al., 1991
Paranoid thinking	First offenders	Selzer, Vinokur, and Wilson, 1977
Attention-deficit hyperactivity disorder	First offenders	Wiezcorek, Miller, and Nochajski, 1991

groups were found to be similar in having higher levels of verbal hostility, irritability, resentment, assaultiveness, and sensation-seeking and were less well-adjusted than the nonoffender group.

Jonah and Wilson (1986) compared DWI offenders with nonoffenders and found the DWI group to be more resentful, more verbally hostile, impulsive, self-deprecatory, and to have more of an external locus of control. Cavaiola and DeSordi (1999) also found first-time DWI offenders to manifest more of an external locus of control when compared with a nonoffender comparison group. Wilson and Jonah (1985) found that DWI offenders scored higher on measures of thrill-seeking and assaultiveness than nonoffenders; however, they did not differ with regards to depression, verbal hostility, or external locus of control. McCord (1984) and Selzer and Barton (1977) also found higher levels of aggressiveness in male DWI offenders.

Reynolds, Kunce, and Cope (1991) compared a group of first offenders with a group of repeat offenders and did not find either group to be sensation-seeking. However, the repeat offenders were found to be less expressive emotionally and less flexible in finding stimulation than first offenders. In an earlier study, Reynolds (1988) had found that repeat offenders had a low psychological need for affiliation and tended to be more introverted. McMillen and colleagues (1992) studied DWI offenders arrested for being involved in accidents or other moving violations and found them to have higher levels of hostility. They were more likely to be sensation-seeking and also had consumed more alcohol per occasion than nonoffenders.

As has been noted in prior research, the personality traits of DWI offenders and high-risk drivers are not often substantially different from one another. For example, Wilson (1991) performed a cluster analysis of 238 convicted DWI offenders and 285 high-risk drivers who had a previous history of accidents or traffic violations. Four subtypes were found (hostile/responsible, deviant, well-adjusted, and irresponsible), which were derived from three factors: thrill-seeking, hostility, and personal adjustment. Wilson (1992) compared four groups of Canadian drivers. The first group was composed of DWI offenders, the second group was composed of drivers who had been involved in three or more accidents in the past three years, the third group had accumulated nine or more demerits (or points) on their licenses, and the fourth group was a randomly chosen control group.

The DWI group and high-risk driving groups were again found to be similar in several dimensions (i.e., locus of control, depression, assaultiveness, and responsible values).

Murty and Roebuck (1991) concluded from their research that DWI offenders were likely to be young, working-class males with hostile temperaments, high levels of risk-taking behavior and a history of prior arrest records. Nolan, Johnson, and Pincus (1994) also found DWI offenders to be "aggressive, hostile, sensation-seeking types" (p. 39) who were more likely to display other high-risk driving behaviors. In a prospective study of high-risk drivers (here defined as someone with either four traffic convictions/crashes in a one-year period or five convictions in a two-year period) Donovan, Umlauf, and Salzberg (1990) found that 11.4 percent of these high-risk drivers had been arrested for a DWI. These drivers were then compared to a DWI offender group and insignificant differences were noted regarding levels of hostility, sensation-seeking, and other personality traits. Vingilis and colleagues (1994) also studied a group of high-risk drivers who had been seriously injured and admitted to trauma units. Of this group, 23 percent had positive BAC levels. When examined on several personality dimensions (e.g., assaultiveness, verbal hostility, resentment, impulse expression, and sensation seeking), negligible differences were noted between those with a positive BAC versus those who had not been drinking.

The aforementioned results comparing DWI offenders and high-risk drivers are similar to earlier studies performed by Perrine (1970) and Zelhart, Schurr, and Brown (1975) who also noted insignificant differences between DWI offenders and high-risk drivers on several personality dimensions, including hostility and aggressiveness. Zylman (1976) contends that high-risk drivers and DWI offenders may be two subgroups within the larger population of high-risk drivers who seem to manifest similar personality traits—which enhances their driving risk whether they drink or not.

In summarizing the body of research literature on psychological characteristics of DWI offenders, it appears that the majority of studies have noted few differences between first-time DWI offenders and repeat offenders. Perhaps the statement by Perrine, Peck, and Fell (1989) best summarizes this contention, that "most first offenders are problem drinkers who have simply not yet been caught for their second

DUI offense" (p. 73). There also appears to be an overlap in psycho-social traits between individuals with DWI offenses and those individuals who have poor driving records, i.e., those who are considered to be "at risk" drivers (McDonald and Pederson, 1990). Of the traits that have received the most attention in the research, it appears that the following are the traits most often investigated:

1. sensation-seeking
2. hostility
3. verbal hostility
4. resentments
5. locus of control (external)
6. impulsivity
7. low frustration tolerance
8. lack of assertiveness

It may be more useful for the counselor working with DWI offenders to not look at these lists of traits as mere labels, but to view them in light of how they may correlate with the DWI offense itself. For example, Wieczorek, Miller, and Nochajski (1991) provide a causal explanation for how sensation-seeking may account for a propensity toward a DWI offense by studying the correlation of these two traits with multiple-location drinking (i.e., drinking in one location and then traveling to another location to drink). Here, sensation-seeking is a trait defined by a demand for varied, intense, novel, and/or complex experiences or sensations with the intent of being willing to take risks to achieve these experiences or sensations (Zuckerman, 1990). The Wieczorek, Miller, and Nochajski (1990) study did find that sensation-seeking significantly contributed to multiple-location drinking. These authors conclude that multiple-location drinkers are more likely to become bored with their surroundings (hence the elevation they found on the Boredom Susceptibility Scale), and are therefore more likely to travel from place to place seeking novel stimulation and more exciting places to drink.

Hostility may be a more complex trait to associate with DWI offenses. For example, Miller and Windle (1990) suggest that a hostile drinker may cause stressful events such as arguments with family members, which in turn could result in the hostile drinker leaving the situation and driving while intoxicated to another location. Hostile drinkers may therefore be unwelcome in one situation and will then move to another location (Wieczorek, Miller, and Nochajski,1991). It is also noted that hostility is often correlated with alcohol and drug dependence (Walter et al., 1990), as would be the case with the stereotype of the "nasty drunk." It is also possible, however, that the hostility so often observed in DWI offenders is partly the result of having been arrested for a DWI offense and mandated to treatment/counseling or education programs. This anger is often viewed as part of their reaction to the fines, penalties, and treatment process (Cavaiola, 1984).

Locus of control is another personality trait that has been researched widely with alcoholics and, to a lesser extent, with DWI offenders. The locus-of-control concept suggests that individuals who are considered to have an "internal" locus of control usually consider themselves to be more in control of their lives and responsible for what befalls them, whereas those with an "external" locus of control tend to view themselves at the recipients of luck, fate, or powerful others. Therefore, individuals with an external locus of control would tend to view a bad grade on an exam as bad luck, while those who are internal, given the same bad grade, would attribute this to their lack of study or effort. So too, with an event such as a DWI, the "external" would tend to deny responsibility for the arrest, instead attributing the DWI offense to bad luck or that the police were "out to get them." What is noteworthy is that the majority of studies mentioned tend to characterize DWI offenders as being more external. In the Cavaiola and DeSordi (1999) study, however, it was noted that on the Drinking-Related Locus of Control Scale, which is composed of items pertaining to drinking behavior, DWI offenders tended to portray themselves as more internal or in control of their drinking, while on the Rotter Locus of Control Scale, they tended to portray themselves as having a more external locus of control.

PSYCHIATRIC CORRELATES

A number of studies have investigated correlations between DWI offenders who may manifest other psychiatric symptomotology. Here, the majority of research points to factors such as depression, psychopathic deviance, and attention-deficit hyperactivity disorder as being manifest in several DWI offenders. What is also noteworthy in this line of research is that prior studies have shown that psychiatric symptomatology is more prevalent among those individuals who manifest an alcoholic diagnosis than among the general population (Helzer and Pryzbeck, 1988; Herz et al., 1990; and Penick et al., 1988). Therefore, there certainly is an overlap between those DWI offenders who are also alcoholic and who manifest psychiatric symptoms. Prior studies have indicated that levels of psychopathology may be higher in individuals with multiple DWI offenses (Steer and Fine, 1978), again suggestive of the overlap in the DWI population with the population manifesting alcoholism. However, another interesting finding (Nochajski, Wieczorek, and Miller, 1996) is that DWI recidivism appears to be more a function of a combination of heavy drinking, drug use, and risk-taking behavior than a function of psychological distress per se. Deviance and impulsivity factors did show a relationship to both drug use and recidivism.

In research examining the relationship of DWI offenders with psychiatric disorders, Sutker, Brantley, and Allain (1980) studied 500 DWI offenders using the Minnesota Multiphasic Personality Inventory (MMPI) and found two subgroups. The first was characterized by elevated social deviance or social nonconformity and heavy drinking, while the second group was characterized by elevations in pessimism and depressed affect. Finch and Smith (1970) found that 24 percent of drivers involved in fatal accidents manifested symptoms of antisocial personality disorders. In a study of problem-drinking young men, Nochajski and colleagues (1991) concluded that the problem-drinking driver has more antisocial tendencies and is less self-conscious about his social interactions than other problem-drinkers. Finally, Soltenberg and colleagues (1999) found that among men who had manifested alcohol dependence prior to age twenty-five and who had a family history of alcohol problems were at increased risk for fighting while drinking, police involvement, abuse or dependence on other drugs, and drunk driving.

Pristach and colleagues (1991) administered the SCL-90-R scale (Derogatis, 1983) to eighty-one first offenders and 103 repeat offenders. The SCL-90-R is a self-report inventory of psychopathology or psychological distress. All participants were grouped according to whether they met the criteria for alcohol dependence. The results indicated that for the nondependent DWI offenders there were no significant differences found on the SCL-90-R, with the exception of the obsessive-compulsive scale. Here, the first offenders scored in a more pathological range. For those offenders who were classified as alcohol dependent there were no significant differences noted between groups; however, both groups did score as being more pathological than a nonpatient comparison group.

Windle and Miller (1989) found higher levels of depressive symptoms in alcohol-dependent women compared to alcohol-dependent men. In a later study derived from the same sample, Windle and Miller (1990) examined the levels of drinking and depressive symptomatology among 461 first-time DWI offenders and performed longitudinal follow-ups over an eighteen-month period. They found upon short-term follow-up that higher levels of drinking were associated with lower levels of depressive symptoms; however, a longer follow-up revealed that higher levels of drinking were associated with higher levels of depression. Selzer, Vinokur, and Wilson (1977) found increased levels of depression in a DWI-offender sample when compared with a nonoffender control group; however, the DWI group did not score as extreme as the alcoholic comparison group. Similarly, the DWI group manifested more paranoid thinking and lower self-esteem than the control group but less than the alcoholic group. In a later study, Selzer and Barton (1977) again found that DWI offenders fell somewhere between alcoholics and control drivers with regard to depression, self-esteem, and self-control. Nochajski, Miller, and Parks (1994) found that repeat DWI offenders were more likely to report depressive symptoms, sensation-seeking behaviors, childhood risk factors, and health problems than first offenders. Donovan et al. (1985) found that both high-risk drivers and DWI offenders exhibited higher levels of depression and emotional maladjustment when compared to a nonoffender sample. Cavaiola, Wolf, and Lavender (1999), in comparing a group of first-time DWI offenders with repeat offenders and a comparison group of nonoffenders, found that both DWI groups had higher elevations on the Psychopathic Deviate Scale, MacAndrews Alcoholism Scale, and the Overcontrolled Hostility Scale than the nonoffender comparison group. There were insignificant differences found with regard to depression. Surprisingly, the first and repeat offenders did not differ with regard to blood alcohol levels at the time of their arrest, nor did these groups differ with regard to other criminal activity.

Although several studies have linked early onset alcoholism with attention-deficit hyperactivity disorder (e.g., Tarter et al., 1977), few studies have linked DWI offenses to individuals who may have been diagnosed with ADHD as children. Wieczorek, Miller, and Nochajski (1991) found that multiple-location drinkers were greater sensation seekers, heavier drinkers, more hostile, and more likely to report symptoms of ADHD than single-location drinkers. Individuals with ADHD are often found to engage in many high-risk behaviors/sensation-seeking behaviors as adults—which sometimes results in their exhibiting higher rates of criminal activity (Fischer et al., 1990; Gittleman et al., 1985; Weiss and Hechtman, 1986). However, few studies have examined the interrelationship between ADHD and DWI offenses.

SUMMARY AND CONCLUSIONS

The research literature reviewed in this chapter points to several correlates of DWI offenders with certain personality types and psychiatric symptomatology/disorders. In summarizing this information, it appears that the majority of DWI offenders manifest some degree of hostility, whether it be verbal, covert, overt, or overcontrolled. They also seem to manifest sensation-seeking traits, which also implies a low tolerance for boredom and frustration. DWI offenders also seem to have a propensity to blame others for their problems, as implied by their manifestation of an external locus of control. In addition, a few studies suggest that DWI offenders typically have low self-esteem and tend to have antiauthoritarian attitudes or perhaps a disdain for rules in general.

With regard to psychiatric symptomatology, most studies find that DWI offenders are more "emotionally maladjusted" when compared to their nonoffender counterparts from the general driving population. However, in further defining this maladjustment, it appears that depression, social or psychopathic deviance, and attention deficit hyperactivity disorder seem to top the list of psychiatric correlates. Obviously, an overlap exists between the aforementioned personality characteristics and some of the psychiatric disorders. For example, antiauthoritarian attitudes and psychopathic deviance have very common characteristics and may even be viewed to exist on somewhat of a continuum, ranging from attitudes against authority to breaking with social convention to breaking laws—and, in doing so, violating the rights of others. Indeed, psychopathy is often characterized as a mixture of overt antisocial behavior and personality attributes such as superficial charm, unreliability, lack of guilt, need to engage in thrill-seeking behavior, impulsiveness, poor frustration tolerance, lack of insight, and a failure to learn from experience (American Psychiatric Association, 1994; Babiak, 1995; Cleckley, 1976; Hare, 1993). The overlap of these traits with many of the aforementioned traits of DWI offenders is striking. Another example of such an overlap would be low frustration tolerance and low tolerance for boredom with attention-deficit hyperactivity disorder.

In examining some of the psychopathology noted within the DWI offender population, it seemed unusual that none of the studies we reviewed mentioned a correlation between bipolar disorder and DWI offenses. This was surprising for several reasons; first, correlations between bipolar disorder and alcoholism have been noted in the literature (e.g., it was speculated that Ernest Hemingway fit both diagnostic categories) and second, because bipolars often engage in quite extreme risk-taking behavior, especially when in the manic phase of their illness. Future research is needed to further investigate this area.

What is noteworthy, and will be described in more detail in Chapter 3, is that many of the personality and psychiatric traits explored in this chapter often are said to correlate with traits of those who are diagnosed as alcoholics. One might readily note the overlap between these aforementioned traits and those described as being part of the "alcoholic or addictive personality" (Nakken, 1997). Does this imply, however, that all DWI offenders are indeed alcoholic, as some researchers suggest? Or are we dealing with different typologies when discussing first offender versus repeat offenders? For example, are there some DWI offenders who fit the personality type of the angry, antisocial offender versus the depressed, hard-luck-story offender, as suggested by Donovan and Marlatt (1982); Fine, Scoles, and Mulligan (1975); or Steer, Fine, and Scoles (1979), who indicate that there are possibly several different subtypes of DWI offenders?

The next chapter will focus on the drinking patterns of DWI offenders and how they compare to those of alcoholics and non-alcoholics, as well as social and demographic correlates of those who are convicted of DWI offenses.

Chapter 3

Profile Differences Between DWI Offenders and Alcoholics, and Other Demographic Variables

As more and more DWI offenders are mandated into alcoholism treatment facilities, demands for more effective treatment models must be met. Counselors are being exposed more frequently to angry, hostile DWI clients. As a result, these clients have often been described as being resistant to treatment (Cavaiola, 1984), although Miller and Rollnick (1991) more recently have concluded that in many instances treatment resistance may be a manifestation of other processes at work. For example, utilizing the Prochaska-DiClemente Transtheoretical Model a process is described in which the client may experience various stages prior to reaching a point of accepting the need for change (this is discussed in more detail in Chapter 7). Prior research, however, may have supported the notion of treatment resistance in DWI offenders, since it generally indicates that practically nothing works in preventing recidivism with repeat offenders. McGuire (1980, p. 102) states that "with the first offender nearly any kind of program seems to work but with the repeat offender, very little seems to have an effect." Panepinto and colleagues (1982), however, conclude that the fact of being mandated to treatment lends itself to rage. If counselors are to effectively treat this difficult population it is essential to examine available treatment approaches, attitude biases, and the assumptions made by treatment professionals about this population. Because DWI treatment programs often emphasize early identification, diagnosis, and rehabilitation, a tremendous opportunity exists to provide early intervention with a population that, if left untreated at this stage, would probably progress to more severe problems over time.

Research finds that there are several important variables within the DWI population that distinguish them from alcoholic populations and nonoffenders or "normal" control groups. As a group, DWI offenders often present with distinct characteristics. For example, DWI offenders tend to be male, aged twenty-two to thirty-five, employed, married, and usually have at least a twelfth-grade education. Their drinking occurs primarily on weekends at bars, social gatherings, and parties with friends (Selzer, 1969). They generally do not view themselves as people who get into trouble with the law. McGuire (1980) found repeat offenders to be heavier drinkers, more impulsive, less restrained, socially less aggressive, disliking social contacts, and more likely to suspect others of being hostile toward them.

Since DWI offenders are referred to the alcoholism field for rehabilitation, researchers have compared DWI offenders to alcoholics in treatment and have found differences. Moskowitz, Walker, and Gomberg (1979) concluded than the average DWI offender tends to have more intact resources than the alcoholic in treatment. The DWI offender generally does not experience the great range of consequences usually seen with the alcoholic in residential care. Alcoholics who enter residential treatment display combinations of economic, emotional, employment, family, and marital problems; the DWI population does not generally report these problem areas. Ninety-two percent of alcoholics in treatment report family problems, whereas 30 percent of the DWI population report family problems. DWI offenders are generally healthier, with only 20 percent reporting physical problems compared to 40 percent of the alcoholic population. Job-related problems among the DWI population are reported to be about 2 percent, whereas 14 percent of alcoholics disclose having trouble on the job. Thirty-two percent of alcoholics in treatment state that they have financial problems, whereas 7 percent of DWI offenders admit problems in that area. Divorce or separation is imparted by 50 percent of the alcoholics in treatment in comparison to 22 percent to 40 percent of DWI clients who express marital problems.

These findings have significant implications for program design. Considering the interventive nature of the countermeasure program, it is reasonable to assume that there would be differences between the

DWI client profiles and the profiles of alcoholics in treatment. Panepinto and colleagues (1982) conclude that "he or she has not usually progressed to a later stage of alcoholism. Not only does this contribute to alcoholic denial, but it also demands a different treatment response" Moskowitz, Walker, and Gomberg (1979) also note in their research that the DWI driver exhibits behavioral trends that have not reached the severity of most alcoholics in treatment. It is little wonder, then, that nothing seems to work in treating the repeat offender. Panepinto and colleagues (1982) suggest that providers consider these profile differences when designing treatment strategies. Alcoholism facilities use traditional approaches in treating this client. Educational materials, lectures, films and pamphlets are designed for the average alcoholic in treatment. Counselors, groups and the therapies utilized are modeled on the type of alcoholic who most likely enters treatment. Therefore, the information and therapy usually found in alcoholism facilities would tend to reinforce the average DWI client's denial. Information must be used in a manner so as to not lead to reinforcement of rationalization and denial.

Based on these profile differences, the alcoholism counselor can begin to develop treatment strategies relating to the DWI client. Panepinto and colleagues (1982) also make the following treatment observations based on profile differences:

Productive areas to focus on in treatment would be those problem areas specific to the DWI population. Focusing on job-related problems, for instance, would usually not prove fruitful since DWI offenders do not report significant job difficulties. The most productive areas would be to demonstrate the progressive nature of alcoholism, family and marital problems and repetitive nature of alcohol-abusing behavior. Difficulty in controlling behavior that has been proven to be stressful, harmful, dangerous and unpleasant are indicators of a significant pattern of alcohol abuse. Perhaps by recognizing these differences we can adopt treatment strategies that are more effective in treating DWI clients. Modalities that address these specific issues may help in reducing recidivism and provide a less frustrating relationship between the alcoholism treatment community and the DWI clients. Cavaiola (1984) also states that counselors need to develop innovative treatment modalities and techniques in order to work with this population.

DEMOGRAPHIC VARIABLES

Several of the studies mentioned here and in Chapter 2 point out demographic and social variables that appear to distinguish the DWI offender population from both alcoholic groups and nonoffender groups. The following is a summary of some of this research.

General Demographics

Several studies investigating demographic variables find that DWI offenders generally tend to be younger than the general driving population (Donovan, 1980; Donovan et al., 1985; Donelson, 1985; Mercer, 1986;) male (Hyman, 1968; Norstrom, 1978; Wieczorek, Miller, and Nochajski, 1992); and single, separated, or divorced (Hyman, 1968; Waller, 1967; Yoder and Moore, 1973), yet other studies find that older DWI offenders are often married (Selzer, Vinokur, and Wilson, 1977; Moskowitz, Walker, and Gomberg, 1979). They tend to be of lower socioeconomic status (Donovan et al., 1985) employed in lower-middle-class occupations, and less well-educated, usually having completed only high school (Donovan, 1980; Donovan and Marlatt, 1983; Donovan et al., 1985; Vingilis, 1983).

Gender Differences

In further exploring gender differences, it is estimated that women represent only 11 percent of the total annual number of DWI arrests (Maguire and Flanagan, 1991). Some studies have noted a trend of increasing arrests for DWI among women (Popkin et al., 1988; Shore et al., 1988), with an estimated 4 to 5 percent increase in the number of female DWI arrests in the past decade (Valerius, 1989). Recent studies have pointed to differences in alcohol metabolism between men and women; therefore, it is not surprising to find that women have a higher risk of fatal driving crashes than do men at the same blood alcohol levels (Zador, 1991). As cited by Jones and Lacey (1998), during 1982, women with BACs of .10g/dl or more were involved in 12.3 percent of fatal crashes. This percentage had increased to 15.7 percent in 1996, which represents a 28 percent increase in the number of women involved in alcohol-related fatal crashes. There is some evidence, therefore, which suggests that women are at higher risk (50 percent) than males for both alcohol-related crashes and crash fatalities when their BACs are .10g/dl and higher.

The question arises, then, as to why DWI offenses and alcohol-related fatalities have increased among women. It is conjectured that, as women have had more opportunities to work outside the home, their rates of drinking and driving have increased, thereby putting them at greater risk for DWI offenses. However, their patterns of DWI arrests still differ from men. For example, Shore and colleagues (1988), in investigating the day of the week of DWI arrests, found that women's DWI arrests were spread evenly throughout the week, as opposed to men, whose DWI offenses usually tend to cluster on the weekend.

In investigating DSM-III-R criteria for Alcohol Dependence, Wieczorek, Miller, and Nochajski (1992) found that men tended to manifest more of the nine alcohol dependence criteria when compared to women, suggesting that the current legal system tends to detect women DWI offenders who are less severely alcohol dependent. However, the research in this area has yielded somewhat equivocal results. For example, Franklin (1989) and Sutton (1993) argue that the majority of female DWI offenders are problem drinkers. McCormack (1985) and Shore and McCoy (1987) indicate that women with certain demographic characteristics (e.g., middle aged and separated/divorced) have a greater likelihood of being arrested for a DWI or an alcohol-related crash.

Parks and colleagues (1996) studied 812 women who had been convicted of DWI offenses. Utilizing multiple measures, including the Diagnostic Interview Schedule (DIS) and Drug Abuse Screening Test, they found that 24.5 percent could be diagnosed as alcohol dependent (utilizing DSM-III-R criteria), 43.1 percent were diagnosed as manifesting alcohol abuse, and 32.4 percent were determined to manifest no diagnosis. Of the abuse and dependent groups, 18.6 percent and 49.7 percent, respectively, also were found to have drug problems. A greater percentage of the women in the dependent group were unemployed, had a criminal history, and reported having a family member with an alcohol or drug problem and a DWI arrest. Those in the no-diagnosis group were more likely to be married and to be older than the women in the dependence group. Reynolds, Kunce, and Cope (1991) found, in comparing male and female DWI offenders on the

Michigan Alcoholism Screening Test (MAST), that female repeat offenders had the highest MAST scores (M = 6.00), when compared to first-time male offenders (M = 4.39), first-time female offenders (M = 4.59), or repeat male offenders (M = 4.65). Yet, despite the literature which suggests that women DWI offenders may be more likely to be problem drinkers or alcoholics, they tend to respond better to treatment and are less likely to become recidivists. Wells-Parker and colleagues (1991) found females arrested in Mississippi were more likely to be unmarried, divorced, older, and white, with no prior DWI and fewer arrests for public drunkenness than males. Also, although there were no differences found on Mortimer-Filkins scores, the women in this group were half as likely to become recidivists.

Racial Differences

Relatively few studies have investigated the racial differences in DWI offenses and alcohol-related crashes. Some of the studies that have investigated this variable have had difficulty in separating the effect of race with socioeconomic status. In reporting on the 1986 National Roadside Breathtesting Survey, Lund and Wolfe (1991) determined that 5.9 percent of African Americans had a blood alcohol content of .10g/dl or more, compared to 2.7 percent of Caucasians, and 4.4 percent of Hispanics. In a study of North Carolina crash data, Popkin and Council (1993) found 51 percent of non-Caucasian drivers and 49 percent of Caucasian drivers had blood alcohol levels over .10g/dl, which was insignificant. James (1990) studied racial differences of DWI offenders in Washington state and found that non-Caucasian drivers comprised 10.5 percent of the total DWI population in that state. Among this group of drivers, 11 percent were Asian, 33 percent were African American, 36 percent were Native American, and 20 percent were "unknown." James had also compared the Washington sample to the general population and concluded that Asian Americans were underrepresented in the DWI population. There were five different profiles derived from his research:

1. Non-Caucasian female homemakers
2. African-Americans in the military
3. Unemployed blue-collar non-Caucasians
4. Asian-Americans in unstructured jobs
5. Older, unemployed, non-Caucasians from unstructured jobs

Ross and colleagues (1991), in reviewing the literature on DWI statistics, concluded that African Americans and Hispanic Americans were overrepresented in the DWI population. However, although these groups may be overrepresented in DWI convictions, a recent study (Jones and Lacey, 1998) suggests that Caucasian male drivers between the ages of twenty-one to thirty-four constitute the largest percentage of the population involved in alcohol-impaired fatal crashes.

Criminal History

Argeriou, McCarty, and Blacker (1985), in studying 1,406 DWI offenders, found that more than 75 percent of these offenders had been arraigned for one or more criminal offenses and 50 percent had been arraigned for criminal offenses other than the DWI or motor vehicle-related offenses. Sixty-eight percent of the DWI recidivists were found to have criminal records. Beerman, Smith, and Hall (1988) found that the number of both minor crimes (e.g., shoplifting, disorderly conduct, disturbing the peace) and major crimes (e.g., assault, homicide, grand larceny, forgery) were the best predictors of DWI recidivism. Wells-Parker, Cosby, and Landrum (1986) also found that DWI offenders with prior criminal arrest records were the ones most likely to have a subsequent DWI offense. Nochajski and colleagues (1993), in a study of the impact of treatment on DWI offenders, found that those who had a history of arrests for crimes other than DWI were more than twice as likely to be rearrested for a subsequent drinking and driving offense.

DRINKING BEHAVIOR AMONG DWI OFFENDERS

Borkenstein (1974) estimates that in a city with a population of 1 million individuals there are 4 million instances a year of people driving with blood alcohol levels that exceed the legal limit. However, only a fraction of these drivers are ever arrested for DWI. It is estimated that approximately only 1 in 200 drinking drivers are ever arrested (Beitel, Sharp, and Glauz, 1975). With this in mind, it is important to realize that the DWI offenders who are referred to treatment may represent a skewed population of drinking drivers. Perrine (1990) makes this point, in distinguishing between "the Quick," "the Caught," and "the Dead" (see Chapter 2). Of these groups, it is only "the Caught" and "the Dead" that researchers ever get to study in any depth. Furthermore, Wilson and Jonah (1985) found that overall alcohol consumption was the single most powerful predictor of impaired driving. Although this conclusion may not appear to be all that surprising, what is noteworthy is that the drinking frequency-amount variable appears to outweigh all the other predictors of DWI offenses (e.g., personality, social, and demographic variables). For example, in a study of 2,000 Canadian drivers, Wilson and Jonah were able to discern three groups. The first group reported that they would drink, but did not drive after drinking. The second group reported that they drove after drinking on one or more occasions but they did not drive while impaired. The third group admitted that they drove while impaired on one or more occasions. This latter group demonstrated different drinking habits and driving behaviors that were more likely to be influenced by peers. This group of impaired drivers was considered to be a small but socially deviant group that was quite different from the larger population of average drinkers. These results were supported in research by Perrine, Peck, and Fell (1989) and Perrine (1990), which found that approximately 10 percent of males from the general population, 40 percent of first-time DWI offenders and 60 percent of repeat offenders drink five or more beverages containing alcohol per occasion as their usual amount.

Selzer, Vinokur, and Wilson (1977), in comparing a group of DWI offenders with a group of alcoholics and a group of nonoffender controls, found there were negligible differences between the DWI group and the control group with regard to the frequency of alcohol intake, which was significantly lower than the alcoholic group. With regard to total amount of alcohol consumed, however, the alcoholic group had consumed significantly more when compared to the other two groups. However, the DWI group had consumed significantly more than the control group.

Bell and colleagues (1978) compared a group of drinking drivers with a group of alcoholics in detoxification. The DWI offenders were less likely to report threatened job loss because of their drinking (2 percent versus 14 percent); that their spouses had threatened to leave because of their drinking (4 percent versus 26 percent); that there were fewer attempts to quit drinking (30 percent versus 70 percent); or that they had previously attended Alcoholics Anonymous (5 percent versus 56 percent). The DWI offenders were also less likely to define themselves as problem drinkers (22 percent versus 82 percent) or that they had been warned by a physician that drinking was harming their health (2 percent versus 22 percent).

Weeber (1981) points to the fact that DWI countermeasure programs may fail because many DWI offenders are indeed problem drinkers who are in need of more professional care or perhaps more intensive treatment. In comparing first-time DWI offenders with repeat offenders, Weeber found that although these two groups were similar on several variables, they differed with regard to drinking behavior. Surprisingly, repeat offenders appeared to drink less often; however, it appeared that once these individuals drank, they drank heavily. Not surprisingly, these repeat offenders had more arrests for public intoxication. Both groups tended to be weekend drinkers.

McMillen and colleagues (1992) studied DWI offenders arrested for being involved in accidents or other moving violations and found them to have higher levels of hostility. They were more sensation-seeking and also had consumed more alcohol per occasion than nonoffenders. Packard (1987) performed a study comparing a group of first-time DWI offenders and a group of outpatients receiving treatment for alcoholism. Interestingly, there were insignificant differences noted on several demographic variables (age, sex, marital status, employment status, and education). However, there were significant differences noted with regard to drinking-related variables (e.g., blackouts, personality changes, work problems, interpersonal problems, loss of control over drinking, alcohol tremors, and familial alcoholism). In each instance, the outpatient group had significantly higher percentages of these problems. The only drinking indicator in which the DWI group had scored as experiencing significantly more problems was with regard to legal difficulties.

What is interesting, however, in spite of the aforementioned research, is that BAC at the time of the DWI arrest does not seem to be a significant indicator of an alcoholism diagnosis or problem drinking. Wieczorek, Miller, and Nochajski (1992) found weak or insignificant correlations between alcohol-related problems (as measured by the Mortimer-Filkins Test, a face-to-face interview, and clinical evaluation) and blood alcohol content at the time of the DWI arrest. Cavaiola, Wolf, and Lavender (1999) also found insignificant differences in blood alcohol levels at the time of arrest between a group of first-time DWI offenders and a group of repeat offenders. (For a more in-depth discussion of this see Chapter 5 on assessment issues.) What is noteworthy, however, is that BAC distributions of fatally injured drivers showed that 80 percent had a BAC in excess of .10g/dl, with 64 percent having a BAC in excess of .15g/dl and approximately 40 percent with a BAC in excess of .20g/dl (Simpson and Mayhew, 1992).

DRUG USE AMONG DWI OFFENDERS

Some studies have addressed the issue of drug use other than alcohol. For example, in an early study, Selzer and Barton (1977) compared a group of convicted DWI offenders with a group of alcoholics and a control group of licensed drivers. The DWI offenders reported significantly more use of marijuana, stimulants, and LSD than either of the other two groups; however, they used substantially less sedatives and tranquilizers than the alcoholic group. These results may fit in with some of the personality variable research that characterizes DWI offenders as sensation-seeking, since their drugs of choice tend to heighten experience rather than sedate it. Nochajski, Augustino, and Wieczorek (1997) studied a group of DWI offenders who had completed a treatment program in order to investigate correlates of recidivism. In a prior related study, Dowling and McCartt (1990) found that DWI offenders who were referred to a long-term drinking driver treatment program were slightly more likely to receive a repeat DWI, than those offenders who were not referred to treatment programs. Nochajski, Augustino, and Wieczorek (1997) point out, however, that the Dowling and McCartt study did not take into account those DWI offenders who did not complete treatment or who dropped out of treatment, which certainly could have accounted for the differences they found. Nochajski, Augustino, and Wieczorek found that a no-treatment group was less likely to rearrested when compared to those who had dropped out of treatment; however, the treatment completers were least likely of the three groups to be rearrested, suggesting better outcomes for those who complete treatment. There were three groups of those who went through the screening evaluation, a no-treatment group, an alcohol-only group, and a drug-treatment group that was found to be younger, and they also had more infractions on their driving records. This latter group was found to have higher recidivism rates. When assessed with the RIASI, a screening instrument used specifically for screening DWI offenders (see Chapter 5), the drug group was found to have endorsed more items related to hostility, sensation seeking, psychiatric distress and health-related risk problems.

ESTIMATES OF ALCOHOLISM

Estimates of alcoholism among the DWI population have also yielded equivocal results. For example, in a study of DWI offenders in Michigan (Mortimer et al., 1971; Filkins et al., 1973), it was estimated that 2 to 10 percent of DWI offenders were problem drinkers, whereas in a California sample 50 to 80 percent were determined to be problem drinkers. Vingilis (1983) estimates that approximately 50 percent of DWI offenders can be considered alcoholic, while Wieczorek, Miller, and Nochajski (1989) found that 51 percent of a sample of DWI offenders who were referred for alcoholism evaluations were indeed alcohol dependent when assessed using DSM-III-R criteria. In comparing first and repeat DWI offenders, it has been estimated that 62 percent of first-time DWI offenders were alcohol abusers while 84 percent of repeat offenders were alcohol dependent (Wieczorek, Miller, and Nochajski, 1990. Other estimates of the incidence of alcoholism range from 20 percent (Kelleher, 1971) to 80 percent (Selzer and Barton, 1977). Selzer (1969) studied ninety-six drivers who were responsible for fatal accidents. Of that group, thirty-six were determined to be alcoholics. Other important differences show up when the two groups are compared. Research into drinking behaviors reveals significant variations. A high proportion of DWI offenders report that they do not drink daily. When tested on the Michigan Alcoholism Screening Test (MAST) another difference is noted: 54 percent to 74 percent of the DWI clients tested scored more than 5 points (interpreted to be indicative of alcoholism) (Selzer, 1971), but 99 percent of the alcoholics in treatment scored more than 5 points. Forty-one percent of DWI offenders and 82 percent of alcoholics report drinking seven or more drinks at a sitting. Selzer, Vinokur, and Wilson (1977) had also administered a brief version of the MAST (Pokorny, Miller, and Kaplan, 1972) to a group of alcoholics, DWI offenders, and a control group of nonoffenders. Thirty-nine percent of the DWI group had scored 6 or more (indicative of alcoholism) and 19 percent had scored 5 (borderline alcoholism), while in the alcoholic group, 99 percent had scored 6 or more. In a similar study, Selzer and Barton (1977) estimated that 68 percent of the 306 DWI offenders they studied were probably alcoholic (15 percent had fallen within the "borderline or possible range"), although these offenders were less psychosocially impaired than the alcoholic comparison group.

In a landmark study, Fine, Scoles, and Mulligan (1975) studied 1500 convicted first-time DWI offenders. Having administered the Alcohol Impairment Index to all participants, these offenders were grouped into one of three groups: Group 1 typically consumed alcoholic beverages once or twice a week; Group 2 typically drank at least twice weekly and consumed an average of five quarts of beer, or one fifth of wine, or two pints of liquor; and Group 3 usually consumed alcoholic beverages on a daily basis with daily intake being at least five quarts or more of beer, or one fifth of wine, or three pints of whiskey. The results indicated significant impairment in those participants who were under forty years old, with the most extreme amounts of drinking taking place between ages twenty to twenty-four. Reported levels of alcohol intake and impairment were comparable for Caucasians (47.4 percent of total participants) and African Americans (49.5 percent of total participants). It was also noted that the heaviest drinking patterns were found in the family of origin of Groups 2 and 3. What was most noteworthy, however, was that 54.4 percent of these first offenders reported levels of alcohol impairment which coincided with inclusion in Group 2 or 3, whereas it is estimated that in the general population (Callahan, Cisin, and Crossley, 1969), only 12 percent can be classified as "heavy drinkers" (i.e., those who consume as much as five or more drinks on nearly a daily basis).

When DWI offenders were asked if they might have a drinking problem, three times as many first-time offenders as the general driving population answered "yes," while sixteen times more multiple offenders responded "yes." In addition, three times as many multiple offenders versus first-time offenders were likely to indicate that they had a drinking problem (Perrine, Peck, and Fell, 1989). What was noteworthy was that these self-reports of problematic drinking had correlated with results obtained on the Mortimer-Filkens Test and Alcohol Dependency Scale for these groups. Saltstone (1989), in comparing groups of alcoholics, incarcerated DWI offenders, non-incarcerated DWI offenders, and criminals (convicted of offenses other than DWI), found that both alcohol and personality variables needed to be taken into account in order to distinguish these populations. Saltstone contends that there is substantial overlap between the DWI population (especially the incarcerated DWI offenders) and the criminal and alcohol populations.

SUMMARY

Although this chapter is not an exhaustive list of research in the area of profile differences between DWI offenders, alcoholics, and nonoffenders/nonalcoholics, the studies that we have presented here are representative of a significant portion of the research in this area and certainly do point to some of the common denominators that are characteristic of the DWI offender population. As was indicated in Chapter 2, the importance of this research lies in one's ability not only to understand this population more thoroughly, but also in being able to utilize this information for purposes of screening/assessment and treatment matching/planning.

Before concluding this section, however, it should be pointed out that in various attempts to define the DWI population, there are certain limitations to being able to accurately characterize this group of individuals. These limitations include those pointed out by Perrine (1990), in his description of the "Quick," the "Caught" and the "Dead," which suggests that not all drinking drivers necessarily are arrested or convicted, nor do they end up in screening or treatment programs. From personal communications with police officers, attorneys, and judges, we know of many instances in which drinking drivers are not arrested but are driven home (or worse yet, allowed to drive home while under the influence!), because of their social standing in the community, or because their wealth enables them to "buy" out of the arrest. In these situations, the charges are reduced to a nondrinking-driving offense, or dropped. It was outrageous situations like these, as well as increased drinking and driving-related fatalities, that resulted in Mothers Against Drunk Driving monitoring the courts and taking a stand against these injustices. Therefore, when looking at the social and demographic characteristics as discussed in this chapter, we must be cautious in the interpretation of these findings. As Perrine (1990) points out, it appears that we are certainly dealing with a skewed population when studying the population of convicted drinking drivers.

By combining the information presented in Chapter 2 and Chapter 3, the reader should have a fairly accurate picture of characteristic profiles of most DWI offenders and repeat offenders and the challenges that face the treatment field in attempting to devise treatment strategies that will be effective and meaningful to all clients.

Chapter 4

Assessment and Diagnostic Issues

The purpose of this chapter is to explore some of the difficulties inherent in the evaluation, assessment, and screening of DWI offenders. Therefore, this chapter will present an overview of some prior research in this area, and will also provide some recommendations based upon what has been discovered about assessment strategies with this population. The chapter that follows will provide the reader with an overview of various assessment tools that have been used, what the advantages and disadvantages are of each of these measures, and recommendations for how to devise a battery of measures that might be used.

As Fine, Scoles, and Mulligan (1975) state, "DWI offenders lack insight into the severity of their drinking problems and their lack of motivation to obtain treatment indicates that some form of compulsion (or compulsory program) will be required" (p. 424). Herein lies the problem of assessment strategies with DWI offenders. Basically, most DWI offenders are not willing participants in the evaluation process; therefore, the task of coming up with an accurate assessment of their status with regard to drinking behavior, drinking and driving behavior, and psychological status is very difficult to say the least.

Historically, DWI programs began to proliferate during the late 1960s and early 1970s when the National Highway Traffic Safety Administration (NHTSA) funded thirty-five Alcohol Safety Action Programs (ASAP). One of the charges of these ASAP programs was to determine what types of education and rehabilitation strategies would be most efficacious in educating or treating DWI offenders (Fitzpatrick, 1992). Along with these ASAP programs, there was a greater demand for evaluation and assessment of DWI offenders. These assessments were often requested by the courts, other branches of the judicial system, or were conducted by the ASAP programs as a means of determining who required more intensive treatment.

As DWI countermeasures programs were taking shape in most states, there was a demand for effective assessment tools that could be used with this population. Today, most states do require that convicted DWI offenders participate in some type of assessment and screening (see Chapter 6 on countermeasures programs). The goal of such screening is usually to determine which of those offenders might be at higher risk for recidivism and, therefore, these screenings have usually been linked to whether the DWI offender will be referred to specific types of education programs or treatment programs.

In theory, if one were to screen a DWI offender who presents with symptoms of alcoholism, then this offender might be more appropriate for alcoholism treatment or, at very least, a more intensive level of treatment. Unfortunately, what may be recommended in theory, is not what may take place in practice. For example, given the problems inherent with many of the screening tools, it was possible for many of these "at risk" DWI offenders to fall between the cracks of the assessment system and thereby escape detection. This could be accomplished merely by falsifying their responses to interview questions or to direct alcohol-problem types of questionnaires or screening measures. Some controversy exists as to whether mandated treatment is effective at all, and whether people should be coerced into treatment (Dunham and Mauss, 1982; Fagan and Fagan, 1982). In view of these concerns, therefore, it is important that screening programs or those performing assessments use rational decision-making methods (Miller, Whitney, and Washousky, 1984).

PROBLEMS WITH CURRENT MEASURES

Without getting into too many specifics about any particular measure or screening test, (these will be covered in the following chapter), there have been several problems noted with many of the assessment tools currently being utilized. Many of these screening measures have proven to be ineffective with DWI offenders for many reasons. For example, DWI offenders may not be truthful in their responses to the test or the test or questionnaire may not detect offenders who have problems other than those that are alcohol-related, assuming they were honest on the screening measure (Nochajski et al., 1993). Another problem often encountered in the screening process is one of "test sensitivity" versus "test specificity." Sensitivity refers to the concept that an individual who manifests a particular condition will successfully be identified by the measure he or she has taken. In other words, if a self-admitted alcoholic were to take XYZ Alcoholism Screening scale, then if this scale is indeed "sensitive" it will identify this individual as an alcoholic. If he or she were to be undetected by the XYZ Alcoholism Screening Scale, then that would be referred to as a "false negative."

Test specificity refers to the ability of the assessment instrument to correctly classify those individuals not having that condition. Therefore, if Mrs. Jones is a member of a nonalcoholic control group and takes the XYZ Alcoholism Screening Scale, then if this scale indeed possesses specificity, Mrs. Jones will not test as being an alcoholic. If she *were* to test as being an alcoholic, then she would be considered a false positive. Naturally, the goal of any of these measures is to limit the number of both false positives and false negatives.

Without straying too far from our purpose, the goal of any measure is to be both reliable and valid. A test is considered to be reliable when the results can be duplicated over and over again, i.e., the test results are considered to be consistent. A test is considered to be valid when it is true to its purpose, i.e., an alcoholism-screening measure is capable of detecting alcoholism. Face validity, for example, refers to the concept that the test items correspond to what it is measuring. Therefore, a screening test for, say, airline pilots, will have items which pertain to flying planes, e.g., weather, navigation, instrument readings, etc.

The issue of test selectivity versus sensitivity is important in terms of how test developers will determine cutoff scores. For example, the Michigan Alcoholism Screening Test (Selzer, 1971) utilizes a cutoff score of five (which is considered a borderline score) and a cutoff of six (which is considered to be suggestive of alcoholism). Based upon the normative data on this scale, if one were to increase or decrease these cutoffs it would result in changes in sensitivity and specificity. For example, if the cutoff of a score of 6 were increased to 8, then it is hypothesized that there would be less sensitivity, i.e., those with the condition are NOT detected, thereby resulting in more false negatives. Conversely, if the cutoff score of 6 were decreased to 3, then the specificity would be significantly reduced, thereby resulting in more false positives. Debate often occurs over whether different cutoff scores should be utilized with DWI offenders. On the MAST, for example, it has been suggested that various cutoff scores be utilized, especially given the high rates of false negatives that are often found when testing criminal justice populations and DWI offenders. Brown (1980) had suggested that a cutoff score of 8 be utilized when screening DWI offenders, presumably in order to reduce the number of false positives. In this study, the mean MAST score for the 70 male DWI offenders was 11.87 (SD = 9.86). The mean score for a control group of non-DWI licensed drivers was 1.60 (SD = 1.27).

Another issue with current measures utilized with DWI offenders is their use of non-obvious versus obvious items. For example, the MAST (Selzer, 1971) has been widely used as a screening measure for clinical settings, such as hospitals, rehabilitation centers, and outpatient clinics, and it has also been used to detect the presence or absence of alcoholism in DWI offenders. In looking at the items of the MAST, one can easily discern that these are "obvious items." For example, "Do you ever feel guilty about things done while drinking?" or "Has your physician ever told you that you should cut down on drinking?" are obvious in what they are asking and looking for. Respondents are told to answer "Yes" or "No" to these MAST items. Naturally, someone who is trying to escape detection on the MAST can simply answer "No." False responses to obvious alcohol-problem items is a problem for screening tools such as the MAST, the Mortimer-Filkins, and the Alcohol Use Inventory, as well as several other measures that rely on a more direct approach. Indeed, a misclassification rate as high as 58 percent has been reported on the MAST by Zung and Ross (1980).

Nonobvious measures rely mostly on prior research to determine those characteristics or traits of the population being studied, in order to arrive at a determination of whether that individual matches the profile of individuals with that condition or not. Such would be the case with something like the MacAndrews Alcoholism Scale of the Minnesota Multiphasic Personality Inventory. The MAC scale consists of fifty-four items, which have been derived from a factor analytic method. This refers to a statistical procedure by which items that were able to discriminate between self-admitted alcoholics and nonalcoholics were included among the fifty-four items of the MAC scale. What is interesting about these items is that they have very little relevance, if any, to alcoholism or drinking behaviors. For example, items such as "I like to cook" or "I like to read newspaper articles about crime" are among some of the MAC items. When the MacAndrews scale was developed, it was administered to many self-admitted alcoholics and it was determined that they would respond to questions such as these in a particular direction (all MMPI items are answered "True" or "False"). Some say that the MAC scale does not measure alcoholism per se, but perhaps a predilection toward alcoholism. Others, however, criticize the MAC scale as measuring neither and instead find the MAC to be sensitive to sensation-seeking behavior as well as a predilection to other addictions, such as smoking or food addictions, thereby claiming that the MAC lacks sensitivity. A study by Otto, Lang, and Megargee (1988) indicates that it is quite possible for alcoholics to escape detection with the MMPI when they were asked to dissimulate or purposely produce a false profile. (The authors of this research even cite "driving under the influence screenings" [p. 453] as one of the conditions under which one might seek to avoid detection.) Of the six alcoholism scales studied in this research, the MAC scale "appeared to be the best alcoholism scale under dissimulation conditions in that it was the only one that differentiated the medical patients and alcoholic profiles at a better-than-chance rate" (p. 456).

SOLUTIONS TO THE SCREENING DILEMMA

Basically two trends, therefore, have emerged in the assessment/ screening literature which warrant mention and explanation. The first trend points to the use of the "multitrait-multimethod matrix" approach that was first advocated by Campbell and Fiske (1959). In their landmark study, which involved performing a meta-analysis of several assessment studies, these researchers found that no one assessment tool was effective in making an accurate assessment. Instead, they determined that using a multimethod approach was the most efficacious and far superior to assessment based upon clinical interview alone. Therefore, in assessing DWI offenders it is recom-

mended that more than one assessment strategy and/or measure be utilized in making any screening determination. Here, for example, both
obvious and nonobvious measures might be used in conjunction with
one another and also in conjunction with the clinical interview or intake information that would be gathered in a face-to-face interview.
The second trend in the screening field, therefore, has been to combine
both obvious and nonobvious test items. Such would be the case with the
Substance Abuse Subtle Screening Inventory-III (SASSI) (Miller, 1994)
and the Research Institute on Addictions Self-Inventory (RIASI)
(Nochajski and Miller, 1995). The problem with the SASSI was that
it was not developed specifically for DWI offenders but rather can be
utilized with a variety of individuals who may manifest alcohol or
substance abuse problems. The RIASI was developed on a population of convicted DWI offenders and assesses "a variety of characteristics that have been found to highly correlate with alcohol or drug
problems" (p. 2).

There are also controversies regarding whether an effective screening measure for DWI offenders in fact exists. Popkin and colleagues
(1988) reviewed several DWI screening instruments and deemed that
none were suitable for implementation in their present state. For example, given the obvious nature of the MAST items in determining
alcohol problems, the MAST is especially susceptible to false response by those who wish to avoid detection. The problem with the
Mortimer-Filkins is that it is lengthy to administer (taking an hour or
more) and the scoring takes additional time and skill to properly
score and interpret. The RIASI was developed taking into account
many of the aforementioned problems noted in earlier screening
measures (the RIASI will be discussed in greater detail in Chapter 5
along with some of the other measures mentioned in this chapter).

As was alluded to earlier, many DWI screening programs have
adopted a "matrix" system of treatment referral decision making. An
example of the matrix system had been devised and advocated by
Dowling and McCartt (1990), utilizing measures or observations
such as scores from the MAST, Mortimer Filkins, blood alcohol content at the time of arrest, or showing up intoxicated at the screening
session. A number of screening programs will often use a combination
of such indicators to determine who should be referred for further
treatment. For example, in New Jersey, first offenders are referred to a
sixteen-week educationally oriented program for further assessment if

they score above 17 on a direct alcohol behavior/problem-type questionnaire, if they had a blood alcohol level over .20g/dl at the time of the DWI arrest, if they have had any prior, related convictions (e.g., refusal to submit to a chemical breath test), or if there is a combination of other indicators (e.g., a BAC of .15g/dl to .19g/dl and a high score on the questionnaire). These matrix systems are advantageous in that they use a multitrait, multimethod approach, which had been advocated by Campbell and Fiske (1959); however, this approach also has certain limitations. For example, studies have pointed to the limited utility of blood alcohol content in making treatment determinations (Wieczorek, Miller, and Nochajski, 1992; see Chapter 5 for a more in-depth discussion of these limitations). Also, one cannot assume that measures obtained on the obvious or direct alcohol measures are necessarily valid indicators of the offender's present drinking status. In a study conducted by Kruzich and colleagues (1986) 490 soldiers who were convicted of DWI offenses were assessed utilizing a multimethod approach that included BAC levels, commanding officer's ratings of the soldier, blood hematology and chemistry profiles, the MacAndrews and F scales of the MMPI, the Vaillant Alcoholism questionnaire, and the Mortimer-Filkins questionnaire. Based upon these various measures, the authors concluded that 88 percent of these DWI offenders could be identified as warranting a diagnosis of alcohol abuse or alcohol dependence. Almost half of this 88 percent were diagnosable as being alcohol dependent according to DSM-III-R st criteria. What was noteworthy in this study was the multiple-regression analysis, which revealed that among the variables most powerful in classifying these soldiers according to diagnosis were: the Vaillant Alcoholism questionnaire, BAC at the time of the DWI arrest, the Mortimer-Filkins questionnaire, GGT levels, the commanding officer's appraisal score, years of education, years of military service, blood HCT levels, the MacAndrews Scale scores, and prior alcohol-related arrests/treatment. In another somewhat similar study (Babor, Kranzler, and Lauerman, 1989), which was not conducted with DWI offenders, but which sought to provide an early screening of alcohol problems, several measures were utilized. These measures included a diagnostic interview, a physical exam with laboratory blood and chem profiles, a personality measure, and the MAST and MacAndrews scales. The findings of this study suggested that the alcohol-specific measures were best at identifying advanced cases of alcohol dependence (i.e., those requiring inpatient treatment) and were not very good at distinguishing female problem drinkers. The study also concluded that when the measures were used in combination with one another, accurate assessment improved. In other words, no single measure or procedure was suitable for early identification of harmful drinkers. These results also have important implications for the early screening and detection of first offenders who may be in the early phases of a substance-dependence disorder.

Another assessment strategy that has been utilized in some screening measures is to employ a "lie" scale or some other measure of test response distortion or defensiveness. This would be the case with a measure such as the MMPI and the MMPI-2, which contain several validity scales (e.g., L, F, and K validity scales, the subtle-obvious scales) and the SASSI-2 and SASSI-3, which contain a defensiveness scale. It is therefore possible to ascertain, if someone were to score low on particular alcohol or drug scales, whether that person may have been approaching the inventory in a defensive manner or in such a way as to downplay problems. This information can be useful in the screening process and counselors can then question clients on why they responded in the way they did and try to ascertain what they may be trying to hide. In a study using the MMPI-2 to compare first time DWI offenders and multiple offenders with a nonoffender group, it was found that both DWI offender groups had higher elevations on the validity scales, suggestive of defensive responding. Both DWI groups had also scored significantly higher on the MAC-R (Revised) scale; however, the first offenders scored higher than the multiple offenders ($M = 24.05$ versus $M = 22.49$). The first offenders had just reached the cutoff score (24), which is considered suggestive of an alcoholism propensity, while the multiple offenders fell below this suggested cutoff (Cavaiola, Wolf, and Lavender, 1999). Therefore, it becomes imperative to take validity measures into account when interpreting any scores on these inventories.

CONCLUSIONS

In summarizing the information covered in this chapter, it becomes obvious that assessment and screening of DWI offenders is no easy task, and that there are many problems and complexities involved in performing an accurate assessment or in obtaining accurate information. Several strategies have been devised for trying to manage some of the problems that have been pointed out; however, each of these strategies also have various advantages and disadvantages. For example, although a matrix system is advised as perhaps being one of the best approaches to come up with an accurate assessment, the dilemma becomes which measures and cutoff scores to utilize or include in the matrix system. We recommend that any measures utilized employ both obvious and nonobvious indicators or alcohol/substance use disorders and that other observations be utilized as well, such as blood alcohol content at time of arrest, number of arrests (both drinking and nondrinking related offenses, such as careless driving), any prior history of treatment or twelve-step involvement, police reports at the time of the DWI arrest, familial history, as well as any psychiatric history all become grist for the assessment mill. Obviously, counselors will often not have all this information at their disposal when making a treatment referral decision, nor can the counselor count on the accuracy of self-report with regards to much of this information (e.g., family history). Yet the task of screening DWI offenders fairly and accurately is not an impossible task. The recent development of the RIASI holds much promise in improving counselor accuracy in making assessments. The SASSI-3 is also a screening instrument that is deserving of further research exploration with the DWI population. These assessment tools will be discussed in more detail in the following chapter.

It is important that counselors not become frustrated by the complexities and administration time for some of the asessment measures that will be presented in the following chapter. What is essential to remember is that using a variety of assessment measures along with clinical judgment is superior to clinical judgment alone in making a screening and referral decision. All too often, we have heard counselors say, "I can spot an alcoholic a mile away." Although clinical intuition is an important tool to have at your disposal, it is best and ethically more sound to have several tools at your disposal, not just intuition alone. As the saying goes, "When the only tool you have is a hammer, everything looks like a nail."

Fortunately, a great deal of research is being conducted that will help counselors in being able to discern which are the most reliable and valid tools to use with this population. Much of this research has been devoted to finding which measures and cutoff scores are best at predicting recidivism. Another area of research has been devoted to using assessment tools for treatment matching purposes. Both of these areas represent a common ground where the research and the treatment fields can unite in the goal of reducing DWI recidivism.

Chapter 5

Assessment and Diagnostic Measures and Tools

This chapter is intended to provide a brief overview of some of the current assessment and screening instruments that have been utilized with the DWI population, and in some instances with criminal justice and alcoholic populations, for purposes of differential diagnosis. As you will see, each of the following measures has its advantages and disadvantages and each appears to be useful depending on the screening situation. The latter part of this chapter includes some suggestions for conducting a biopsychosocial interview with DWI offenders, along with some points that are important to look for when making an assessment. The various types of screening instruments to be discussed will be divided into the following categories: structured interview format, direct measures, and indirect measures.

STRUCTURED INTERVIEW FORMAT

Various assessment settings may use a standardized structured interview as part of their evaluation. These structured interviews differ from traditional intake formats or databases in that they contain specific questions which can then be used with a list of criteria, such as the DSM-IV, in order to determine if the individual being screened meets the criteria for that particular disorder. Or, in some instances, the questions of the structured interview provide an in-depth picture of the client's behavior (e.g., with regards to alcohol or drug use). The overall advantages of structured interviews is that they provide a standardized format by which all clients can be asked the same questions, in the same sequence, thereby providing the counselor with comparable information and data. It does not leave to chance that certain questions will be omitted or will not be asked due to forgetfulness. The other main advantage is that unlike a database or biopsychosocial intake form, which would differ, naturally, from agency to agency, the use of a structured interview allows for more uniformity. Although the main advantage of uniformity may have more research implications than it does clinical implications, it can be an advantage for the counselors to compare their results with prior research studies. The other advantage of the interviews being reviewed is that they provide the counselor with some interesting techniques for gaining a better picture of the client. For example, the Comprehensive Drinker Profile's use of the "card sort" technique (see below), or the Timeline Follow-Back, which makes use of several memory aids to assist the client in recalling what they may have had to drink on specific days or occasions. The common disadvantages of the structured interviews usually focus on the time it takes to interview the client and to score and/or interpret the information obtained.

The following is a partial list of some of the current structured interviews that have been utilized in DWI and Substance Use Disorder research and in clinical settings with these populations. Wherever possible, we have attempted to either list the name, address, and phone number of the publisher or to provide a reference for obtaining more information about that particular interview.

Diagnostic Interview Schedule (Robins et al., 1982)

The DIS is a structured interview that has been used extensively in epidemiological research, clinical research in psychopathology, and for diagnostic evaluations. The DIS is simple to administer, in that it requires very little decision making on the part of the interviewer, who merely reads off a series of questions to the client in a structured format. Each of these questions corresponds to an axis diagnostic category, which includes the substance-use disorders. The advantage of the DIS is that it is easily administered and it takes approximately forty-five minutes to complete with the client. The disadvantage of this type of structured interview with DWI offenders would be the possibility of false responding, since the questions pertaining to substance-use disorders are easily discernible and can be easily faked. As indicated earlier, the DIS is used most often in research settings, although it can be used clinically as well.

Structured Clinical Interview for DSM-III-R (SCID) (Spitzer et al., 1990) Published by: American Psychiatric Press, 1400 K Street, Washington, DC 20005. Phone: 1-800-368-5777

Unlike the DIS, the SCID requires that the person conducting the interview have clinical experience and sound clinical judgment for decision-making purposes regarding interpretation of the meaning of the client's responses. Each section of the SCID corresponds to one of the major diagnostic categories of the DSM-III-R and begins with a few "probe" questions. If the client reveals no information suggestive of a particular disorder on these probe questions, the interviewer skips to the next section. With regard to DWI offenders, the sections corresponding to the substance-use disorders of the DSM-III-R would be utilized. Again, the advantage of the SCID is that it is designed to utilize the objective criteria of the DSM to render a diagnosis. The SCID also can yield information pertaining to the severity of a particular symptom, however, its disadvantages lie in its being time-consuming, and the effectiveness may be determined by the skill and clinical experience of the interviewer. There also have been studies which have shown that the age, gender, and race of the interviewer and client may affect information that is disclosed during the interview (Buros, 1988).

Addiction Severity Index (ASI) (McLellan et al., 1992)

The ASI also falls within the framework of a structured clinical interview; however, the ASI obviously assesses substance-use disorders only. The ASI can be administered by a technician in about sixty minutes and assesses seven problem areas that are consequential to substance abuse: medical status, employment and support, drug use, alcohol use, legal status, family and social status, and psychological status. The questions are about both recent and lifetime use and events related to the use of drugs and alcohol. The ASI yields two sets of scores: severity ratings (which are subjective ratings of the client's need for treatment) and composite scores (which essentially is a measure of problem severity during the past thirty days). Unlike the DIS and SCID, which have been used extensively in clinical research, the

ASI is primarily used to identify problem areas for treatment planning and outcome evaluation (Dodgen and Shea, 1997). The ASI provides an excellent overall picture of the client's drinking/drug use and problems that have resulted from such use. The main disadvantage of the ASI when utilized with the DWI population is given the obvious nature of the items, clients can falsify their responses.

Comprehensive Drinker Profile (CDP) (Marlatt and Miller, 1984) Published by: Psychological Assessment Resources Inc. P.O. Box 998 Odessa, FL 33556. Phone: 813-968-3003

The CDP is also a structured interview that covers many areas related to the client's drinking behavior. The CDP was designed for individuals who are entering treatment programs, as it provides a means of assessing the nature and severity of their drinking and is therefore helpful in the treatment planning process. The CDP is unique in that it utilizes a "card sort" modality for several of the subsections. For example, under "Beverage Preferences" the client would be given a group of cards with the names of various alcoholic beverages (e.g., beer or ale, wine, scotch, vodka, rum, liqueurs or cordials, brandy, sparkling wines, etc.). The client would then be asked to rank-order their preferences for these beverages. In another card sort item, the client is given a group of cards containing the names of drinking settings (e.g., a bar or tavern, restaurant, social clubs, outdoors, home, etc.). They would then be asked to rank-order their estimated frequency for drinking in these particular settings. The CDP begins by collecting basic demographic information and then goes on to explore drinking history. Under this section, there are questions pertaining to the development of the drinking problem, present drinking pattern, a drinking pattern chart, quantity/frequency summary, episodic pattern chart, pattern history, alcohol-related life problems (here the questions of the MAST are orally presented), and relevant medical history. This section also explores past and present drug use (both prescribed and illicit drugs).The third section of the CDP contains questions pertaining to motivational information, such as reasons for drinking, effects of drinking, other life problems (which includes another card-sort task, in which a list of current problems related to drinking are indicated, one per card—e.g., aggression or fighting, fatigue or tiredness, financial problems and health problems, suicidal thoughts, and work problems).

There are also subsections which assess the client's motivation for treatment and a self-rating of drinker type—for example, "Total Abstainer," "Light Social (Nonproblem) Drinker," "Moderate Social (Nonproblem) Drinker," "Heavy Social (Nonproblem) Drinker," "Problem Drinker," and "Alcoholic."

The main advantage of the CDP is its ability to provide the counselor with a thorough look at the person's drinking behavior, the types of settings they may drink in, the psychological/emotional effects of drinking that the drinker experiences, and so on. The MAST provides a summary of drinking-related problems and can be scored to determine whether the person's drinking-problem behavior is indicative of alcoholism. The CDP also provides information pertaining to how the clients view their drinking and their motivation for treatment. The disadvantages of the CDP are the length of time to administer the interview (as it is estimated to take anywhere from one to two hours), the length of time to score those items that are able to be scored (e.g., MAST items, the Quantity-Frequency Summary Data), and then to interpret the overall CDP results. As with the other structured interviews, the possibility of false responding with the DWI offender population is a disadvantage. The use of the card sort, however, is helpful in providing somewhat of a "forced-choice" type of format, which induces the client to respond, rather than saying simply that they do not drink anymore or other evasions.

Timeline Follow Back (TLFB) (Sobell and Sobell, 1992; Sobell, Toneatto, and Sobell, 1994)

The TLFB is included in this section on structured interview procedures, although it can be self-administered in a questionnaire-type format. It essentially is a method of drinking estimation that attempts to gain information regarding the client's daily drinking behavior by the use of various memory aids. These memory aids include:

1. A standard daily calendar
2. Key dates (such as birthdays, holidays)
3. A standard drink conversion chart, which aids the client in reporting their drinking in terms of standard drinks
4. "Black" and "white" days (here referring to significant periods of heavy or light drinking)

5. Discrete events and anchor points (such as arrests, illnesses, loss of employment)
6. Boundary procedures (e.g., establishing highest and lowest drinking periods)
7. Exaggeration technique (a technique used to accurately identify a more precise estimation of the number of drinks, for example, "You said you drank a lot of beer. Is a lot five or fifty?")

The advantages of the TLFB are that it can be administered rather briefly—usually in thirty minutes or less—and that it provides a detailed estimation of the client's drinking behavior, which then allows for an analysis of patterns such as antecedents to drinking, consequences, and relapse triggers. Concurrent validity has been established in comparing the TLFB to the Alcohol Dependency Scale and the Short Michigan Alcoholism Screening Test, which revealed significant correlations for higher levels of overall consumption. The TLFB also has high test-retest reliability across multiple populations of drinkers (Sobell, Toneatto, and Sobell, 1994). The main disadvantage of the TLFB, as with other interview techniques, is that accuracy cannot be expected from clients who are interested in denying their drinking history or avoiding self-disclosure. Therefore, the utility of the TLFB will naturally depend on how willing the client is to admit to alcohol consumption.

QUESTIONNAIRES AND INVENTORIES

As can be seen from scanning Chapters 2 and 3 on personality and profile studies with DWI offenders, the vast majority of research in this area has utilized various types of questionnaires and inventories to assess the DWI offender population. These types of measures provide the advantages of being self-administered, which can save both time and expense; they are also standardized, which ensures consistency in administration and scoring. For many of these measures, reliability and validity have been established. The disadvantages of some of the measures that will be discussed lie in the obviousness of the test items. An obvious test item, for example, "Has your spouse or family ever complained about your drinking?" can easily be "faked" by someone who is avoiding detection, as could be the case with most mandated clients. Therefore, some of the question-naires and inventories to be discussed have utilized two strategies. The first is to provide obvious items, but then to provide test-taking attitude scales, which are designed to detect either a "fake good" (i.e., someone who is trying to portray himself or herself in a more favorable light, usually by means of non-self-disclosure and/or defensive responding) or "fake bad" (i.e., someone who is trying to present himself or herself as being more pathological or distressed by endorsing a variety of test items). The Minnesota Multiphasic Personality Inventory (Hathaway and McKinley, 1989) is an example of an inventory that contains scales which determine test-taking attitudes. The second strategy for dealing with the problem of falsification is to provide nonobvious items. These nonobvious items are usually derived from the various profile studies that were discussed in Chapters 2 and 3. For example, nonobvious in-dicators of a predisposition toward DWI recidivism would include items pertaining to hostility, sensation-seeking, prior criminal history, or antiauthoritarian attitudes. The critiques of this approach point to the possibility of false positives (i.e., that a person manifesting these traits may not necessarily be a consistent drinking driver). To counter this ar-gument, however, the proponents of nonobvious measures would point to the fact that DWI recidivism is probably best predicted by both a cer-tain style of drinking behavior combined with several demographic and personality measures. This provides a better means to differentiate the individual who is more likely to commit a subsequent DWI offense ver-sus the person who perhaps was at a celebration of some sort and had too much to drink on that occasion. The key differentiating terms are "pro-file" (referring to demographic and personality characteristics), and "pattern" (referring to a particular drinking or drug-using style). The fol-lowing are some of the measures currently being used clinically as well as in research studies with DWI offenders.

Michigan Alcoholism Screening Test (MAST) (Selzer, 1971)

The MAST is probably the most widely used alcohol screening measure. It contains twenty-five weighted, "Yes-No" response format questions pertaining to drinking habits, alcohol abuse/dependence, symptoms, and other drinking-related problems. The MAST takes about five to ten minutes to complete and can be administered in a struc-tured interview format or the respondent can answer the items in pencil-and-paper format. If the latter format is utilized, it is usually preferable to review the test items with the respondent for sake of clarity. The content of the questions tends to relate to adverse consequences associated with drinking (e.g., medical, legal, family, and social problems) and some items also reflect involvement with medical or social service agencies as a result of drinking (e.g., "Have you ever been in a hospital because of drinking?" "Have you ever gone to anyone for help about your drinking?" or "Have you ever been a patient in a psychiatric hospital or on a psychiatric ward of a general hospital where drinking was part of the problem?"). Scoring is quick and easy, with each question being given a weighted score of 0, 1, 2, or 5. For example, "Have you ever gotten into fights when drinking?" are given a weighted score of 1 if answered affirmatively, while "Have you ever attended a meeting of Alcoholics Anonymous?" or "Have you ever had delirium tremens (DTs), severe shaking, heard voices, or seen things that weren't there after drinking?" is given a weighted score of 5 if answered affirmatively. Questions such as "Has drinking ever created problems with you and your spouse?" or "Have you ever lost a job because of drinking?" are given a weighted score of 2. Selzer (1971) indicates that scores of 3 or less are considered nonindicative of alcoholism, while scores of 4 are "suggestive of alcoholism" (or borderline) and scores of 5 and above are considered "indicative of alcoholism" or more definitive in indicating alcohol dependence. The wording of the MAST questions is such that it assesses lifetime experiences with alcohol. The MAST does not focus on the quantity of alcohol an individual consumes nor frequency of drinking. Neither does the MAST focus on any other concomitant drug use. The normative data on the MAST was conducted with several different groups: 103 control subjects, 116 hospitalized alcoholics, 99 DWI offenders, 110 individuals arrested for drunk and disorderly behavior, and 98 high-risk drivers who had their licenses revoked for excessive accidents and moving violations. These participants were generally Caucasian males between the ages of twenty-five and forty-four years old. There is also a brief version of the MAST (Selzer, Vinokur, and van Rooijen, 1975) that consists of thirteen of the original twenty-five items.

Criticisms of the MAST have pointed to several factors. For example, the MAST has been criticized by some women's groups because the normative studies were done with males. Recovering alcoholics have also been critical of the MAST because there is no way to differentiate between those who are active alcoholics and those who are in recovery, because the MAST does not distinguish between past and present drinking behavior (Marion et al., 1996). Nochajski and colleagues (1995) point out that MAST tends to focus on symptoms and factors that are associated with late-stage alcohol dependence, which may make the MAST inappropriate for young DWI offenders, who tend to manifest less severe problems with alcohol. Another criticism of the MAST is that it is easy for respondents to escape detection if they choose to do so, merely by responding negatively to all the questions. Therefore, if you have DWI offenders who are set on not disclosing anything about their drinking behavior, they would most likely end up with a score of 2, since the only question they probably would answer affirmatively is "Have you ever been arrested for drunk driving after drinking?" It is interesting that this particular item would yield a score of two (if answered affirmatively), regardless of whether the person taking the test has been arrested for one DWI offense or multiple offenses. Ostensibly, a person who had refused the breathalyzer might deny having been arrested altogether and could receive a total MAST score of 0. In comparing a group of first time DWI offenders with a group of multiple offenders and a comparison group of nonoffenders, slight but significant differences were found on the MAST, in the expected direction, with the control group scoring the lowest (M = 3.36), followed by the first offenders (M = 4.74), with the highest MAST scores being obtained by the multiple offenders (M = 5.54). In comparing five different standardized alcohol screening measures, Lapham and colleagues (1995) found that the MAST had identified the highest percentage of the 2,317 first-time DWI offenders as alcoholic, which raises the issue of false positives. Jacobson (1983) and Moore (1972) have indicated that the MAST is likely to yield a high rate of false positives. Vingilis (1983), in criticizing this aspect of the MAST, stated, "a first time DWI offender, feeling badly about his drinking, and endorsing none of the other questions, could obtain a score of 5." This also makes a strong case for utilizing the MAST in conjunction with a thorough clinical interview and other measures.

Mortimer-Filkins Questionnaire (Mortimer, Filkins, and Lower, 1971). Available through the National Highway Traffic Safety Administration, Traffic Safety Programs, Office of Traffic Injury Control Programs (NTS-11), 400 Seventh Street, NW, Washington, DC, 20590. The NHTSA can also be accessed through their Web site at <nhtsa.dot.gov>. A self-instructional guide is available, which walks the counselor through the steps of learning to use the Mortimer-Filkins, titled: *Procedures for Identifying Problem Drinkers (PIPD): A Screening and Assessment Package for Courts and Treatment Agencies: A Self-Instructional Guide (DOT HS 806-988).*

Unlike the majority of measures surveyed in this chapter, the Mortimer-Filkins questionnaire was developed specifically with the DWI population in mind. The Mortimer-Filkins has also been used widely in research studies, however, because of the length of time for administration (forty-five to ninety minutes depending on whether the questionnaire and interview are given separately or in conjunction with one another), it has not enjoyed the same degree of popularity in clinical settings as some of the other measures discussed in this chapter. The scoring procedure is somewhat complicated at first; however, once counselors become familiar with the scoring system, it is not as difficult to score. Another drawback of the Mortimer-Filkins is that it does not contain validity scales to ascertain whether the test taker may be faking "good" or "bad." The instrument has been normed on alcoholic inpatients, alcoholic outpatients, incarcerated offenders, and a heterogeneous control sample.

The questionnaire portion of the Mortimer-Filkins consists of fifty-eight items (which are responded to in "True-False," "Yes-No," and short answer format). It takes about fifteen minutes for the client to fill out, and is self-administered. The items of the questionnaire portion naturally include questions related to drinking problems such as: "How many drinks can you handle and still drive well?" "Does drinking help you to make friends?" "I have had periods in which I carried on activities without knowing later what I was doing." "Does drinking help you to work better?" and "Drinking seems to ease personal problems." The questionnaire also includes items that make inquiry into family and marital problems (e.g., "My home life is as happy as it should be" or "Are your relatives upset with the way you live?"); recent stress (e.g., "Have you recently undergone a great stress such as something concerning your job, your health, your finances, your family or a loved one?"); abnormal problems (e.g., "Do you feel you have abnormal problems?" "I often feel as if I am not myself"); sadness or depression (e.g., "Are you often sad or down in the dumps?" "I wish I could be as happy as others seem to be"); general dissatisfaction, (e.g., "I am satisfied with the way I live," "My daily life is full of things that keep me interested" or "My friends are much happier than I am"); sleeping problems, (e.g., "I have trouble sleeping" or "I am often afraid I will not be able to sleep"); worry or fear (e.g., "Do you have a lot of worries?" or "Do you often feel afraid to face the future?"); boredom (e.g., "Are you often bored and restless?"); resentment, (e.g., "Do you think that your creditors are much too quick to bother you about payments?" or "I wish people would stop telling me how to live my life"); and inability to cope (e.g., "Are you bothered by nervousness [irritable, fidgety or tense]?" or "I sometimes feel that I am about to go to pieces.") Each of these questions are scored depending on the direction they are answered in and this score is then added to the interview score. Scores of 16 and above on the questionnaire portion of the Mortimer-Filkins are considered to be indicative of "problem drinkers," scores of 12 to 15 are considered to be indicative of "potential problem drinkers" and scores of 11 and below are considered to be indicative of "social drinkers;" however, counselors administering the test are cautioned that a low score (e.g., a zero, 3 or 4), along with a high blood alcohol content at the time of the arrest, could be indicative of someone who either falsified their responses or misunderstood the questions. What is noteworthy on the questionnaire portion is that not all the questions obviously pertain to drinking. Presumably based upon prior research, the Mortimer-Filkins also measures "neurotic attitudes . . . and the emotional and behavioral profile of the problem drinker" (pp. II-13-14). The PIPD manual goes on to state, "Problem drinkers are more likely than most people to:

- be isolated, living alone and possibly divorced or separated
- (if married) be having marital problems, including threats of separation or divorce
- be having problems with other family members, especially parents or children
- have a history of alcoholism in the family, especially near relatives

- have undergone great stress recently, such as a death of someone close, or crises in health, work, finances, or family life
- have undergone stress for a continued period without breaks or
  vacations
- feel that their problems are abnormal and to feel anxious, worried, depressed and overwhelmed by the demands of society
- feel persecuted and unfairly treated by others
- feel guilty, sinful and immoral because of their failures
- be unable to make enough income to meet basic needs
- be heavy smokers and to use other drugs to counter the effects
  of alcohol
- have had their driving license revoked, suspended or limited for
  motor vehicle violations
- have been previously arrested, often for drinking-related offenses
- sleep poorly, and perspire heavily in their sleep
- feel that drinking helps them to ease their problems and be
  more like other people, and to help them make friends and get
  started in doing things
- have asked for help for these problems, especially from community social service agencies" (Mortimer and Filkins, 1986,
  pp. II-13-14)

Some of the aforementioned items constitute a neuroticism scale
that measures general maladjustment, which is thought to correlate
with individuals who receive DWI offenses. The questions that make
up the neuroticism scale are less transparent than the drinking problem
portion of the questionnaire. Overall, the Mortimer-Filkins is considered to be less obvious than the MAST (Miller and Windle, 1990).

The interview portion of the Mortimer-Filkins can take anywhere
from thirty to forty-five minutes. Naturally, the more experienced the
interviewer, the quicker the interview can be completed. The interview portion consists of sixty-nine main questions, some of which
have additional items. Only fifty-two items are scored, however. (The
highest possible score on the interview therefore is $52 \times 4 = 208$.)
Scores of 40 and above are considered to be indicative of "problem
drinkers," while scores of 25 to 39 are considered to be indicative of
"potential problem drinkers" and scores of 24 and below are consid-

ered to be indicative of social drinkers. Again, as with the questionnaire portion, counselors are cautioned that if a client were to score low on the interview, while having other information suggesting problem drinking (e.g., a high blood alcohol level at time of arrest), then this could suggest a problem drinker who might have falsified or misunderstood the questions. The interview begins with some demographic questions but then moves on to questions regarding general health, health problems related to drinking, other criminal history, drinking habits and patterns, family and/or marital life, work/employment history, and social life.

Once the questionnaire and interview portions are scored, it is then recommended that the counselor review all "Critical Records," which would include BAC at the time of the arrest, the client's motor vehicle record, and criminal history. It is highly recommended that these records be reviewed whenever possible in order to check for other indicators of problem drinking (e.g., a high blood alcohol content at the time of the arrest) other motor vehicle arrests that might have been drinking related but were not charged as such (e.g., reckless driving, careless driving, etc.), and also to check the criminal record for alcohol-related convictions such as drunk and disorderly offenses or any offense involving out-of-control behavior. These items would then be reviewed along with the scores of the questionnaire and interview in making a recommendation for driver education, outpatient or inpatient alcoholism treatment, marriage or family counseling, or mental health counseling.

There have been various criticisms levied against the Mortimer-Filkins. As was alluded to earlier, some critics feel that the instrument is too lengthy and the scoring too complex. Others point to the tendency of the Mortimer-Filkins to focus on late-stage alcohol problems, which may not be appropriate indicators for younger problem drinkers who may not, for example, have experienced health problems related to drinking, marital problems, or perhaps even job problems in the same way that an older problem drinker might (Nochajski, Miller, and Wieczorek, 1992).

Also, there is the noted problem of asking direct questions regarding drinking behavior, which may lend to false responding. There were also some difficulties noted in the original cutoff scores recommended when the test was first developed. For example, cutoff scores of 56 and above were initially considered to be indicative of problem drinkers, while scores above 36 were considered indicative of potential problem drinkers. Miller, Whitney, and Washousky (1984) then recommended using cutoffs of 50+ for problem drinkers, 40 to 49 for "presumptive problem drinkers" and 39 and less as indicative of "social drinkers." In their research, when these cutoffs were utilized in conjunction with BACs, they were found to be the two best discriminating variables in whether the decision to recommend treatment was made. When the Mortimr- Filkins scores were high, there was no perceived need to require additional corroborating information with which to make a treatment referral decision. Others have noted that the problem with the Mortimer-Filkins arises when the client's score is "borderline," in which case it becomes difficult to make a determination whether a serious alcohol problem exists (Miller and Windle, 1990). In a more recent study (Anderson, Snow, and Wells-Parker, 2000), the Mortimer-Filkins was found to have predictive efficacy in being able to predict DWI recidivism when compared with several other measures (depending on what cutoff scores were utilized). This finding was counter to an earlier finding by Wendling and Kolody (1982), which indicated that the Mortimer-Filkins had poor predictive validity.

MacAndrews Alcoholism Scale (Revised) of the Minnesota Multiphasic Personality Inventory-2 (MAC-R) (MacAndrew, 1965, 1981) The MMPI-2 is available through National Computer Service, Inc., 5605 Green Circle Drive Minneapolis, Minnesota 55343-4400. Phone: 1-800-627-7271.

The MAC-R is an alcoholism scale derived from the MMPI. The MMPI-2 consists of 567 items, of which 49 items comprise the MAC-R. This scale was originally developed to be a subtle, or covert, scale designed to distinguish those with alcohol problems or an alcohol or addictive vulnerability from those without such a vulnerability. Therefore, although the original MAC scale included two direct or obvious items regarding drinking practices, these were eliminated from the MAC-R. Some of the items included are: "I have few or no pains." (True); "I was fond of excitement when I was young." (True); "I would like to wear expensive clothes." (True); "I pray several times a week." (True); "I used to keep a diary." (False); "I cannot keep my mind on one thing." (False); "I have never been in trouble with the law." (False). As one can readily see, none of these items relate directly to alcohol or other addictive behaviors. How then, does the MAC-R scale work?

When the MAC scale was originally developed, its purpose was to distinguish male alcoholics from nonalcoholic psychiatric patients. Two hundred alcoholics were compared to 200 psychiatric patients and forty-nine items (such as the ones mentioned above), were able to distinguish the alcoholic group from the nonalcoholic group. Each item answered in the direction noted above in parentheses is scored as 1. Scores above 28 are considered "strongly suggestive of substance abuse (including alcohol). Scores between 24 and 27 are considered suggestive of such abuse, but there will be many false positives. . . . Scores below 24 strongly contraindicate a substance abuse problem" (Graham, 1990, p. 153). It is strongly suggested, however, that the clinician seek other corroborating evidence of a substance abuse disorder and not just to make a determination based upon the MAC-R (Graham, 1990). Both reliability and validity have been established.

In one longitudinal study, (Hoffman, Loper, and Kammeier, 1974), MMPIs of alcoholic males who sought inpatient treatment were compared with MMPIs that they had taken some thirteen years earlier. The MAC scores of those men who required alcoholism treatment were compared to a group who did not become alcoholics and significant differences were noted in the MAC scores. Some research indicates that drug addicts will also score higher than psychiatric patients but not different from alcoholics (Fowler, 1975; Kranitz, 1972; Graham, 1978). In addition, Graham (1978) also found that pathological gamblers scored similarly to both drug addicts and alcoholics on the MAC. There are no contraindications of using the MAC with women and adolescents (Wisniewski, Glenwick, and Graham, 1985; Wolfson and Erbaugh, 1984); however, some studies indicate that African-American nonalcoholics, for some reason, tend to score in the positive range, thereby yielding false positives (Graham and Mayo, 1985; Walters, Greene and Jeffrey, 1984; Walters et al., 1983).

In studies with the DWI population, the MMPI and the MAC have shown to reveal particular patterns. For example, Sutker, Brantley, and Allain (1980) found there were four common profiles noted that were characterized by elevations on the depression, psychopathic deviance, and mania scales in various combinations with one another. It is not surprising to find that these elevations were similar to those that would be found in the general alcoholic population. Lapham, Skipper, and Simpson (1997) used four standardized measures (MAC, Alcohol Use Inventory [AUI], MAST, and Skinner's Trauma Scale [STS]) in assessing risk for recidivism in a group of 1,384 first offenders. After a four-year follow-up period, it was found that 21 percent had been rearrested for a DWI. The best predictors of recidivism were a MAC score of 23 or above, elevated scores on the AUI scales, young male status (age thirty or under) and a blood alcohol level at time of first arrest of 0.20 percent or above. In further analyzing the data utilizing a stratified analysis, the MAC was the single best predictor of recidivism. These researchers conclude that "screening programs for DWI offenders should carefully evaluate personality factors in making referral and sentencing recommendations" (p. 528).

In another study comparing first-time offenders with multiple DWI offenders and a nonoffender comparison group (Cavaiola, Wolf, and Lavender, 1999), significant differences were noted on the MAC-R, as well as on the depression, psychopathic deviance scale and K scale (which is a validity scale). Unexpectedly, the first offender group had scored the highest on the MAC-R (24.02) when compared to the repeat offenders (22.49) or the nonoffenders (19.98). Also unexpectedly, the nonoffenders had scored higher on the depression scale than either of the DWI groups. The two DWI offender groups had scored significantly higher on the psychopathic deviance scale. The significant elevation on the K scale suggests that the DWI offenders may have attempted to present themselves in a more favorable light, which could account for the unexpected differences noted. In spite of the attempt to "fake good," it appears that the MMPI and MAC-R scales were still able to differentiate the DWI offenders from the nonoffender group.

Although the MAC-R is thought to be less likely to be faked, given that it is an indirect measure, some studies suggest that respondents can fake or dissimulate, if motivated to do so. For example, Otto and colleagues (1988) performed a study in which they had a group of adult male alcoholic inpatients and a group of nonalcoholic medical patients take the MMPI twice. In the first condition, they were told to respond honestly; in the second condition, they were told to fake their responses. Under the first condition, the MAC and other alcoholism scales of the MMPI had a "hit rate" (i.e., success rate) of about 83 percent in correctly picking out the alcoholics from the nonalcoholic matched control group. However, under the "faking" or dissimulation condition the "hit rate" dropped to 65 percent. Although the MAC scale was found to be superior to the other alcoholism scales examined, there was still a high false negative rate under dissimulation conditions. What was noted, however, was that the MMPI dissimulation or validity scales were able to pick up on the false responding. Therefore, it was concluded that although alcoholics may be able to decrease apparent pathology when motivated to do so, and to avoid detection by MMPI dissimulation scales when they are faking good, it is rare that they can do both, which fortunately bodes well for the MMPI as a measure for screening alcoholics.

In a later study, however, Levenson and colleagues (1990) found high rates of "false positives" in a sample of 1,117 males. Of this sample, four groups were identified; (1) current drinkers reporting problems, (2) former drinkers reporting problems (3) current drinkers reporting no problems and (4) abstainers. When the MAC scores of these groups were compared, current or past drinkers with problems had mean MAC scores around the criterion level of 24 when compared to the nonproblem drinkers and abstainers. When compared with regard to arrest history, arrestees with drinking problems had the highest MAC scores (25.02), while nonarrestees without drinking problems had the lowest scores (21.95). However, both arrestees without drinking problems (23.19) and nonarrestees with drinking problems (23.42) had nearly identical mean MAC scores, which were near the alcoholism positive criterion level (24).

Among the nonarrestees without drinking problems, 36 percent had MAC scores of 24 or above, and 32 percent had MAC scores of 27 or above (of this group, the authors note that only two had reported any drug-use history). Therefore, the dilemma of the high false-positive rate was unexplained. Levenson and colleagues (1990) concluded that the MAC scale is not an alcoholism scale per se, but rather measures "cluster of personality traits" (p. 461), which might include rebelliousness and a pleasure-seeking, social orientation. Although these traits are not unlike those described as being central to the DWI offender population, the false-positive rate in this study suggests that there may be individuals who test positively on the MAC who are not alcoholic. Therefore, caution is advised in using the MAC-R and to utilize this scale in conjunction with other measures.

Before leaving this section on the MAC-R, it should be pointed out that there are several other alcoholism/addiction scales that are derived from the MMPI-2. The Addiction Acknowledgement Scale (AAS) and the Addiction Potentiality Scale (APS) are two such scales, which were added around the time that the original MMPI was revised. The AAS consists of those items built into the MMPI that relate to alcoholism or addiction symptoms (e.g., acknowledgement that addictive substances has played a negative role in one's life), while the Addiction Potentiality Scale is somewhat similar to the MAC-R in determining if the respondent's APS profile is similar to self-admitted alcoholics or addicts. A recent study (Rouse, Butcher, and Miller, 1999) indicates that when a group of substance abusers were compared with nonsubstance abusing psychotherapy clients, all three scales (AAS, APS, and MAC-R) were more elevated for the substance abusers. Discriminant analysis found that all three scales were effective screening instruments; however, the AAS was the best single predictor and a combination of the AAS and MAC-R provided the best overall discrimination.

One of the problems, however, with the MAC-R is that since it is contained within the MMPI-2, the use of this test is restricted to psychologists who have demonstrated training in administering and scoring this instrument. Although it is possible that the MAC-R questions could be taken out of the MMPI-2 and scored independently, the counselor would then not have available to them the wealth of other data that is derived from scoring the entire MMPI-2, such as the clinical scales and validity scales.

Research Institute on Addictions Self-Inventory (RIASI) (Nochajski and Miller, 1995; Nochajski et al., 1993). Information on the RIASI is available from the Research Institute on Addictions, 1021 Main Street, Buffalo, New York 14203. Phone: (716) 887-2575.

Unlike some of the other measures discussed in this chapter, and similar to the Mortimer Filkins, the RIASI was developed specifically for the purpose of screening the DWI population. The RIASI was developed specifically to address many of the problems inherent in some of the previously described measures. For example, the

RIASI addressed the problem of false responding by employing "non-obvious" indicators of alcoholism/substance use disorders. Also, the RIASI makes use of the prior research on personality factors common to those with alcohol and drug problems by including scales that measure traits such as sensation-seeking, hostility, and so on. One of the other advantages of the RIASI is that it is easily administered and has a simple scoring procedure. Currently there are both Spanish and English versions.

The current version of the RIASI, consists of fifty-two items that assess a variety of "proximal" (e.g., current alcohol consumption, beliefs about alcohol, preoccupation with drinking, and family history of alcohol or drug problems) and "distal" characteristics (e.g., sensation-seeking, hostility, depression, anxiety, and interpersonal competence) that are highly correlated with alcohol and drug problems (Nochajski, Walter, and Wieczorek, 1997). A cutoff score of 10 positive responses has been utilized, which maintains a relatively high degree of sensitivity and specificity. Those drinking drivers receiving a score of 10 or more are then referred to a state-approved agency for further evaluation and treatment. The RIASI has had an interesting history from the time it was first conceptualized and has gone through some revisions based on information from a number of pilot studies. Some of the RIASI items were derived from scales such as the Diagnostic Interview Schedule, the Preoccupation with Alcohol Scale, and the Negative Assertion Scale. The initial pilot study for the RIASI used questions from the Sensation Seeking Scale, the Buss-Durkee Hostility Inventory, the Childhood Risk Checklist, the Alcohol Beliefs Scale, the Locus of Control Scale, an anger scale, and the somaticism, obsessive-compulsive, anxiety, depression, and psychoticism scales of the SCL-90-R. From this pilot study, eighty-eight items were found to successfully discriminate those individuals who met the alcohol-dependent or alcohol-abuse criterion, based on the DSM-III-R, and thirty-eight items that identified individuals who were repeat DWI offenders. In a subsequent pilot study, these items were tested in a statewide survey of convicted DWI offenders. The results indicated that forty-five items could most accurately identify problem drinkers or drug abusers from all of the various subgroups. Three distal items were later added, with an additional proximal item targeting tolerance. In addition, a three-item lie scale was also added, comprising the current version of the RIASI. Some of the items included are as follows: "I smoke or use tobacco products," "I was referred for a liver test, or a blood test for liver enzymes" (examples of health questions); "When I don't get my way, I sulk or pout," "I don't like to break rules, even if I think they are wrong," or "I often feel like a powder keg ready to explode" (examples of hostility questions); "I like to gamble for money," "I sometimes do dangerous or risky things just for fun," or "I like people who are sharp and witty even though they may sometimes hurt other peoples' feelings." (examples of sensation-seeking questions); "I have experienced a major stressful life event in the past twelve months," "I often have feelings of nervousness," or "I have feelings that something bad will happen to me" (examples of anxiety questions); "A drink or two gives me energy to get started," "After seven or more drinks, I feel happier," or "When I have a problem I try to make it go away by drinking" (examples of alcohol beliefs) (Nochajski and Miller, 1995).

The RIASI has been empirically compared to several of the existing screening measures. For example, when the RIASI was compared to the MAST (Nochajski et al., 1993) under two separate conditions (in the first condition participants were told that their scores would determine treatment recommendations, while in the second condition the scores carried no treatment implications), the RIASI was found to be superior in discriminating those DWI offenders who met the DSM-III-R criteria for alcohol dependence. The RIASI has also been compared with the Mortimer-Filkins (Nochajski, Miller, and Parks, 1994) and was found to be more effective in successfully screening DWI offenders who met a DSM-III-R diagnosis for alcohol dependence or alcohol abuse, regardless of whether their scores would determine treatment recommendations.

The RIASI was also found to be even more effective than using a combination of screening measures (or Matrix system [Dowling and McCartt, 1990]), such as the MAST, Mortimer-Filkins, blood alcohol content at the time of arrest and showing up intoxicated to the screening session. A number of screening programs will often use a combination of such indicators to determine who should be referred for further treatment.

One recent study (Nochajski, Walter, and Wieczorek, 1997), found that fifteen items (composed of both proximal and distal items), of the

RIASI were predictive of recidivism, (i.e., first offenders who later had a subsequent DWI offense). A cutoff score of 4 positive responses from among the fifteen items was utilized to successfully predict DWI recidivists. When compared to the matrix indicators, this recidivism subscale of the RIASI was found to be a better predictor of DWI recidivism.

Overall, the RIASI is one of the most promising DWI screening tools available today. As indicated earlier, there is no cost for its use, it is easy to administer, it does not require extensive, specialized training to administer or score, it is brief, both reliability and validity have been established, and the research that has been conducted thus far on the RIASI has been extremely favorable. There are no readily discernible disadvantages to this assessment tool.

Substance Abuse Life Circumstances Evaluation (SALCE) Published by ADE, Inc. 20 West Washington St. Suite 12B, Clarkston, Michigan 48016 (1983, 1986).

The initial version of the SALCE was published in 1983 and was based upon the Criteria for Diagnosis of Alcoholism developed by the Criteria Committee of the National Council on Alcoholism. This measure was developed specifically for DWI offenders, and it assesses drinking behavior on a continuum ranging from "non-problem social drinking" to "severe problem drinking" and/or "alcohol addiction." However, the SALCE was not designed to distinguish alcoholics from nonalcoholics, but rather to "characterize an individual's need to alter his/her use of alcohol or other drugs. More specifically, the test's function is to identify behavioral, attitudinal and clinical indicators of this need."

The SALCE consists of eighty-five True-False and Likert Scale questions and it was designed to be used along with an interview, similar to the Mortimer-Filkins. However, the eighty-five items can be self-administered. When the SALCE is scored, there are five possible categories that the respondent could fall under, D1 = No use, D2 = use with no reported problems, D3 = use with minimal problems, D4 = substance use with problems, and D5 = substance use with physical or psychological symptoms of addiction. A validity measure ascertains test-taking attitudes (e.g., is the respondent open, honest, guarded, or defensive?) The computerized test report also contains treatment recommendations based upon the category that the

DWI offender falls under. The SALCE takes about fifteen minutes to complete. Scoring takes about five minutes for computer analysis and about twenty minutes for the interview (Lacey, Jones, and Wilisnowski, 1999). The SALCE is easily administered and computer-scored, although the disadvantage to the computer-scoring is the expense (which includes a $450 one-time administration fee) and the cost is $10 per test. Both reliability and validity have been established.

In a recent study comparing several screening measures (Lacey, Jones, and Wilisnowski, 1999), the SALCE was found to have the highest sensitivity, having correctly identified 92 percent of the problem drinkers in comparison to the MAST, the Mortimer-Filkins and the Driver Risk Inventory (DRI). However, the SALCE was also found to have the least selectivity, identifying only 57 percent of the nonproblem drinkers correctly. In this study, the MAST, Mortimer-Filkins, and DRI had only identified approximately 80 percent of the problem drinkers correctly, which clearly suggests that the SALCE was superior in being able to identify problem drinkers. However, these three measures had fewer false negatives. For example, the Mortimer-Filkins and the DRI correctly identified about two-thirds of the nonproblem drinkers and the MAST had correctly identified the nonproblem drinkers in 85 percent of the cases.

Driver Risk Inventory-II (DRI) Developed by Lindeman and Scrimgeour (1999) and available through Behavior Data Systems, P.O. Box 32308, Phoenix, Arizona 85064.

The DRI is considered to be one of the most psychometrically sound instruments for DWI screening, in that reliability has been well-established and validity of the DRIII is based on its comparison to other established measures (Lacey, Jones, and Wilisnowski, 1999). The DRIII consists of 140 items, which, similar to the RIASI, were empirically selected by item analysis. These items ask direct questions about alcohol and drug use and driving practices. The DRI has been normed for both men and women and it is available in both English and Spanish versions. It can be administered in pencil-and-paper format, individually, or in a group setting or it can be administered online for computer-scoring.

The computerized report yields five independent scales: truthfulness, alcohol, drugs, driver risk, and a stress coping abilities scale.

For each of these scales, the respondent is classified according to "risk level" by means of a four-point scale ranging from low risk to high risk. The truthfulness scale provides a measure of response bias or faking. The driver risk scale assesses risky driving practices and irresponsible driving, which is unique to this particular scale and seems to follow from some of the research literature that notes correlations between DWI offenders and high-risk drivers. The computerized evaluation report also flags "critical items" questions and provides the counselor with treatment recommendations. The cost of the DRI comes to approximately $7 per test with discounts available for volume purchases or purchases for research purposes. Although the DRI-II has not been utilized extensively in reserach studies to date, the authors have performed several validation studies with rather large populations. The reliability and validity of the DRI have therefore been well established. The other advantage of the DRI is that the test authors have compiled a large database of all of the DRI-I and DRI-II test administrations that were computer scored. This will allow for future predictive studies to be performed. The study by Lacey, Jones, and Wilisnowski (1999) mentioned in the description of the SALCE (see the previous section), is one of the most comprehensive studies available that compares several screening measures. This study found that the DRI had fairly good sensitivity, correctly identifying 80 percent of the problem drinkers and was also very good in its selectivity (i.e., by correctly classifying approximately 66 percent of the nonproblem drinkers).

Substance Abuse Subtle Screening Inventory-II (SASSI) (Miller, G. A., 1994a) The SASSI is available through the SASSI Institute, P.O. Box 5069, Bloomington, Indiana 47407. Phone: 1-800-726-0526. Also available through The Psychological Corporation, 555 Academic Court, San Antonio, Texas 78202-2498. Phone: 1-800-211-8378 or Website: www.PsychCorp.com

The SASSI was first introduced back in 1985 by Dr. Glenn A. Miller. The SASSI-II was released in 1994 and the SASSI-III was released in 1998. The SASSI was developed as a screening tool to assess individuals with chemical dependency. It was designed purposely to deal with the issues of falsification of responses that is often found in individuals mandated to treatment. Reliability and validity of this measure have been established (Miller, G. A., 1994a). It is of interest to note that although the SASSI was not developed specifically for use with the DWI population, one of the standardization samples utilized was composed of DWI offenders.

The SASSI has two main sections. The first part consists of items that ask direct questions regarding alcohol and drug use and related problems. There are twelve questions pertaining to alcohol use and another set of fourteen items pertaining to general drug use (not regarding specific drugs). These questions are referred to as the Face Validity-Alcohol (FVA) and Face Validity-Drugs (FVOD), because the items pertain directly to alcohol and drug-taking behavior and related problems. Clients respond to these questions on a four point Likert scale ranging from 0 = Never, 1 = Once or twice, 2 = Several times, 3 = Repeatedly. Questions include: "Taken a drink or drinks to help you express your feelings or ideas?" "Got into trouble on the job, in school, or at home because of drinking?" "Become nervous or had the shakes after having sobered up?" "Taken drugs to improve our thinking and feeling?" " Taken drugs to help you feel better about a problem?" or "Spent your spare time in drug-related activities (e.g., talking about drugs, buying, selling, taking, etc.)?" Responses to the Face Validity items are then added and separate FVA and FVOD scores are obtained.

The second part of the test consists of sixty-two True-False format items, which contain six of the subscales of the SASSI. Included are the Obvious Attributes Scale (OAT), Subtle Attributes Scale (SAT), Defensiveness Scale (DEF), a Supplemental Addiction Measure (SAM), Family versus Controls (FAM), and Correctional (COR) subscales. Several of the items from this section of the SASSI were taken from the Psychological Screening Inventory (Lanyon, 1968). This section of the SASSI can be hand scored utilizing transparent scoring templates for the various subscales. The entire inventory can be scored and interpreted in about fifteen to twenty minutes. The six scales of the SASSI each yield a separate score, which is then plotted on a score sheet (one side is for adult males, the other side is for adult females). The score sheet is set up in such a way that one side provides a graph of the various subscale scores, which are then converted to standard T scores on the graph, and the other side provides "Decision Rules," which works similar to a decision tree. (For those not familiar with decision trees, they are usually set up in such a way as to ask the test scorer/interpreter several sequential questions, e.g., "Is either the FVA or FVOD T-score greater than 80?" If "yes," then the client is classified as "Chemically Dependent;" if "no," the test scorer goes on to the next decision rule. Another example: "Is OAT or SAT T-score 70 or more?" If the answer is "yes," then this individual would be classified as chemically dependent. There are several other questions of this type as one goes down the decision tree.)

Basically, one could be classified as chemically dependent if one has a high score on the FVA or FVOD scales, which means that the client had responded affirmatively to a number of items pertaining to alcohol or drug use and problems related to such use. (Please note, however, that these scales make no distinction between recent use versus lifetime use. Glenn Miller (1994b) points out that initially respondents were asked about their use six months prior to date of taking the SASSI; the caveat was that probationers or parolees would be reluctant to report actual alcohol or drug use for fear of incriminating themselves as having violated their probation or parole. Therefore, questions covering lifetime experience with alcohol or drugs are asked.) Respondents can also be classified as chemically dependent based upon their scores on the six subscales of the SASSI. For example, if both the OAT and SAT T-scores are above 60, then the respondent is classified chemically dependent. It is noted in the decision tree that a person could be classified as chemically dependent if they receive a high score (>60) on the DEF subscale, high scores on either the OAT or SAT (also >60), and a high score on the SAM (>60). Although this seems rather complicated, the Decision Rules are well-displayed and easy to use.

As was indicated above, there are six scales to the second part of the SASSI-II. Each scale purports to measure a different constructs. For example, according to Glenn Miller (1994a, pp. 5-2 to 5-4), the OAT scale "reflects the individual's tendency to endorse statements of personal limitation, particularly those that are commonly and stereotypically associated with substance abusers (e.g., impatience, low frustration tolerance, grandiosity, etc.)" Clients who score high on this scale are endorsing "character defect" types of items, while low scorers are reluctant to admit to problems or personal shortcomings. Examples of items of the OAT scale are as follows: "Sometimes

I have a hard time sitting still" (True); "Some crooks are so clever that I hope they get away with what they have done" (True); "I have not lived the way I should" (True). The SAT scale was designed specifically as a measure of avoidance of self-disclosure. This scale therefore, attempts to get at more subtle or pervasive personal patterns or styles. Respondents scoring high on the SAT may have difficulty in recognizing or admitting their substance use disorder. Examples of items from the SAT include the following: "My troubles are not all my fault" (False); "I like to obey the law" (False); "I break more laws than many people" (True); "I smoke cigarettes regularly" (True); "At times I have been so full of pep that I felt I didn't need sleep for days at a time" (True).

The DEF subscale was designed to measure test-taking defensiveness. High scores on the DEF may reflect "unconscious denial or more deliberate efforts at concealment" (Miller, G. A., 1994a, p. 5-10), or high scores may "contain a flavor of self-righteousness or superiority to others in intellectual understanding or moral virtue" (pp. 5-10, 5-11). Some of the items of the DEF include: "I can be friendly with people who do many wrong things" (False); "I think carefully about all my actions" (True); "I have sometimes sat about when I should be working" (False). The SAM scale was developed as an adjunct to the DEF scale and, jointly with the DEF, addresses the issue of defensive responding. High scores on this scale also correlate with individuals who have personality traits similar to those who are chemically dependent. Some of the items of the SAM are: "I have never been in trouble with the law" (False); "I have not lived the way I should" (True); "I have used alcohol or 'pot' too much or too often" (True); or "I have neglected obligations to family or work because of drinking or using drugs" (True). These latter items are examples of some of the more direct items on this section of the SASSI.

The FAM scale was developed to distinguish respondents who were known to be family members of substance abusers from a control group. The FAM subscale is considered a supplementary scale of the SASSI and is not utilized in the "Decision Rules." Although the FAM scale purportedly measures "co-dependency," it is recommended that counselors use this scale cautiously (Miller, G. A., 1994a) because co-dependency characteristics (e.g., low self-esteem, low assertiveness, compulsive behaviors, stress-related illness) can result from other problems or family dynamics than just chemically dependent contexts. Items from the FAM scale include: "I have never done anything dangerous just for fun." (True), "I always feel sure of myself." (False), "I have never broken a major law" (True). The last of the subscales is the COR scale. This scale was developed in response to requests from criminal justice programs for a tool that would assist in making a differential chemical dependency diagnosis, given the extremely high correlation between illegal behavior and chemical abuse/dependency. Individuals scoring above the cutoff of 11 are responding in a manner similar to those in the criminal justice validation sample and are therefore "more than twice as likely to have a broad range of legal problems than those who score below the cutoff" (p. S-7) (Miller, 1994a). When the COR was developed six data samples were utilized, which included probationers, male and female parolees, incarcerated individuals, and DWI offenders.

Unfortunately, to date, not many studies have utilized the SASSI for DWI screening purposes, perhaps owing in part to the expense and scoring procedures. One recent study (Myerholtz and Rosenberg, 1997) had compared scores on the MacAndrews Alcoholism Scale of the MMPI, the Michigan Alcoholism Screening Test, the CAGE, and the SASSI in a population of DWI offenders and found that each measure had yielded similar reliability scores. However, given the lack of a validation standard, no conclusions could be made regarding the accuracy of these measures in screening DWI offenders. Hopefully, more empirical research utilizing the SASSI will be forthcoming. Given the nature of the test items, which include both direct and indirect questions, it appears that it can be a useful measure in the DWI screening process.

Alcohol Use Inventory (AUI) (Wanberg, Horn, and Foster, 1990) The AUI is available through National Computer Service, Inc., 5605 Green Circle Drive, Minneapolis, Minnesota 55343-4400. Phone: 1-800-627-7271.

The AUI was first introduced for clinical use in 1975 and has been updated since that time to its current version (Horn, Wanberg, and Foster, 1987; Wanberg and Horn, 1983; Wanberg, Horn, and Foster, 1990). The AUI provides counselors with a demographic description of the client, a profile summarizing the scale scores, and a summary description of critical items that the client had endorsed. Reliability and validity for this instrument have been established and psychometric properties and standardization procedures are reported in the literature (Horn, Wanberg, and Foster, 1987).

The AUI consists of 228 questions and respondents are asked to choose from among two to five answers or choices, the one that best describes what they believe to be true regarding their drinking behavior. Therefore, the accuracy of the AUI interpretation is dependent on the respondent's willingness to disclose information in a forthright manner. The AUI questions are similar to those that would be asked in any clinical interview and therefore the AUI can be administered as a structured interview or it can be given to the client to fill out in a self-administered questionnaire format. The authors (Wanberg, Horn, and Foster, 1990) caution that either approach has its advantages and disadvantages; for example, an interview format allows the counselor to question responses in more depth, while the questionnaire format is perhaps more objective and less subject to response bias. Naturally, it is recommended that the AUI be utilized in conjunction with a clinical interview.

The AUI is based on the theory that alcoholism is a multifaceted and multidetermined disorder; therefore, the AUI explores several aspects of alcohol use and alcohol-related problems. The AUI consists of twenty-four scales, which are broken down into three major levels: the primary scales, second-level scales and third-level scales. There are seventeen primary scales, which are organized into five sets, or "domains of expression," which pertain to use of alcohol and include:

1. Benefits from use (e.g., does the client perceive alcohol as enhancing mental abilities, social relationships, or the ability to cope with stress, anxiety, or depression?)
2. Styles of use (e.g., measures gregarious drinking, amount of drinking, compulsive behaviors associated with drinking, and sustained or episodic patterns)
3. Negative consequences of use (e.g., any disruptions in physical or psychological functioning, emotional control, social roles)
4. Concerns about use (e.g., has the client sought help for drinking, any worries, guilt, or shame associated with drinking)

5. Acknowledgment that use is causing problems (e.g., the extent
to which the client reports that drinking is central to unresolved
personal problems and readiness to seek help)

The second-level scales consist of six scales, which are derived from
the primary scales but are not merely combinations of the primary
scales, and therefore yield distinct data regarding the mood-enhancing
perception of drinking, obsessive-compulsivity associated with drinking, disruptions such as blackouts, severe hangover symptoms, delu-
sions, loss of control, interference with sleeping and eating habits,
anxiety about drinking, and finally, receptiveness to treatment for these
problems. The third-level scales provide a broad picture of involvement
with alcohol based upon items drawn from the other two levels.

When computer-scored (by National Computer Services) the AUI
yields a profile that includes demographic information, information
about drug-use behavior (there is a checklist of different drug types,
amount of use over the past twelve months, and the respondent is
asked whether they feel they have a problem with that drug), alcohol
use, and a chart indicating the client's scores on each of the scales described above. The interpretative report also provides a summary of
the conditions that are apparent in the client's alcohol use behavior, a
DSM-III-R diagnostic impression is made based upon the respondent's profile, and finally treatment recommendations are made, in
terms of particular treatment strategies that might be employed with
that particular client (e.g., structured, educational, confrontative, etc.)
and what areas need to be addressed in treatment (e.g., client's concerns, marital problems, vocational problems, medical problems).

Although the AUI has not been utilized extensively with the DWI
population, perhaps owing to the expense involved with administration and computerized scoring, it has been used favorably in one research study in particular. Lapham, Skipper, and Simpson (1997) had
used four standardized alcohol screening measures (the MAC, AUI,
the MAST, and the Skinner's Trauma Scale [STS]) in assessing risk
for recidivism in a group of 1,384 first offenders. After a four-year
follow-up period, 21 percent had been rearrested for a DWI. The best
predictors of recidivism found were a MAC score of 23 or above, an
elevated score on the AUI scales, age and gender (i.e., being a young

male, age thirty or under), and a blood alcohol level at time of first arrest of 0.20 percent or above.

Drug Abuse Screening Test (DAST) (Skinner, 1982; Gavin, Ross, and Skinner, 1989)

The DAST is a twenty-eight item self-report questionnaire that is based on the Michigan Alcoholism Screening Test (MAST). It takes about five to ten minutes to complete and can be administered as a structured interview or can be self-administered by the client. The items of the DAST focus on the negative consequences of drug use and are posed in a "Yes-No" format (e.g., "Do you ever feel bad about your drug abuse?" "Has drug abuse ever created problems between you and your spouse?" "Can you get through the week without using drugs (other than those required for medical reasons)?" "Have you ever been arrested for possession of illegal drugs?") Each question is scored either "0" or "1" depending on the direction of the response; therefore, the highest possible score is a 28. Similar to the MAST, cutoff scores are utilized that suggest whether the client may manifest a substance-use disorder. In comparing DAST scores for individuals who sought addiction treatment the means were as follows: for alcohol problems only (4.5), for drug and alcohol problems (15.2), and for drug problems only (17.8) (Skinner, 1982). The psychometric properties of the DAST have been well established (Staley and El-Geubaly, 1990). The DAST has not been used extensively with the DWI population. Its advantages and disadvantages are similar to those reported for the MAST; for example, the DAST only asks about lifetime use and does not assess the client's current level of use. Also, the DAST can lead to false negatives, given the propensity towards falsification or resistance to self-disclosure in those clients wishing to avoid detection.

Drug Use Screening Inventory (DUSI) (Tarter and Hegedus, 1991)

The DUSI consists of 149 "Yes-No" items and takes about twenty minutes to administer in either a structured interview or self-administered questionnaire format. Respondents are asked to recall their behavior over the past year, which differs from the MAST or DAST, both of which ask about lifetime experience. There are ten domains that are assessed, which are as follows: substance use, behavior patterns, health status, psychiatric disorder, social competency, family system, school performance/adjustment, work, peer relationships, and leisure/recreational activity. Scores are obtained for each domain according to (1) problem severity, (2) an overall problem index score is obtained by adding up all the positive responses and averaging the scores across all ten domains, and (3) a relative problem density, which is a computation of the percentage of each domain, thereby revealing which domain is the most troublesome for the client.

The DUSI is said to be appropriate for individuals from age sixteen through adult. The DUSI had high face validity; however, there are no norms established for reliability or other types of validity. One of the advantages of the DUSI is that is does cover a variety of areas; however, this can be a disadvantage in that some domains may not be relevant for most adults (e.g., school adjustment). For DWI offenders, the questions pertaining to substance use bear striking similarity to the questions of the DAST and are subject to the problems of false responding, as there are no validity checks for false responding built into the instrument. The DUSI is recommended as a screening tool to assess and monitor treatment changes and for follow-up assessment (Tarter and Hegedus, 1991).

THE BIOPSYCHOSOCIAL ASSESSMENT

Any counselor who has worked with the DWI offender population is well aware that traditional intake or assessment formats that are readily applicable with most substance-dependent inpatient or outpatient clients are perhaps not as helpful when it comes to doing an intake assessment with DWI offenders. If anything, traditional alcohol or drug treatment databases often miss the mark, or are geared toward clients who usually manifest a variety of symptoms and problems. It is not unusual for the DWI offender to enter an intake session with the contention that they have only one problem—that being the DWI offense itself. Therefore, to spend time trying to make inquiry into other alcohol or drug-related problems often seems to be an exercise in futility. However, the majority of treatment programs will require that some intake assessment be conducted along with any of the aforementioned questionnaires or inventories.

Please keep in mind that we are not naïve enough to suggest that DWI offenders will necessarily respond openly or honestly to these questions; however, there may be ways to get at some useful information, depending on how questions are posed or framed. A case in point, most biopsychosocial intakes will ask whether there is any history of alcoholism or drug addiction in the client's family. This naturally is an example of a direct question, the purpose of which is readily discernible. Even if DWI offenders are not aware of genetic risk factors for substance-use disorders, they certainly know that role modeling could also be a red flag and will usually reply that there is no one in their family of origin with such a history. Another problem with this question involves the issue of what constitutes "alcoholism" or "drug addiction." DWI offenders may use a wide variety of definitions, which will then determine their response to the question. Therefore, if they define alcoholism as daily drinking and the inability to maintain a job, family, or home, then they would not be likely to define an early stage or functional alcoholic family member as an "alcoholic." Other ways to get this information will be discussed later in this section.

In devising an intake or biopsychosocial format, it is also advised that one look through some of the structured interview formats that were discussed earlier in this chapter. For example, the Diagnostic Interview Schedule (DIS) or Structured Clinical Interview for DSM (SCID) both contain excellent questions pertaining to problematic alcohol or drug use. The Mortimer-Filkins Questionnaire also contains some excellent questions that could be incorporated into an intake format specifically for the DWI population.

With the aforementioned issues in mind, we recommend that some of the following areas be addressed in the biopsychosocial intake. Many of the areas that we have addressed in our intakes with DWI offenders have been based on prior research in these areas, as you will see as you go through the following suggested biopsychosocial areas. For the sake of counselor credibility, it is important to begin with the DWI offense(s) itself:

I. The DWI Incident
    A. Gather facts pertaining to the DWI offense (e.g., When did the DWI take place? [Date and time of day.] How did the

DWI incident happen? Was there an accident? If there was an accident, did it result in injury to person or property? What brought the client to the attention of the police? Where did the DWI take place? Was it close to home, close to the drinking location? Were there multiple drinking locations?)

B. What were the clients' drinking and/or drug use like prior to the DWI incident? Also, were they taking any prescription medication? Does their blood alcohol content, as indicated in the police report, correspond with what the individuals claim they were drinking? Keep in mind, however, that blood alcohol content may be misleading. Wieczorek, Miller, and Nochajski (1992) point out three limitations or difficulties with BAC measures. First, the BAC at the time of the arrest is only a single measure and, therefore, provides no information about alcohol dependence, only about alcohol consumption prior to the arrest. Second, the BAC, at the time of the arrest, may be lower than the peak BAC since the breathalyzer may have been given during the ascending or descending BAC curve. Third, there are individual differences noted in alcohol absorption, which can vary with body weight and whether the person drinks on a full stomach (Chan, 1987).

C. What were the circumstances leading up to the DWI arrest? For example, was the client drinking at a celebration of some sort? Does the client consider his or her drinking to be typical or atypical? Was there any emotional distress or stressors present prior to the arrest (e.g., an argument with a loved one, a death or other significant loss, etc.)? Also, did the client perceive that he or she was too impaired by alcohol or drugs to operate a motor vehicle or did it feel okay to be driving?

II. Drinking and Drug Use History

A. Chronological History: Including alcohol, what substances have been used, in what quantities? Any fluctuations in pattern? Any periods of abstinence? Any attempts to stop, quit, or slow down use, and what initiated those changes? Any treatment attempts? If so, why was treatment initiated and what was the outcome? Similarly, if the client had been in a DWI program prior to this, what did he or she get out of the program, if anything, and why didn't the program work?

B. Recent Use: It is important to ask what the client's alcohol and/or drug use was like around the time of the DWI incident—not just in the hours leading up to arrest, but in the days, weeks, or months prior to the arrest. How did the DWI arrest change or affect (if at all), the client's level of alcohol or drug use? Here, the Timeline Follow Back (TLFB) method can be used effectively.

C. Problems Associated with Use: Here a MAST or DAST can be used to structure your questions. Although you may not get forthright responses, it is important to ask these questions "for the record" and also for liability reasons.

III. Coping Styles and Personality Characteristics

A. How does the client cope with stress in general (e.g., if he or she has had a bad day at work or at home)? What types of stressful events bother him or her the most?

B. What stressors have been created by the DWI arrest? Here it is important to explore how the DWI and subsequent loss of license effect this client's life, livelihood, relationships with others, and so on. How did he or she deal with this stress?

C. Personality Traits: How do the clients describe themselves? Are they risk-takers? Are they more conventional types of individuals? What are the riskiest things they have done? Are they prone to anger outbursts? Do they hold onto resentments? Are they prone to depressive reactions? You will hear some of this information as you are asking about other areas of functioning (e.g., when you ask about educational history, you should get a sense as to how a person dealt with stress or adversity, or in employment history, how a person deals with a difficult boss or co-worker).

D. Leisure Activities: What do the clients do to relax? Do they have balance in their lives when it comes to leisure activities or ways to unwind? Alcoholics and addicts naturally lack this balance and obviously will turn to substances at times of stress.

IV. Family and Social Life

A. Current Living Situation: Is this person single, married, separated, divorced, widowed? Who are the significant people in his or her life at present? Any recent losses? What were these significant others' responses to the DWI arrest (e.g., were they critical, angry, supportive, etc.)? Who was not told about the DWI, were there people that purposely were not told about the DWI arrest, and if so, why?

B. Family of Origin: What was the typical or acceptable use of alcohol while the client was growing up? For example, at family barbecues, holidays, celebrations, Sunday dinners, weekday dinners, on weekends? Were there any fluctuations in the described use of alcohol? What about in extended family, such as grandparents, aunts, uncles, other blood relatives? Did drinking ever interfere with any family function such as holidays, celebrations, and so on? Is there any history of medical illnesses such as diabetes, liver trouble, stomach problems, respiratory problems related to smoking, any family history of cancer or heart disease? Any history of psychiatric problems? Any treatment for psychiatric, alcohol, or drug problems?

C. Social: Explore friendships or lack thereof. Who are the significant people in the client's life. How did they react to the DWI arrest?

V. Educational and Employment History

A. Usually the educational and employment histories can be combined with a series of chronological questions, which would include information about where the clients went to school, their school performance, their behavior in school, whether they completed school or dropped out, and whether they received schooling or training beyond high school. Also, in young DWI offenders it is important to look at whether alcohol or drug use interfered with grades or the completion of school (e.g., many young people who leave college in their freshman year do so due to poor grades resulting from alcohol or drug abuse). Also, it is important to look for possible signs or symptoms of Attention-Deficit Hyperactivity Disorder, as prior research does suggest a correlation between ADHD in childhood or young adulthood and alcohol and drug dependence (see Chapter 2).

B. Employment History: Here it is best to begin with questions about the types of jobs held, for how long, reasons for leaving, and job satisfaction or dissatisfaction. Is the client presently employed? Has the client achieved the goals he or she set out to achieve, educationally or occupationally? If so, why or why not?

VI. Legal History

A. What other legal involvement has this person experienced other than the DWI arrest(s)? In the Mortimer-Filkins Test Manual it is recommended that a criminal history be obtained if at all possible in order to objectively validate this history.

B. Have there been other motor-vehicle offenses? If so, what type and when did they occur? Given the research on high-risk drivers, we know that it would not be unusual to see careless or reckless driving offenses or multiple accidents.

C. Is there any family history of criminal behavior? Again, prior research indicates that DWI offenders may have a family member (such as a parent) with a DWI history or a history of other legal problems.

VII. Medical History

A. Any history of illnesses? Accidents? If so, explore the details (some estimates indicate that approximately one-third of those patients occupying hospital beds are admitted for alcohol or drug-related problems, although you may never see an alcohol or drug diagnosis on the patient's chart).

B. Any current illnesses? Look for history of diabetes, gastritis, pancreatitis, and Hepatitis C (as it could relate to prior IV drug use).

C. Has the person had a recent physical exam? If so, the counselor may want to request these records, especially if blood work was done, in order to see if the liver enzyme readings are within normal limits (SGOT, GGTP levels are examples). If there were elevations, were these addressed by the examining physician?

The aforementioned areas are just a few of the areas that might be addressed in a biopsychosocial assessment with a DWI offender. Naturally, this list of areas and questions is by no means complete, as each counselor will find various ways of addressing these areas and ways to ask these questions in such a way as to get the most out of the interview with the DWI offender.

What we have hoped to accomplish in this chapter is to provide the reader with an overview of some of the various measures and assessment tools available in screening or evaluating DWI offenders. As was pointed out in Chapter 4, there are many problems inherent in trying to assess the typical DWI offender, however, as we have advocated, counselors must employ several assessment strategies. With the exception of those screening situations in which the DWI offender may be seen for only one session, it is also important to view assessment as an ongoing process, especially for the counselor who will be treating the DWI offender on an ongoing basis, perhaps over the course of several weeks or months. It is important that counselors also remain open-minded and flexible to new information that becomes available as the assessment process ensues.

Chapter 6

Alcohol Countermeasures

Kami R. Venema

The act of operating a motor vehicle while under the influence of alcohol is a violation of the law in every state in the country. However, not all states address DUI/DWI violations in the same way. Surprisingly, some states—Idaho, Nebraska, South Dakota, Washington, and Wyoming—do not have an official DWI offender program at all. Yet that does not mean those states are not concerned with reducing alcohol-related moving violations. In fact, several of the states that do not have an official program still offer driver education classes to address the problems associated with drunk driving. In various ways, from the name they assign the act itself to the treatment recommendations they provide for offenders, each state has determined how it will deal with this issue.

The following chapter attempts to give a general overview of the various ways states address drinking and driving. Legislation, which dictates how each state imposes sanctions, is the first important piece of the puzzle. As a natural consequence, blood alcohol concentration comes into play in determining whether or not a violation has occurred. Next comes the assessment and referral criteria, which are both critical in evaluating treatment needs for each identified offender. Although DWI offender programs vary a great deal, a basic knowledge of the main types of treatment offered, length of treatment, and associated costs is necessary as a frame of reference. The efforts to prevent

Kami R. Venema, MA, is a doctoral student in psychology at Widener University and holds a master's degree in psychological counseling from Monmouth University.

recidivism, an important area of focus for state offices dealing with DWI, cannot adequately be addressed without mentioning the various technological innovations available. Finally, which programs will have the greatest impact on drunk driving in the future? In examining existing programs, experts and researchers have come to some interesting conclusions regarding what should be done to reduce DWI.

DETERRENCE VERSUS TREATMENT

Amid the national debate surrounding drunk driving is the issue of deterrence versus a treatment approach to DWI offender programs. Many experts in this field argue as to which approach is more effective—treatment or deterrence. Deterrence generally refers to the measures established to reduce the incidences of an undesired behavior, often through fear of punishment. Treatment, however, utilizes therapeutic interventions to change the attitude and behavior of the offender. Furthermore, researchers often examine treatment in terms of education versus other forms of treatment, such as counseling. Unfortunately, the question of treatment versus deterrence has often been approached as orthogonal or an "either-or" issue. Research suggests that treatment and deterrence both offer different effects and mechanisms that are effective in reducing drunk driving, which supports bringing the two ideas together (Nichols, 1990). This could explain why many states have based their program on a blending of the two. DeYoung (1997) for example, in a study comparing first and second offenders, found that combining alcohol treatment with driver's license restriction or suspension was associated with lower DWI recidivism rates.

LEGISLATION

Legislation common to all fifty states includes zero-tolerance laws and implied consent. Zero-tolerance laws make it illegal for drivers under the legal drinking age to have any amount of alcohol in their system. The legal blood alcohol concentration (BAC) limits for zero-tolerance laws are generally set between 0.00 and .02g/dl. Violation of these laws often results in rather stiff penalties. Offenders often face suspensions and fines for breach of the zero-tolerance law, in addition to those resulting from conviction of the original offense. Some states, such as Alaska and Colorado, include possession of alcohol (open containers) as grounds for license revocation even if driving was not a factor.

Implied consent, on the other hand, applies to all drivers regardless of age. According to this law, by operating a motor vehicle the driver has agreed to a chemical test to determine blood alcohol content. If a law-enforcement officer suspects that an individual has been driving while under the influence, he or she can require a chemical test of breath, blood, or urine. Refusal to submit to such a test most frequently results in the immediate revocation of driving privileges. In some states, refusal of a BAC test can result in civil charges and fines. Currently, Hawaii, Massachusetts, and Rhode Island are the only states in which BAC refusal is not admissible in court as evidence in a DWI criminal procedure. Other states not only admit refusals, but make it impossible to decline. For example, in Nevada, drivers cannot refuse a breath, blood, or urine test. According to that state's implied consent law, blood may be forcibly drawn if the driver refuses, even if it is the driver's first offense. Although each state has enacted legislation allowing for drivers to be arrested and their licenses suspended based only on the failure or refusal of a BAC test, enforcement of impaired-driving laws still relies heavily on behavioral observations, rather than on BAC measurements.

What is noteworthy, however, is even with the implied consent law, there are proportionately fewer arrests for driving under the influence of mood altering chemicals other than alcohol, even though most state laws include mention of drugged driving in their statutes. There are problems, however, when it comes to driving under the influence of these mood-altering chemicals. Certainly, a person who drives under the influence of heroin would be considered to be driving while impaired, yet what about a person who is driving under the influence of Percoset (a narcotic pain killer), which he or she takes with a physician's prescription for back pain? Or what about the person who is receiving methadone (a synthetic opiate) as part of a heroin detoxification program or to maintain heroin abstinence? Several states specify that no one should drive under the influence of narcotics, and in all of the aforementioned cases a person could be charged with driving under the influence. However, what about an individual whose driving is impaired by an over-the-counter cough medicine that contains an antihistamine? (Antihistamines do depress the central nervous system.) Perhaps because our society tends to label drugs as "good" (i.e., prescription medicines, over-the-counter preparations) versus "bad" (e.g., heroin, cocaine, marijuana), that this may account for the lower rates of DWI arrests in which drugs are the chemical that one is driving under the influence of.

BLOOD ALCOHOL CONCENTRATION

An elevated blood alcohol level and the refusal to take a BAC test has become, for many states, the primary objective determination of guilt when investigating cases of DWI. Although Massachusetts and South Carolina have presumptive standards of .08 and .10g/dl respectively, the remaining forty-eight states all have numeric standards by which they determine legal limits of blood alcohol concentration. Because BAC level is such a critical part of this process, it has been an area of manipulation in the battle to reduce drunk driving.

Although the .10g/dl BAC remains the standard used by most states, the .08g/dl level is the legal limit in 16 states and is being championed as a standard by prominent individuals, groups, and organized emergency-room physicians. Some proponents of lower blood alcohol concentration standards argue that alcohol impairment is evident—in terms of deteriorating attention, "task tracking," peripheral vision, and reaction times—by the time BAC reaches .04g/dl (Liddle, 1999). Several states have even considered lowering the legal blood alcohol concentration by half, to as low as .04g/dl. Although no state has lowered the limit for all drivers beyond .07, a Maine law lowered the legal blood alcohol limit from .10 to .05g/dl for people convicted of DWI. A study of the proportion of fatal crashes involving drivers with prior DWI convictions, from the six-year period before enactment of the law to the six-year period following enactment of the law, revealed a 25 percent decline in the involvement of this group compared with the other New England states (Hingson, Heeren, and Winter, 1998).

Early in 1998, a House Committee failed to accept a Senate-passed proposal to lower legal intoxication to a blood alcohol level of .08g/dl. Although bill proponents believed they had lost because of heavy industry pressure, opponents complained the bill infringed on the rights of states to set their own drunk-driving laws ("Senate passes," 1998). In

September 1998, Vice President Al Gore attempted to achieve a similar goal by announcing incentive grants totaling more than $71 million for states to help deter drinking and driving. Of that total, $49 million came in the form of incentives for states to enact and enforce laws making the operation of a motor vehicle by a person with a .08g/dl blood alcohol concentration a drunk-driving offense ("Incentive grants," 1998).

Beginning in 1999, twenty-three states introduced over fifty bills aimed at establishing stricter DWI limits. Many of those proposals included penalties for drivers caught with relatively small amounts of alcohol in their bloodstream. Washington State legislators considered a bill that called for a $500 fine and a thirty-day license suspension for people who operated a vehicle while alcohol "impaired," a BAC of .02g/dl to .08g/dl (Liddle, 1999). Currently, several states have measures in place to penalize drivers who may not exceed the legal limit, but are nonetheless impaired.

SANCTIONS

Each state has assigned similar types of punishment for DWI offenders. For the most part, typical penalties include fines, license suspension, and jail sentences. The severity of these sanctions, however, is often left to the discretion of the sentencing judge. Certain courts may be notoriously harsh on DWI offenders, while others may be more lenient depending on the circumstances. For example, several states give numerous hours of community service in place of incarceration, reserving jail time for multiple offenders. Table 6.1, compiled using data from various state Web sites and driver's-license manuals, shows the types and ranges of penalties a DWI offender may face in each of the fifty states. It is important, however, to keep in mind the ever-changing nature and subjective dispensing practices of legal sanctions. Today's maximum fine could be tomorrow's minimum; and, each court is given the freedom, within limits, to assign particular penalties as it deems appropriate.

As a result of the court monitoring programs instituted by Mothers Against Drunk Driving (MADD), several states had passed legislation which makes it illegal for courts to plea-bargain a drinking and driving arrest down to a lesser charge such as reckless driving or careless driving. This applies, however, to those arrests in which proper police procedures have been followed and a blood alcohol level ex-

TABLE 6.1. Penalties for DWI Offenders

State	BAC Limit*	Fine ($)	First Offense Jail	Suspension
Alabama	0.08	500-2,000	<1 yr	90 days
Alaska	0.08-0.10	>250	72 hrs	>30 days
Arizona	0.10	>250	>10 days	90 days
Arkansas	0.10	>150	24 hrs	120 days
California	0.08	390-5,000	Varies	120 days
Colorado	0.05-0.10	300-1,000	5 days-1 yr	N/A
Connecticut	0.10	500-8,000	48 hrs	90 days-1 yr
Delaware	0.10	230-6,000	Varies	1 yr
District of Columbia	0.10	300-10,000	Varies	180 days
Florida	0.08	250-500	<6 mos	180 days-1 yr
Georgia	0.08	300-1,000	Varies	1 yr
Hawaii	0.08	150-10,000	Varies	90 days
Idaho	0.08	<1,000	<6 mos	90-180 days
Illinois	0.08	<1,000	<1 yr	1 yr
Indiana	0.10	500-10,000	Varies	<180 days
Iowa	0.10	>1,000	48 hrs	180 days
Kansas	0.08	>200	48 hrs	30 days
Kentucky	0.10	200-500	2-30 days	90 days
Louisiana	0.10	100	Varies	90 days
Maine	0.08	400-2,400	Varies	90 days
Maryland	0.07	0-300	Varies	180 days
Massachusetts	0.08	500-5,000	<2.5 yrs	1 yr
Michigan	0.07-0.10	100-500	<90 days	<730 days
Minnesota	0.04-0.10	<700	<90 days	30-60 days
Mississippi	0.10	>200	Varies	90 days-1 yr
Missouri	0.10	<500	<6 mos	<90 days
Montana	0.10	100-500	1-60 days	6 mos
Nebraska	0.04-0.10	200-500	Varies	60-180 days
Nevada	0.10	200-5,000	2 days-6 mos	90 days
New Hampshire	0.08	350-1,000	Varies	90 days-2 yrs
New Jersey	0.05-0.10	250-400	12-48 hrs	180 days-1 yr
New Mexico	0.08	300-5,000	<1.5 yrs	1 yr
New York	0.05-0.10	500-1,000	<365 days	>80 days
North Carolina	0.08	100-2,000	24 hrs-2 yrs	1 yr
North Dakota	0.10	>250	Varies	91 days
Ohio	0.10	200-1,000	>3 days	180 days-3 yrs
Oklahoma	0.10	<1,000	10-365 days	180 days
Oregon	0.08	565-5,000	>48 hrs	1 yr
Pennsylvania	0.10	300-10,000	48 hrs	30 days-1 yr
Rhode Island	0.10	100-10,000	Varies	90-180 days
South Carolina	0.10	>200	48 hrs	180 days
South Dakota	0.10	<1,000	<1 yr	30 days
Tennessee	0.10	>350	48 hrs	1 yr
Texas	0.10	2,000-10,000	Varies	90-180 days
Utah	0.08	700-5,000	48 hrs	90 days
Vermont	0.08	750-2,500	Varies	90-80 days
Virginia	0.08	200-2,500	Varies	1 yr
Washington	0.08	685-5,000	24 hrs-1 yr	90 days
West Virginia	0.10	100-500	24 hrs	180 days
Wisconsin	0.10	150-300	Varies	180-270 days
Wyoming	0.10	200-750	Varies	90 days

State	BAC Limit*	Fine ($)	Second Offense Jail	Suspension
Alabama	0.08	1,000-5,000	48 hrs-1 yr	1 yr
Alaska	0.08-0.10	>500	20 days	>1 yr
Arizona	0.10	500	90 days	1-3 yrs
Arkansas	0.10	>400	>7 days	16 mos
California	0.08	390-5,000	48 hrs	1.5 yrs
Colorado	0.05-0.10	500-1,500	90 days-1 yr	90 days
Connecticut	0.10	500-8,000	10 days	1-2 yrs
Delaware	0.10	230-6,000	60 days	1.5 yrs
District of Columbia	0.10	300-10,000	90 days	1 yr
Florida	0.08	500-1,000	<9 mos	5 yrs
Georgia	0.08	300-1,000	48 hrs	1 yr
Hawaii	0.08	150-10,000	48 hrs	1 yr
Idaho	0.08	<2,000	10 days-1 yr	1 yr
Illinois	0.08	<1,000	<1 yr	3 yrs
Indiana	0.10	500-10,000	5 days	1-2 yrs
Iowa	0.10	>1,500	7 days	1 yr
Kansas	0.08	500-2,500	5 days	1 yr
Kentucky	0.10	350-500	7 days-6 mos	1 yr
Louisiana	0.10	200	Varies	1 yr
Maine	0.08	400-2,400	7-12 days	1.5 yrs
Maryland	0.07	0-300	48 hrs	1 yr
Massachusetts	0.08	600-10,000	30 days-2.5 yrs	2 yrs
Michigan	0.07-0.10	200-1,000	2-365 days	1-5 yrs
Minnesota	0.04-0.10	700-3,000	30 days	180 days
Mississippi	0.10	>600	Varies	1-2 yrs
Missouri	0.10	<1,000	<1 yr	5 yrs
Montana	0.10	300-500	7-180 days	90 days-1 yr
Nebraska	0.04-0.10	200-500	Varies	180 days-1 yr
Nevada	0.10	200-5,000	10 days 6 mos	1 yr
New Hampshire	0.08	350-1,000	10 days	180 days-3 yrs
New Jersey	0.05-0.10	500-1,000	48 hrs - 90 days	2 yrs
New Mexico	0.08	300-5,000	Varies	1 yr
New York	0.05-0.10	<10,000	<7 yrs	1 yr
North Carolina	0.08	1,000-2,000	7 days-2 yrs	4 yrs
North Dakota	0.10	>500	4 days	1 yr
Ohio	0.10	300-1,500	>10 days	1-5 yrs
Oklahoma	0.10	<2,500	1-5 yrs	1 yr
Oregon	0.08	565-5,000	>48 hrs	3 yrs
Pennsylvania	0.10	300-10,000	30 days	1 yr
Rhode Island	0.10	100-10,000	10 days	1-2 yrs
South Carolina	0.10	>1,000	48 hrs	1 yr
South Dakota	0.10	<1,000	>3 days	1 yr
Tennessee	0.10	>600	45 days	2 yrs
Texas	0.10	2,000-10,000	30 days	180 days-1 yr
Utah	0.08	700-5,000	240 hrs	1 yr
Vermont	0.08	750-2,500	48 yrs	1.5 yrs
Virginia	0.08	200-2,500	48 hrs	3 yrs
Washington	0.08	925-5,000	30 days-1 yr	2 yrs
West Virginia	0.10	500-1,000	6 mos-1 yr	10 yrs
Wisconsin	0.10	300-1,000	5-180 days	1-5 yrs
Wyoming	0.10	200-750	7 days	1 yr

TABLE 6.1 *(continued)*

State	BAC Limit*	Fine ($)	Third Offense Jail	Suspension
Alabama	0.08	2,000-10,000	60 days-1 yr	3 yrs
Alaska	0.08-0.10	>1,000	60 days	>3 yrs
Arizona	0.10	Varies	4 yrs	3 yrs
Arkansas	0.10	>900	>90 days	2.5. yrs
California	0.08	390-5,000	30 days	3 yrs
Colorado	0.05-0.10	Varies	Varies	2 yrs
Connecticut	0.10	500-8,000	120 days	2-3 yrs
Delaware	0.10	230-6,000	3 mos	2 yrs
District of Columbia	0.10	300-10,000	90 days	2 yrs
Florida	0.08	1,000-2,500	<1 yr	10 yrs
Georgia	0.08	300-1,000	10 days	5 yrs
Hawaii	0.08	150-10,000	10 days	1-5 yrs
Idaho	0.08	<5,000	30 days-1 yr	1-5 yrs
Illinois	0.08	<10,000	1-3 yrs	>6 yrs
Indiana	0.10	500-10,000	Varies	10 yrs
Iowa	0.10	>2,500	30 days	6 yrs
Kansas	0.08	500-2,500	90 days	1 yr
Kentucky	0.10	500-1,000	30 days-1 yr	2 yrs
Louisiana	0.10	300	Varies	730 days
Maine	0.08	400-2,400	30-40 days	4 yrs
Maryland	0.07	0-300	48 hrs	1.5 yrs
Massachusetts	0.08	1,000-1,500	150 days-5 yrs	8 yrs
Michigan	0.07-0.10	500-5,000	1-5 yrs	5 yrs
Minnesota	0.04-0.19	700-3,000	30 days	Indefinite
Mississippi	0.10	>2,000	Varies	3-5 yrs
Missouri	0.10	<5,000	<5 yrs	10 yrs
Montana	0.10	500-1,000	30-365 days	90 days-1 yr
Nebraska	0.04-0.10	200-500	90 days	1-15 yrs
Nevada	0.10	200-5,000	1-6 yrs	3 yrs
New Hampshire	0.08	350-1,000	10 days	3 yrs <
New Jersey	0.05-0.10	1,000	>180 days	10 yrs
New Mexico	0.08	300-5,000	Varies	>10 yrs
New York	0.05-0.10	Varies	Varies	1 yr <
North Carolina	0.08	<2,000	14 days-2 yrs	Indefinite
North Dakota	0.10	1,000	60 days	2 yrs
Ohio	0.10	500-2,500	30 days-1 yr	Varies
Oklahoma	0.10	<5,000	1-10 yrs	3 yrs
Oregon	0.08	565-5,000	>48 hrs	3 yrs
Pennsylvania	0.10	300-10,000	90 days	1 yr
Rhode Island	0.10	100-10,000	6 mos	2-3 yrs
South Carolina	0.10	>3,500	60 days	2 yrs
South Dakota	0.10	<2,000	< 2 yrs	>1 yr
Tennessee	0.10	>1,100	120 days	3-10 yrs
Texas	0.10	2,000-10,000	2 yrs	180 days-1 yr
Utah	0.08	700-5,000	1,000 hrs	1 yr
Vermont	0.08	750-2,500	Varies	3 yrs
Virginia	0.08	200-2,500	30 days	Indefinite
Washington	0.08	1,725-5,000	90 days-1 yr	3 yrs
West Virginia	0.10	3,000-5,000	1-3 yrs	Indefinite
Wisconsin	0.10	600-2,000	30-365 days	2-3 yrs
Wyoming	0.10	200-750	7 days	3 yrs

ceeds the legal limit for that state. Unfortunately, many drinking and driving offenders continue to slip through legal loopholes if proper police procedures were not followed or if the blood alcohol measure could in some way be contested.

ASSESSMENT, REFERRAL CRITERIA, AND INCENTIVES

Critical to any initiative to control drunk driving is the identification of those who will likely drive drunk repeatedly and determine the nature of their underlying problems. This is vital so that appropriate actions, in terms of sanctions and treatment, can be taken. Upon a first conviction, many offenders are automatically referred to alcohol education classes and possibly receive treatment if considered necessary. DWI offenders with an exceptionally high BAC level or multiple offenses are assessed to determine potential alcohol problems. If found to be chemically dependent or at high risk for chemical dependency by a certified alcohol/drug counselor, pursuant to the diagnosis criteria adopted in that state, offenders are either assigned to a treatment agency or given a choice of programs from among state-approved facilities.

Each state has its own battery of assessment tools for determining offender alcohol problems. The face-to-face interview is the most widely used assessment tool; however, the Mortimer-Filkins paper-and-pencil test is also quite popular. Other common tools are the Michigan Alcoholism Screening Tool (MAST), Substance Abuse Life Circumstances Evaluation (SALCE), Addiction Severity Index (ASI) and Driver Risk Inventory (DRI). Some states utilize a locally created tool, such as New Jersey's use of a questionnaire developed at Rutgers University (see Chapter 5 for a discussion of assessment measures).

After assessments are performed, a decision regarding who should be referred for treatment must be made. Some states, such as Nevada and Minnesota, only admit court-mandated offenders, generally those convicted of a DWI offense, into the program. Similarly, offenders who sign diversion agreements can avoid prosecution, incarceration, and a prolonged license suspension in exchange for attending a treatment program. Washington, DC, along with a handful of states that allow offenders to choose treatment as a substitute for jail time, is almost exclusively diversionary in nature. And, although Kansas and Vermont have no criteria for referral to treatment, most states have very specific criteria that must be met, namely a diagnosis of substance abuse, for referral to treatment. Wyoming currently uses the DSM-IV criteria (APA, 1994), while Michigan, Montana, and West Virginia use the American Society of Addiction Medicine Patient Placement Criteria (ASAM, 1998). States such as Florida, New Jersey, and Oregon, however, utilize their own locally developed guidelines based on criteria such as diagnostic indicators, previous driving record, and prior treatment for substance abuse.

In most states, there are additional incentives for entering and successfully completing a DWI offender program. The most common incentive for completing an offender program is reinstatement of the previously confiscated license. If the license is not automatically restored after treatment completion, then the offender is usually able to apply for reinstatement following the suspension period. Other incentives include reduced or suspended jail time and the ability to receive a restricted license, which allows offenders to drive to and from home, work, and a treatment facility.

PROGRAM DESCRIPTIONS

DWI offender programs generally fall under the authority of the Department of Transportation or the Department of Health Services for that state. Many programs, however, are coadministered by the two departments. In several states, the rules and procedures of the DWI offender program are established by the Department of Transportation, but the assessment and treatment of offenders is governed by the Department of Health Services.

As mentioned previously, a number of states have programs that allow certain DWI offenders to be diverted from criminal sanctions by entering alcohol education or treatment programs. Diversion programs, also known as Deferred Prosecution, Deferred Adjudication, Deferred Sentencing, and Pre-Trial Diversion, to name a few, are almost always restricted to first offenders. After successful completion of a treatment or education program, diversion programs generally allow charge dismissal and can prevent or delay information about an offense from appearing on the offender's driving record. Clearly, the biggest problem with this type of program is that many repeat offenders remain first offenders in official records. Supporters argue that, while diversion programs have not proven effective in reducing recidivism, they do serve to relieve a strain on the courts (The Century Council, 1997).

Most states do not have separate procedures for offenders based on frequency of convictions. However, there are a few states that make a distinction between first-time and multiple offenders and the type of treatment they receive. For example, in Mississippi, first-time offenders are sent through an education-based system governed by the Mississippi State Alcohol Safety Education Program. Multiple offenders, on the other hand, are remanded to programs under the direction of the Department of Mental Health. In states with programs similar to the one in Mississippi, first offenders are required to attend education classes, but may not undergo formal evaluation and treatment. Once the offender attends the mandatory classes, he or she is considered to have completed the program. Multiple offenders, however, are required to receive much more rigorous treatment and may be subjected to monitoring following completion of the program. In Alabama, treatment is begun at the least-restrictive model, generally starting at intensive outpatient, and increased to inpatient treatment if the defendant fails to meet treatment goals at the lower level of treatment intensity.

When addressing the question of which treatment will effectively reduce repeated violations, there is no one right answer. When it comes to alcohol treatment programs, the options are quite diverse. The focus of treatment varies by agency and by offender needs, but there are some general themes present in many of the programs. Considering that it was a DWI violation that brought the offender to the attention of the court, it seems logical that one goal found in several state programs is the reduction of recidivism. This is achieved through educational courses focused on alcohol, substance abuse, and driving safety. These programs generally consider themselves education-focused, or information-only programs. For those offenders who have an identified substance abuse problem, or who may be at high risk, programs are concerned with recovery and abstinence, through problem identification, recognizing the destructive effects of alcohol, and improving decision-making. These treatment-focused programs attempt to help clients reach an awareness of their problems while changing attitudes and behaviors.

The length of treatment each offender receives in any state program varies. Driver improvement course requirements can be as short as eight hours, while treatment programs can be as lengthy as one year. The average length of education-based treatment ranges from eight to forty hours across any number of days or weeks depending on the intensity of the program. Treatment programs generally run anywhere from seventy-two hours to one year, but across the fifty states the average length is approximately three to six months.

As one might conclude, as the length of required treatment varies, so does the cost. Although some states provide supplemental funding, the majority of the state programs are supported 100 percent through client funds. In fact, approximately 64 percent are funded this way, with 34 percent of the state programs utilizing some combination of client, state, and federal funding. Only one state, Arkansas, provides 100 percent of the offender program funding. Program costs vary based on the type of treatment provided, assessments performed, paperwork handling fees, and course materials. Clients can expect to spend anywhere from $45 per session to several thousands of dollars for an extended stay at an intensive outpatient facility; however, the average program cost per client is approximately $400. Because the financial burden is frequently shouldered solely by the offender, many programs offer a sliding scale for those who have difficulties making payments. In Massachusetts, clients determined indigent by the court do not pay program fees. In such cases, programs access a state-funded indigency pool for reimbursement. Considering the provisions for indigent clients and the sliding fee scale, it is somewhat surprising that very few programs report suffering from inadequate funding. Those programs claiming a need for increased funding generally site staff shortages and the inability to maintain and coordinate programs as the resulting obstacles.

Individual treatment plans are required in a majority of the state programs. This plan, tailored to the unique needs of the offender, is frequently used in making the program completion determination. Of those states that have a DWI offender program, all require some type of determination to verify program success. Throughout the various programs, these determinations are made by a myriad of people.

Treatment provider program staff, to include certified chemical dependency counselors, case managers, and program directors, have all been tasked with making the final assessment of treatment termination. If program attendance was court mandated, the original sentencing judge or assigned probation officer may be responsible for this determination. In those cases, input from the treatment agency can be incorporated to supplement the court's decision. Programs that are strictly educational in nature may assign this task to the individual class instructor.

As with the source, the basis for the completion determination is equally varied. Educational and treatment-focused programs have very different completion requirements. Education-based programs frequently use participation and class attendance to justify a favorable determination. In addition, the offender may be required to pass a post-test or prove that he or she has met assigned DWI risk-reduction goals. Treatment-focused programs tend to use the attainment of more abstract goals as the basis of successful completion. Evaluators look for compliance with treatment requirements, adherence to any treatment contract, attitudinal and behavioral changes, and offender understanding of the offense in their assessment. California's offender program looks for significant improvement in occupational performance, physical and mental health, family relations, and financial affairs in determining completion status. In some programs, continued sobriety is a condition for a favorable determination. Virtually all programs, whether stated or not, expect all associated fees to be paid and paperwork to be completed before a completion determination will be processed.

Regardless of the state, failure to successfully complete a mandatory treatment program, be it educational or otherwise, has consequences. Most frequently, any and all charges previously set aside as a condition for entering a program are reinstated against the offender. Jail sentences, fines, and suspensions are determined and enforced to the fullest extent of that state's law.

PREVENTING RECIDIVISM

In 1994, 31 percent of the 1.5 million people arrested for DWI were repeat offenders (http://www.ncadd.com, 1999). It is estimated that up to 80 percent of DWI offenders continue to drive while their license is revoked (http://www.ncadd.com, 1999). In an attempt to address the problems associated with conventional legal sanctions, many states have begun to use alternative restrictions, such as ignition interlock devices and home arrest with electronic monitoring, as a substitute for incarceration. Today the technology available to monitor and prevent drinking and driving is virtually limitless.

The breath-alcohol ignition interlock device is a mechanism installed in a vehicle, which is set to lock a motor vehicle's ignition when it registers a specified alcohol setpoint. The standard ignition interlock device contains a mouthpiece, memory sufficient to record date and time of various information, antitampering mechanisms, and a breath sample retest feature. These devices can be rather expensive, which contributes to the limited use, despite the availability in several states. Maine, one of approximately twenty-two states authorizing the use of these devices, has very stringent rules governing their use. Regulations in that state dictate everything from manufacturer certification, to installer requirements, to orientation and training for the device. In fact, Maine's Interlock Program is currently in suspension because there is no longer an approved manufacturer of the device doing business in the state.

There are generally two ways to get an ignition interlock device installed in an offender's vehicle. The first is by court order and the other is by offender request. A court-ordered interlock device is installed in an offender's vehicle for use after the offender's license has been reinstated or while the offender is operating under a limited license. The length of time the device must be in the vehicle varies by state and by sentence. Some courts only require the interlock device be used until the end of the suspension period. Others may insist the device be kept operational until a specified period after the full license reinstatement. In Illinois, the average length of participation in that state's ignition interlock program is estimated to be fourteen months. Several states allow an offender to request the installation of the device in order to facilitate receiving a restricted license or as part of an agreement with his or her auto-insurance provider. Should the requestor meet the qualifications, an interlock device can be installed, and eventually removed, at his or her own expense. In a recent review of the literature on interlock devices, Coben and Larkin

(1999) concluded that in five of the six studies reviewed, interlock devices were effective in reducing recidivism during the time period that the interlock device was installed in the car.

In addition to ignition interlock devices, Michigan employs such innovative sanctions as home-based random breath-video identification systems and remote alcohol testing with voice recognition, as well as electronic ankle bracelets. Arizona, Nevada, Rhode Island, and Minnesota also utilize ankle tethers to prevent recidivism. However, these measures are generally reserved for habitual offenders. Immobilization and impoundment processes are also in place in many states to reduce the number of DWI violations. Immobilization can take the form of a wheel boot or a steering wheel lock as mandated by local courts and implemented by law enforcement officials. The length of time the vehicle remains impounded is at the discretion of the courts, but commonly runs concurrently with the period of license suspension.

Vehicle impoundment is usually executed in the case of offenders with multiple prior convictions. However, early in 1999, New York City Mayor Rudolph Giuliani created controversy by instituting a new basis for vehicle forfeiture. Motorists caught at or above the legal limit at any DWI checkpoint will have their vehicle confiscated immediately, regardless of prior clean record, and are subject to criminal prosecution. According to reports, even if the drivers are found not guilty in criminal proceedings, they may find challenges in the civil court when attempting to retrieve the impounded vehicle (Beals, 1999). Additionally, many citizens were disturbed because of the hardship these immediate seizures created for the family of the offenders. This initiative, justified under the forfeiture provision in the city's administrative code, which allows for the confiscation of instrumentality of crime, remains a source of legal and social debate.

Another alternative sanction has proven less popular. A 1994 report by the National Highway Traffic Safety Administration examined Washington and Oregon laws that provided for a special striped sticker to be placed over the vehicle license plate registration tag of drivers with a suspended license (Voas and Tippetts, 1994). These "Zebra Sticker Laws," as they became known, were intended to provide probable cause for stopping the vehicle in the future by making the vehicle readily identifiable. Although Washington showed little change, the results in Oregon indicated the sticker program was effective in decreasing the rates of accidents, moving violations, and DWI offenses by both drivers who had received stickers and those at risk of receiving a sticker. Although the authors of this report concluded that zebra sticker programs could be effective in reducing rates of additional violations such as DWI, these laws did not receive widespread public acceptance in either state and both allowed their laws to expire when they came up for review (Voas and Tippetts, 1994).

Another sanction that has been investigated recently is the use of "house arrest" as an alternative to jail sentences for multiple DWI offenders (Courtright, Berg, and Mutchnick, 1997). A study of such a program, which employed EM, or electronic monitoring, was found to be more cost effective than jail time. Incarceration has been shown to be an effective tool in preventing DWI recidivism; however, studies of electronically monitored house arrest have not investigated the overall impact on reducing recidivism with long-term follow-up studies.

Unfortunately, although there are many innovative interventions in place to prevent recidivism, the difficulty remains as to how to measure success. It is routinely accepted that for the hundreds that are caught each day, many more go undetected. According to one researcher, fewer than 5 percent of all DWI offenders are arrested in any given year (Nichols, 1990). Although it is possible that interventions have contributed to a decrease in DWI violations, it is more probable that the offenders are just more careful about not getting caught. To be sure, it is difficult to accurately assess recidivism rates given the difficulty of attaining the true magnitude of the initial violation.

After examining the various programs and measures to curb DWI violations, it is important to address the challenges to success and what can be done to overcome them. According to a nationwide survey conducted by the National Highway Traffic Safety Administration (NHTSA) in 1998, several problems exist in the enforcement of laws against drunk driving. It was found that police officers are often overburdened with responsibilities, adjudication is too prolonged, judges assign sentences based on little information, and laws lowering BAC limits have seemed to have little effect (NHTSA, 1998). During the Surgeon General's Workshop on Drunk Driving, held in 1988, various panels recommended remedies that could have prevented some of these difficulties had they been implemented. For instance, they suggested empowering the community to become involved through education and participation in policy development, adopting license suspension procedures that will minimize the amount of time required for field officers to carry out testifying functions, and making alcohol assessments available to the judge prior to sentencing ("Highlights," 1990). In addition, the panels recommended that states should apply "hard" driver's license revocations for a minimum of ninety days for first offenders accompanied with mandatory sanctions such as fines or jail ("Highlights," 1990). More recently, however, research has shown that traditional penalties, even if stringently applied, may not be sufficient. A review of 215 studies conducted by the National Commission Against Drunk Driving found that, compared to traditional legal sanctions, a combined intervention approach consisting of education, licensing sanctions, psychotherapy/counseling, and follow-up supervision reduced recidivism and alcohol-related crashes by 7 to 9 percent. (NCADD, 1999).

So, what might a program of the future look like? An example of an alternative to the more traditional approach to treatment is Chicago's Haymarket House (The Century Council, 1997). This Rehabilitative Confinement Program (RCP), as it is known, combines detention, community service, treatment, and payment of fines or monetary sanctions. Offenders in the Chicago area are remanded to these RCPs in week-long increments, up to four weeks. RCPs are housing facilities with fully supervised detention capacity, where offenders are monitored at all times. Offenders also participate in the Sheriff's Work Alternative Program (SWAP) as a form of community service (The Century Council, 1997).

With so many factors at play: legislation, sanctions, assessment, treatment, evaluation, and potential recidivism, it is not surprising that each state program differs from the next. Legislative bodies pass laws, such as zero tolerance and implied consent, in an effort to gain control over the problem of drunk driving. Whether or not lowering the BAC level will assist in this effort remains an area of debate. Also in contention is the type of approach, be it hard sanctions, diversion, or treatment, that is most effective for reducing drunk driving. Although many researchers say a combination of sanctions and treatment is the best answer, states continue to manage their programs the way they see fit. Factors playing a role in program management include time, cost, resources, and public support, to name a few. Finally, the ongoing struggle to control recidivism will continue to spawn new, creative technology and innovative ideas for offender programs. Considering the countless nuances of this topic, it is important to consider how and why state programs operate as they do in order to improve them in the future. For more information on state and national provisions for drunk driving or to view current research in this area, visit the following Web sites:

> http://www.carsearch.com/links/dmv.html
> http://www.dwidata.org
> http://www.ncadd.com
> http://www.nhtsa.dot.gov

Chapter 7

Resistance Issues in the Treatment of the DWI Offender

This chapter explores specific resistance issues that are salient to working with the DWI offender population. Our goal is to present the reader with some pertinent facts and relevant information regarding resistance to treatment and to discuss how resistance issues may impact the treatment process. We will also present some ideas on how to manage resistance.

It is well known that DWI offenders are not the only population to present with resistance to the assessment and treatment process. Nearly anyone who is mandated to treatment or forced into treatment by another person, agency, or organization will most often resist treatment to one degree or another. As the saying goes, "Minds are like parachutes, they only work when they are open." Unfortunately, the court-mandated DWI offender's mind often is shut tight. What makes the DWI population so difficult to work with is that so often the offender manifests a multitude of defenses when presenting for assessment, education, or treatment. For the alcoholism counselor, the DWI offender will present classic manifestations of denial (e.g., "I wasn't drinking; it must have been the cough syrup I was taking."). There have been instances in which DWI offenders have been videotaped at the time of the DWI arrest. When the videotape was then presented in court, depicting this individual in his or her most drunken state, the DWI offender screamed, "That is not me on that tape; it must be an actor that looks like me!" There are also classic manifestations of minimization (e.g., "I only had three beers. How can that put me over the legal limit?" Or projection, the best known of which is, "Those damn cops were out to nail me; that's why they were just waiting for me to come out of the bar that night." Less common, if ever, we will even hear a DWI offender state, "I admit it; I screwed up. I should not have been behind the wheel of my car after drinking that much." Oftentimes, DWI offenders are grappling with two issues. First, they may be questioning whether they have a drinking problem and second, they may question their culpability in having caused a motor vehicle accident or fatality.

Some studies illustrate this point. Yoder and Moore (1973) found that only 26 percent of first offenders thought they had a drinking problem, whereas 69 percent of the Michigan Alcoholism Screening Test (MAST) scores indicated they did have a drinking problem. Similarly, Cavaiola, Wolf, and Lavender (1999) found that of seventy-seven first offenders and seventy-one multiple offenders, that only 5 percent and 12 percent, respectively, had responded "No" to Question #1 of the MAST, "Do you think you are a normal drinker?" When questioned further about those who responded "No," many indicated that they had stopped drinking after the DWI offense. Therefore, they did not consider themselves "normal drinkers," and did not necessarily considered themselves to be alcoholics or problem drinkers either.

The term "resistance" was first used by psychoanalytically oriented therapists, and it was rare to ever find the term used by behaviorally oriented therapists (Wachtel, 1982). In its more general usage, resistance refers to any client behavior that the therapist or counselor labels as antitherapeutic (Turkat and Meyer, 1982). At one time, resistance was thought to occur on both a conscious and an unconscious level, however, in its more popular usage, resistance usually refers to the unmotivated client who wants nothing to do with change. Lazarus and Fay (1982) state, "Resistant patients are neither people who do not want help nor deliberate saboteurs, but instead people for whom exploration and change are difficult, painful and even dangerous" (p. 200). This may certainly be true of many DWI offenders as well.

Another way to view resistance is presented in the Prochaska-DiClemente model (1982). Although the Transtheoretical Model was initially studied with regard to cigarette smokers, it has been applied appropriately to other addictive behaviors. This model provides a conceptualization for how and why people change. Rather than looking at "resistance" as resulting from various pernicious personality traits such as denial or projection or that clients are basically unmotivated for change (Miller and Rollnick, 1991), the Transtheoretical Model attempts to explain so-called resistance as a process of change which has various stages. This model is often depicted as having six stages; for example, in the *precontemplation* stage, individuals are not yet even considering the possibility of change because they may not see themselves as having a problem or the problems they may be experiencing are viewed as outside of themselves. Therefore, individuals in the precontemplation stage often do not present for treatment, and if they do, they do not do so of their own free will. Such would be the case with many of the DWI offenders who are mandated into an assessment, education, or treatment program.

The second stage is called the *contemplation* stage. Here, the person enters a state of ambivalence, vacillating between reasons for concern versus reasons not to be concerned or reasons to change versus reasons not to change. Although these individuals will present in treatment, they may not appear very motivated, depending on what brought them into treatment. For example, in the midst of a crisis, a person may appear motivated to change, as a means of reestablishing equilibrium; however, once the crisis point has passed, he or she may not see any reason for change. Such would be the case with DWI offenders who seek counseling on their own, in the midst of the DWI crisis; however, if their case were dismissed for some reason, it would be unlikely that such individuals would continue to seek assistance.

The third stage, the *determination* stage, is likened to "a window of opportunity" (Miller and Rollnick, 1991) in which the individual clearly admits to the problem and is determined to do something about it. The next stage, the *action* stage, is when the individual engages in certain behaviors to bring about change, such as going to counseling, going to AA and/or NA meetings, participating in a group, working the Steps, and so on. Since change is not guaranteed, the individual must then take steps to ensure that progress is maintained. Such is the case in the *maintenance* stage, in which the individual may learn new behaviors or skills in order to maintain progress. An example of this would be the individual who avoids certain "people, places, or things" that have become associated with alcohol or drug use or the person who continues to attend AA or NA regularly, although perhaps not as frequently as when first becoming sober.

The last stage, the *relapse* stage, may or may not occur, usually depending on how serious the person is concerning maintenance behaviors. If relapse does occur, however, usually the person reverts to the beginning of these stages. In Prochaska and DiClemente's research with smokers it is noteworthy that the smokers would often go through these stages three or four times before they would quit smoking permanently.

The other important implication of the Transtheoretical Model is that it is important for counselors to match their counseling style with the particular stage presented by the client. For example, with an individual in the precontemplation stage, it is important to provide information or education about what might constitute a problem. For the person in the contemplation stage, it would be helpful for the counselor to try to bring up issues that would help to tip the balance or tip the scales in favor of change. In the determination stage, the counselor helps by providing a good treatment match between the needs of the client and the best possible treatment available to that individual. In the action stage, the counselor's role is to help the individual work on issues that were central to their addiction and to help the addict with the self-diagnosis process and to continue to support the process of identification with other addicted individuals. In the maintenance stage, it is important to help the client develop a viable relapse prevention plan such as that discussed by Marlatt and Gordon (1985).

In a recent study by Wells-Parker and colleagues (2000), motivation to change and self-efficacy ratings were examined in 670 first-time DWI offenders who were court mandated to a four-week intervention program. Utilizing the stages of change for drinking scales (Rollnick et al., 1992) to measure motivation for change, based upon the Miller and Rollnick (1991) transtheoretical model, it was determined that the majority of these DWI offenders could be classified as being in the action stage at both pretest and posttest conditions (at the beginning and end of the four week program). Higher action and self-efficacy scores were related to lower recidivism rates, while those with the highest scores on the contemplation scale had higher recidivism rates. In terms of treatment implications, it was suggested that many DWI offenders may have acknowledged a drinking problem and that they were attempting to take action to change drinking behavior and/or drinking and driving behaviors. It was also noted, however, that many recidivists had both high action and self-efficacy scores, which may suggest that "confident attempts to control drinking and to avoid future drinking and driving events are not enough" (Wells-Parker et al., 2000, p. 237). It was concluded from this study that traditional DWI programs that focus on confrontation of denial may not be effective approaches with those offenders who are in the action stage. Instead, it may be more effective to focus on current drinking behavior and plans to avoid drinking and driving events. In working with DWI offenders, it is equally important to assess what stage they present in as a means of working more effectively with them. Obviously, not all DWI offenders are alike, therefore it is imperative for the counselor to determine what motivation or potential motivating factor exists. This will be addressed in greater detail later in this chapter.

RESISTANCE AND THE DWI OFFENDER

The initial manifestation of resistance on the part of the DWI client is usually one of anger (see Figure 7.1). Furthermore, it is not uncommon for this anger to be directed at the treatment agency or the counselor. In many instances, the referral to the counseling agency represents the first time that the DWI offender is not dealing with a faceless bureaucrat, so unfortunately, the counselor often gets the brunt of months of suppressed anger. Anger is then often expressed at the court system, the judge, the police, and so on. It is recommended that the counselor not challenge these assaults and accusations or get into a debate about "the corruption in the system," a favorite topic of most DWI offenders. No matter which "side" the counselors take, they lose, More importantly, by engaging in debate, usually control of the session is lost and most treatment agencies require that some intake information be collected within the first session or two. Lazarus and Fay (1982) recommend that counselors start out with a logical, supportive, empathetic approach, e.g., "Most people get angry when forced into things they don't want to do" (p. 125). This may help to elicit a less negative reaction from the client. Even though the counselor does not agree

FIGURE 7.1. Stages of Resistance in the DWI Offender Referred to Treatment

---

Stage 1: Anger Stage: Regarding the referral to treatment "How dare *they* order me to treatment," "How dare *they* label me an alcoholic," or "Others may need an alcohol awareness program, not me."

Stage 2: Testing the Limits: Client tests the counselor, the agency, or the legal system. Bargaining most likely to occur in this stage. "Maybe if I miss a few sessions, no one will really notice or care" or "These stupid rules apply to others, not to me."

Stage 3: Compliance Stage: Client cautious in self-disclosures, going through the motions. "I'll do anything you say; let's just get this thing over with."

Stage 4: Anger Stage (Part 2): Client angered by being forced to look at drinking behavior, being forced to look at DWI as a drinking-related event or being forced to take responsibility for behavior.

Stage 5: Self-Depreciation Stage: Client may begin to feel angry at self. Some non-clinical depression may appear. "I was stupid. I shouldn't have been behind the wheel of a car when I had so much to drink."

Stage 6: Surrender/Acceptance: Client is willing to accept responsibility for the DWI offense and accepts the need to address this issue. Willingly accepts the need for counseling, group sessions, or perhaps even active AA attendance.

---

with the DWI offender's projection of blame, it is essential that individual feels that he or she is being heard, otherwise, this will only reinforce resistance. The offender will not be willing to hear the counselor when it comes to discussing ways to prevent recidivism. It is also essential to understand that the DWI offender population tends to manifest an external locus of control (Cavaiola and DeSordi, 1999; Donovan, 1980). Individuals with an external locus of control usually tend to see events happening as a result of chance, good or bad luck, or forces that are beyond their control. They often do not take responsibility for their behavior even when good things happen. It is therefore the rare DWI offender who will enter treatment saying, "I am responsible for my DWI. I messed up and should not have been behind the wheel of a car after drinking."

The anger that is often seen in this initial stage of treatment is based upon this perceived lack of responsibility and is often based on fear. Here, the DWI offender may fear that if one were to take responsibility for the DWI event it would mean needing to face issues regarding the role of irresponsible drinking behavior, the use of poor judgment, or possibly alcoholism. For most DWI offenders, it is "easier" to focus blame elsewhere and to defend their position with anger. What is unfortunate, however, is that often the referral process creates more anger and resistance to treatment.

For example, it will sometimes take months before the DWI offender is adjudicated (sometimes a strategy used by defense attorneys to stall for time by requesting several postponements). Once offenders are in the system, they have already paid fines, have had their licenses suspended, and have gone through various aspects of the judicial system before entering treatment. This is not to say that legal sanctions are not necessary or effective. They are indeed effective and research studies support this contention (Nichols, 1990). Studies also indicate that treatment has also been effective in reducing recidivism (Wieczorek, 1993). What is central to the issue of resistance is that treatment is often looked upon as an afterthought. In some states, DWI offenders are not even told that education or treatment programs are part of the consequences of a DWI conviction until well after their cases have been adjudicated. When DWI offenders are then told that they must participate in such programs, they often report feeling deceived, which naturally results in feelings of anger.

At this point, the DWI client has either signed a written treatment contract or has verbally consented to attend an alcohol awareness or counseling program. In the second stage of resistance, testing the limits, the DWI client begins to test the parameters of this contract. Here, the client may be testing the counselor's sincerity or credibility in enforcing the contract or treatment agreement. Very simply, a treatment contract is not a contract unless it has defined consequences in the event the agreement is broken. For example, the contract should, ideally, specify what consequences will be incurred if the client misses sessions, comes to the session under the influence, and so on. Other examples of "testing the limits"-types of resistance include showing up late for sessions, nonpayment of fees, late cancellation of sessions, or no-shows.

Although these stages will often overlap and manifest themselves in various order, clients will often become compliant at this point in treatment as they enter a compliance stage. This is not unlike the child who first tests parental limits before accepting them. DWI clients will often comply with treatment while not investing much of themselves in the treatment process. They show up, speak when spoken to, yet at the same time their compliance is evident in their lack of self-disclosure. At this juncture, counselors will sometimes become complacent and often settle for this behavior as a treatment gain. Forrest (1982) writes about the importance of confrontation as an integral part of treatment. Here, the counselor provides feedback to the client, continues to stress reality, and redirects the client's attention back to himself or herself. By confronting the client, the counselor avoids being "the patsy," i.e., feeding into the externalization and avoidance behavior (denial, distortions, etc.) of the client, with the goal of trying to create internal conflict within the client. As we all know, individuals who are comfortable are not usually motivated toward change. Miller and Rollnick (1991) stress the point, however, that confrontation does not imply a vicious assault of the client, but rather can take many forms, and counselors should be creative in how they confront the client with reality. Small (1981) provides an excellent description of confrontation:

> The act of bringing the client face-to-face with his reality as you perceive him as a whole person. Confrontation occurs when there is an observed discrepancy between: (a) What a client is saying and your perception of what he is experiencing (b) What he is saying and what you heard him say at an earlier time (c) What he is saying now and his actions in everyday life. (p. 67)

Often in treating DWI clients there exists a discrepancy between what the client is saying and what he or she is experiencing. Beneath the anger or compliance are often other feelings that need to be drawn out through various types of confrontation, prodding, reassurance, and so on.

In the anger stage (Part 2), the client usually responds with anger to the confrontation or this anger may later manifest itself in self-deprecation. These are signs that internal conflict is taking place. This may be the opportune time to begin to explore alternatives with the client and to bring him or her closer to surrender/acceptance as the denial system begins to break down. One of the common elements to these later stages is that the client has invested himself or herself in the treatment process. Even responding with anger at this point may be better than apathy or complacency, for it signals that the client may be emotionally investing in the treatment process. Self-deprecation also signals that there is dissonance or conflict within the client, which also can be a favorable sign prognostically. Obviously, however, not all clients reach these later stages. It is not unusual for many DWI clients to remain locked in the first or second stages and to refuse to examine the DWI event as a drinking-related problem. It is important for the counselor to continually seek supervision and feedback from colleagues in order to examine their reactions to the DWI client and to continually examine better intervention strategies.

MANAGING RESISTANCE

It is often helpful for agencies and counselors to look at ways that they can refrain from adding fuel to the DWI offender's resistance. For example, it is recommended that as much of the treatment plan as possible be shared with the client as early in the treatment process as possible. Zelhart and Schurr (1977) point out that nonvoluntary DWI clients are often antagonistic, angry, frightened, deceptive, and will actively deny having any problem related to their alcohol use. They recommend that treatment planning take the form of a "consensual regimen" between client and counselor. Consensual regimen techniques have been effectively employed with other types of treatment, such as pharmacological therapy, as a means of eliciting cooperation and might include a contract between client and treatment staff, identifying and establishing the goals of treatment as well as the frequency of treatment. Davidson (1976), concludes that when the client and counselor agree on the priorities of counseling and establish clear contracts with achievable milestones or goals, the treatment process moves more smoothly and rapidly. Here it may be important to stress with the DWI client that there is an implicit common goal, i.e. the prevention of another DWI offense. We have yet to work with a DWI offender who did not agree that a repeat offense was undesirable, if for no other reason than to prevent ending up back in the legal system or back in treatment. Miller and Rollnick (1991) also point to the importance of beginning treatment at whatever stage the client presents in, with regard to the

Transtheoretical Model. For example, if a counselor were to use action stage strategies (e.g., deciding on more intensive treatment or recommending attendance at ninety AA meetings in ninety days) with a client who is clearly in the contemplation stage, then one would be certain to encounter greater resistance.

It is also important to stress the significance of a thorough assessment, not only in the early phases of treatment, but throughout the treatment process. Some counselors assume that assessment occurs only in the first session or two. Actually, assessment is an ongoing process in treatment. The resistant client will give up minimal information about himself or herself early in treatment. This does not mean that the questions need not be posed again at a later point in treatment. For example, even using a structured questionnaire such as the MAST (Selzer, 1971), the possibility exists that the DWI client may respond differently at the onset of treatment versus three months later.

Zelhart and Schurr (1977) also recommend that various sources of data be utilized in the assessment process. For example, they suggest including any prior treatment records (e.g., hospital records, motor vehicle reports, DWI arrest reports [including blood alcohol levels at the time of the arrest], and any other legal history, such as incidents of domestic violence). In addition, any biomedical or blood chemistry profile including liver function tests should be included. The use of multiple sources of information is also advocated in the Procedures Manual of the Mortimer-Filkins Questionnaire, which has been widely used in assessment of DWI offenders (Mortimer, Filkins, and Lower, 1971).

In addition, a thorough assessment should also incorporate contacts with family members or significant others (see Chapter 10). Although it is possible and sometimes likely that the family member will manifest the same denial or rationalizations as the DWI offender, it is still important to bring family members in at various points in the treatment process in order to assess their status and reactions. For example, one spouse, who initially was very resistant to coming in for a group session with family members and significant others, later on became one of the group's most outspoken advocates. Other family members who come in feeling angry and resistant will often let this defensive posture down once they learn that the counselor or agency is not out to blame them for the DWI offense. Therefore, it is imperative for DWI treatment programs to incorporate several family meetings or sessions both conjointly and nonconjointly with the DWI offender.

The reason for stressing the aforementioned assessment strategies and urging that they become part of the DWI program is that most DWI offenders obviously will enter the assessment or intake sessions feeling angry and suspicious. Therefore, it is important that the counselor view assessment as an ongoing process. DWI clients and family members often will reveal important information once they feel some trust in the counselor or agency, or sometimes once they see that counseling/treatment is coming to a close. Naturally, there are many DWI clients who remain guarded throughout. When possible, it is helpful to utilize more formal assessment tools with these DWI offenders such as the Substance Abuse Subtle Screening Inventory (SASSI) (Miller, 1994) or the MacAndrews Scale of the MMPI-2 (Hathaway and McKinley, 1989). Both of these measures will be able to give the counselor a measure of the client's defensiveness, yet they can also yield some valuable information in spite of their guardedness (see Chapter 5 for further discussion of these measures).

With regard to managing resistance, it is also important that counselors monitor their own resistance. A case in point, many treatment agencies will work with DWI offenders in group counseling settings. Many DWI groups, however, will offer education only and will not focus on the DWI clients (i.e., their reactions, feelings to the information they are receiving). Since education is vital to the treatment process, it is recommended that separate groups be devoted to didactic sessions (i.e., lectures, films, AA speakers) and that the client be well aware of the demarcation between the didactics and group counseling. Often a form of "counselor resistance" is found when the treatment staff opts to offer education or didactics only and very little in the way of assessment and "talking with" the client (as opposed to "talking at" them). A good example of this occurs when the counselor leading the DWI group bombards them with films. Although media tools can be effective, the counselor must remember that merely viewing a film is a passive experience. For behavior or attitude change to take place, an active, emotionally-engaging experience is usually considered to be more effective. Whitehead (1975) makes a good point by questioning the popularity of the education-only approach, which he concludes is probably a function of our culture's belief in "education as an overall . . . panacea of the twentieth century" (p. 130).

In order to lessen the likelihood of resistance and to increase participation, we found that structured exercises were helpful in the beginning to get the group talking, although not necessarily interacting. Group interaction will take more time to develop and is a more difficult challenge for the counselor. The client's fear may be based on the belief that "If I confront or expose you, then you will confront or expose me." Group facilitation techniques are useful in getting the group to interact. An example of this type of exercise is for group members to pair off and to interview each other on various "safe" topics (e.g., interests, hobbies, work history, special talents, or something about their family), and then talk about what they learned about each other in the large group. These topic areas can later move on to less safe areas such as discussing the DWI incident(s), drinking behavior, family-of-origin drinking attitudes, and behavior.

The counselor working with the DWI offender needs to continually be searching for "weak spots" in the client's defensive armor. For example, one twenty-five-year-old male who, after presenting with the usual denial and rationalizations for his DWI offense, began talking about his dream to become a stockbroker, which he had entertained since high school. It was from this disclosure that this client began to look at reasons why his goal had not been attained (i.e., because of his drinking behavior, the DWI offense, and subsequent loss of license). With his acceptance of this reality, he was then willing to explore alternatives to achieving his goal, which naturally implied that he would need to address his drinking problem as something that had held him back in many areas of his life. While being careful not to label his "drinking behavior" as alcoholic too quickly, he eventually came to this conclusion himself after attending the DWI group and some AA meetings. Another example of identifying the "weak spot" in the defense system involved a thirty-two-year-old woman who came into the DWI group feeling very angry with the courts, her lawyer, motor vehicles, and whomever else became a likely target for her anger. After a few sessions, she had disclosed that around the time of the DWI offense she had been going through a divorce that was not of her choice. From there she began to disclose her anger toward her ex-husband for leaving her and the depression she felt in response to the loss of the marriage. This is an example of what Gilliland and James (1997) refers to as a "transcrisis," when earlier crises will often compound or exacerbate a present crisis state. It also points to the stress that is created by the DWI event itself, as for many individuals this is the first time they have come in contact with the criminal justice system, the police, courts, and so on. Also, the stress of possible job loss, income loss, and telling family members about the arrest puts the individual into a state of crisis arising from these various stressors, which in turn results in feelings of resentment and resistance once the DWI offender enters treatment (Garrett, 1980).

CONCLUSION

Seasoned counselors will tell you that their favorite clients are those who really work hard at changing—clients who are motivated and who will go to any lengths to work on self-improvement. When group counselors think of a satisfying group experience, it is usually one in which all group members are working equally hard together. With the resistant client, the opposite is often the case. The counselor finds himself or herself feeling ineffectual, incompetent, or angry and frustrated. It is important that the counselor not transfer these feelings onto the client, for to do so will merely incite more resistance or a justification for the resistance already present. We also need to be aware of agency resistance as well. For example, treatment agencies often will give the DWI group to their least experienced counselors or to counselor trainees, with the rationale that since this group is the hardest to work with, if they make a few mistakes it is not a big deal. Unfortunately, with this population, mistakes can be quite serious, especially in view of DWI recidivism and the potential fatalities that may result. Therefore, it is important that counselors continue to expand their skills in working with resistant clients and in doing so, they will become more effective counselors with all of their clients.

Chapter 8

Treatment Strategies, Part 1

ISSUES IN TREATMENT

Treatment for drinking drivers can refer to a variety of therapeutic interventions, approaches, and programs. One of the difficulties confronting the treatment field is the lack of a generally accepted definition of treatment. Treatment programs can run the gamut of experiences: intensive outpatient counseling programs, education groups, outpatient counseling, and inpatient programs. A DWI offender could undergo any one of a wide variety of treatment modalities because programs vary significantly based on the defined treatment for a DWI client. Programs differ in the length of time an offender could be required to remain in a treatment program. Intensity levels of treatment for the DWI offender can vary from didactic groups, utilizing videotapes and lecture material, to process-oriented small groups, or individual counseling. The various program staffs offer an array of treatment services: providing Antabuse to clients, family therapy, self-help, relapse prevention, and self-control training, as well as traditional inpatient and outpatient chemical dependency treatment. However, the dominant form of treatment for DWI offenders is the education group. Wells-Parker (1994) found that 53 percent of the programs she studied were education-based modalities. Of the DWI programs studied, approximately one-third were considered to be counseling or psychotherapy types of programs. Less than 3 percent of the evaluated DWI offender programs included family counseling, relapse prevention, behaviorally oriented treatment regimes, or other commonly used elements of treatment in the alcoholism field. Fewer than 15 percent of the programs studied included AA or utilized medications to deter drinking.

There has been a great deal of controversy throughout the years as to whether or not treatment is effective in reducing DWI rates and associated fatalities. There have been many debates throughout the years as to whether deterrence approaches without a treatment component would be just as effective. Some even question whether treatment is effective at all. DWI offenders access treatment through the legal system. Another portion of the controversy surrounding treatment addresses the effectiveness of mandated treatment. The DWI offender represents a large portion of mandated referrals into the treatment system with the numbers rising consistently (Weisner, 1990). One argument as to whether treatment is an effective component of deterrence does not address treatment effectiveness, but rather points to the numbers of DWI offenders arrested. Lewis (1985) estimates that even if all apprehended offenders were mandated into treatment and were completely eliminated from all future crashes, we would see only a 25 percent reduction in crash fatalities caused by alcohol. Therefore, many argue that more of our resources should be allocated for general and specific deterrence programs, particularly roadside checkpoints and increased enforcement techniques, rather than treatment.

Others suggest that any effort made to address this issue must be comprehensive in its approach and include both deterrence measures and rehabilitative treatment programs (Wells-Parker, 1994). Simpson and Mayhew (1991) state that any effective countermeasure strategy aimed at the problem of repeat offenders must include a variety of tactics including primary, secondary, and tertiary prevention programs.

The deterrent effects of legal sanctions have been studied and reviewed throughout the literature. Nichols and Ross (1989), in their research on sanction effectiveness, concluded that license revocations, fines, confinement, and treatment produce some evidence of deterrent effect. However, research has consistently indicated license suspensions to be the most effective form of sanction, for both specific and general deterrence effects. Research shows a general deterrence effect related to license suspensions by population-wide reductions in alcohol-related crashes (Klein, 1989; Bloomberg, Preusser, and Ulmer, 1987). Furthermore, evidence suggests that the positive impact of legal sanctions is greater when combined with treatment. A number of research studies conclude that legal sanctions combined with treatment have more impact on reducing recidivism than sanctions alone (Sadler and Perrine, 1984, Tashima and Peck, 1986). Many researchers conclude that the combination of DWI education and treatment programs with license suspensions are more effective than treatment alone (Nichols and Ross, 1989). Wells-Parker (1994) found that treatment had a greater impact on repeat offenders than sanctions. Due to the limited effectiveness of DWI education and treatment programs alone, researchers in this area recommend these approaches not be used as a substitute for traditional sanctions, particularly license sanctions (e.g., Hagen, 1977; Nichols et al., 1981; Popkin et al., 1983; Mann et al., 1983; Voas, 1986; Sadler and Perrine, 1984; Peck, Sadler, and Perrine, 1985; Tashima and Peck, 1986; Nichols and Ross, 1989). Although there is little doubt in the literature that both treatment and legal deterrence impact the DWI problem, definitive conclusions are difficult to draw. More research is needed to better understand the effectiveness of the strategies used.

One of the problems that has often been encountered in the research literature is that sanctions (i.e., license suspension and treatment or rehabilitative approaches) were viewed as competing approaches to the DWI problem. Most researchers today agree that probably neither approach unilaterally is as effective in preventing DWI recidivism as when combined. As Wieczorek (1993) concludes, "Treatment and sanctions should be seen as complementary approaches to the reduction of alcohol-related accidents. Unfortunately, treatment has been viewed as an alternative and not as an adjunct to punishment and the research literature lacks studies that examine the combined effects" (p. 21).

OVERVIEW OF TREATMENT ISSUES

Overall, it has been difficult to produce conclusive research evidence that demonstrates treatment effectiveness (Annis, 1982; Annis and Chan, 1983). However, this does not mean that treatment does not work. Difficulties stem from within the research field, as well as the treatment field. Often, the terms used in research are not well defined and can vary in meaning from one research study to another. Therefore, it makes it difficult to generalize conclusions from the data. Frequently, studies have suffered from inadequate control groups, questionable assessment procedures, and validity problems with screening and measurement tools (Ross, 1984; Longabaugh and Lewis, 1988; Holden, 1983; McCarty and Argeriou, 1986). Mann and colleagues (1983), however, pointed out that lengthy follow-up periods have been a major strength of most DWI research. Establishing the efficacy of treatment is a vital, yet complicated, issue. Statistical methods have been limited in the ability to study treatment effectiveness. However, more recently, meta-analytic statistical methods have produced interesting and helpful data. By comparing outcomes from many different studies, researchers are able to examine data from a wide array of studies conducted. This technique overcomes the limitations of other methods.

Wells-Parker and colleagues (1995) conducted the best known of these studies. Wells-Parker (1994) described the meta-analytical technique as being "sensitive to similar patterns of results in large numbers of evaluation studies on a single topic even when the results of those studies do not show obvious across-study consistencies" (p. 303). Although treatment was effective by reducing recidivism 8 to 9 percent across all types of offenders and treatments when compared to untreated offenders, she concluded that it was not clear as to the reason for this effect (Wells-Parker, 1994). Many limitations of this study were noted, such as the inability to assess the level of alcohol consumption or level of family stress due to alcohol abuse. However, in spite of the inability to account for the effect, she concluded that "rehabilitation is more effective than sanctions such as license revocation for alcohol-related driving outcomes, including DUI recidivism or crashes involving alcohol" (Wells-Parker, 1994, p. 304). Wells-Parker and colleagues (1989) also found that "the general effects of any intervention will likely be small when evaluated with a heterogeneous sample. In general, when studying diverse groups, it is unlikely that any one intervention strategy will stand out as consistently effective.

Variables within the group such as age, gender, and education influence the effectiveness of the intervention. It is difficult to control for these variables, yet any valid measures obtained through research must include this control in their design. Researchers found that one of the problems with many of the educationally oriented DWI programs is that although knowledge and attitudes toward drinking and driving were improved, drinking outcomes often were not (Brown, 1980a; Brown, 1980b; Nichols, Ellingstad, and Struckman-Johnson, 1979; Vingilis, Adlaf, and Chung, 1981; Wells-Parker, 1989). Data interpretation can also be misleading and often relates to how the problem is perceived. For example, recidivism has been the main focus of measuring the success of treatment. Using this as a measure of treatment success produces interesting debate. The advantage of using this measurement is that it is concrete and unbiased. Others contend that it is not a valid measurement of treatment outcome, as it is not clear what is really being measured (McCarty and Argeriou, 1986; Beerman, Smith, and Hall, 1988). For example, many DWI offenders may continue to drink and drive without being arrested. Does a lower recidivism rate therefore merely reflect that the drinking driver has become more skilled at not getting arrested?

With the emphasis on the maximization of health care dollars, outcome studies are essential. However, the value of treatment cannot be measured in reduced crashes and recidivism alone. Improving treatment outcomes can also help prevent ongoing suffering and disruption of family life. It has also been found that those offenders who attend treatment have a 30 percent less mortality rate (Mann et al., 1994). Even if reducing fatalities by only 50 percent, we would save approximately 1,000 lives a year. The question remains, however, whether treatment is indeed effective and warranted as a means of dealing with the problem of drinking and driving. According to Wieczorek (1993), although the "prevailing wisdom on this matter, presented by Stewart and Ellingstad (1989), is that 'rehabilitative approaches can only have a very small effect on traffic safety, even if maximally effective,' recent research findings cast doubt on this conventional wisdom. A substantial number of alcohol-related fatal accidents may be avoided through effective treatment programs if DWI offenders are a sizable proportion of drivers in alcohol-related fatalities" (p. 5).

Another problem is that treatment programs often do not have well-defined goals or philosophies (Nunnally and Durham, 1975; Fitzpatrick, 1992; Frawley, 1988). Lack of clarity regarding goals and desired outcome influences our choices when developing program content. It is important to stress again that when designing treatment programs it is important to remember that DWI offenders do not necessarily fit the commonly accepted alcoholic profile. It is a widely accepted conclusion that treatment programs for DWI offenders need to be specifically designed to address the diversity within this population. However, DWI offenders are often provided the same treatment as alcoholics who enter treatment facilities. Traditional alcoholism treatment methods continue to be largely applied to this group, although a growing body of research indicates major differences between the DWI offender in treatment and alcoholics, which has potential implications for treatment (Wuth, 1987) (see Chapters 2 and 3 for more complete discussion). Fillmore and Kelso (1987) demonstrated that only 20 percent of the DWI offenders referred to treatment have the same level of problem severity as alcoholics in treatment. Moreover, Hoffman and colleagues (1987) found that the DWI offenders represented a less advanced stage of alcoholism. Fitzpatrick (1992) states that programs fail to consider the goals and philosophies of treatment that have implications for both the development of methods and the evaluation of treatment programs. He goes on to state, "many programs appear to be designed without active consideration of the relative merits of each of these goals for the type of community, the type of offender, and the resources available for treatment" (p. 163). Another view includes improving understanding of effective policies and treatment by examining intermediate outcomes and processes of the treatment program. Measuring the achievement of ultimate goals is desirable, but it does not tell us much about what went right or wrong in treatment. Rossi (1978) states that when programs fail in achieving goals it is unknown whether it is due to inadequate models, and therefore should be discarded, or due to a failure to deliver the program in an effective way. We must have a better understanding of what works in treatment—and why it works—if we are to improve our ability to build effective treatment models.

ETHICAL QUESTIONS

Ross (1984) describes two perspectives within the field when defining the drinking-driving problem. The way in which the problem is defined influences the treatment goals and the measurement of treatment outcome. One definition is that it is an alcohol-abuse problem. The other focuses on the aspect of traffic crashes, fatalities, or highway safety issues. Using recidivism as a measure of successful treatment outcome implies that the goal of a treatment program is to reduce alcohol-related car crashes. This approach may fail to take into account realistic treatment goals and mistakenly mix deterrence issues with treatment issues. For example, if highway safety is the main philosophical goal of treatment, then ostensibly these treatment programs may focus on "harm reduction" strategies. These strategies include refraining from driving after any alcohol intake, calling cabs for rides home, or appointing a designated driver.

On the other hand, if the elimination of alcohol abuse/dependence is the main philosophical goal of treatment, then the DWI event is perceived as a symptom of alcohol abuse or dependence and the focus of treatment would be on abstinence from all mood-altering chemicals. This then raises an important ethical question for treatment providers: who is the "client"? Is the client society at large, thereby making traffic safety the main goal of treatment, or is the client the DWI offender, making the reduction of problems related to alcohol the goal of treatment? These questions then spill over into the ethical issues of treating mandated clients who may not want any part of treatment or counseling. For instance, what are appropriate goals for a mandated client? Should the goals be focused only on prevention of future drinking and driving events, or do programs have the right to include treatment goals focused on the offender's alcohol problems? These ethical dilemmas often create ambivalence within a program and its counseling staff when establishing and evaluating treatment goals. The DWI offender represents the largest proportion of mandated referrals from the criminal justice system into the alcoholism treatment community. Within the past two decades, these numbers have steadily increased (Weisner, 1990). For the most part, the DWI client would not be seeking help for an alcohol or drug problem if it were not for the court mandate into treatment. The conviction that resulted in the referral to treatment is most likely the first major consequence related to a client's alcohol and/or drug use. Except for the arrest, most DWI offenders have never experienced arrest and adjudication. Effective counseling techniques rely on the counselor understanding these two important facts. This issue will be explored more completely in Chapter 9.

PROFILE DIFFERENCES AND DIVERSITY: IMPLICATIONS FOR TREATMENT

DWI offenders referred to alcoholism treatment facilities possess characteristics that differentiate them from alcoholics in treatment.

We see that offenders sometimes fall midway between social drinkers and problem drinkers with regards to their drinking behavior. There are some indications that those DWI offenders who are repeat offenders with high BACs may not be problem drinkers but rather individuals for whom sensation-seeking, criminal-like behaviors are more common (Wieczorek, Miller, and Nochajski, 1990). Panepinto et al. (1982) concluded that most DWI offenders "have not usually progressed to a later stage of alcoholism. Not only does this contribute to alcoholic denial but it also demands a different treatment response." Certainly a percentage of DWI offenders are alcoholics that do respond to the traditional treatment methods. However, many drunk drivers do not fit the alcoholism profile utilized within the treatment field. As discussed in Chapter 2, tremendous controversy exists over the rates and percentages of alcoholics and problem drinkers in the DWI population. We also see that a percentage of the DWI population use drugs other than alcohol alone or in combination with alcohol and drive under the influence (Simpson, 1986; Smiley, Ziedman, and Moskowits, 1981).

This growing body of literature further shows that the DWI population is not a homogeneous group, as earlier assumed. Mann and colleagues (1983) suggest that rehabilitation program failures may be the result of not considering the DWI population's heterogeneous nature. Packard (1987, p. 6) states "given the substantial differences between the two populations sampled, it is evident that treatment interventions need to be tailored to meet the specific characteristics of each group." She goes on to say that a "univariate model of assessment and treatment of persons with drinking problems is no longer viable" (Packard, 1987). McGuire (1982) concluded that programs successful with light drinkers could be ill-suited for heavier drinkers. Gurnak (1989) felt it was critical to identify subgroups of DWI offenders because of the relative influence on rehabilitation outcomes. The diversity of the population must be taken into consideration when designing programs (Panepinto et al., 1982). As early as 1977, attention to the diversity of the population was noted to influence treatment success (Scoles and Fine, 1977). A cluster analysis conducted by Steer, Fine, and Scoles (1979) identified seven types of DWI offenders and concluded that each type required a different type of intervention. Likewise, Donovan and Marlatt (1983) identified five clinically relevant DWI offender types that differentiate offender characteristics. This typology is a means to identify key types so as to determine the most appropriate form of treatment during the assessment process.

- *Cluster 1:* High levels of driving for tension reduction, "heavy drinkers," with frequent episodes of alcohol abuse, and low levels of depression and resentment.
- *Cluster 2:* High levels of assertiveness with low levels of aggression, hostility, and sensation seeking. Low levels of driving for tension reduction. This offender tends to be older, and moderate in drinking style.
- *Cluster 3:* Depression and resentment are at high levels with low levels of assertiveness and emotional adjustment. This cluster possesses moderate drinking patterns.
- *Cluster 4:* This group has the highest driving-related aggression, assaultiveness, sensation-seeking, hostility, and irritability. The individuals in this group tend to be younger and heavier drinkers.
- *Cluster 5:* Highest levels of assertive behaviors, and has low levels of driving for tension reduction. They are younger, less frequent drinkers than cluster 2.

These subtypes could play an important role in the treatment process. A current theory implies that each cluster type would respond to different treatment modalities. This typology requires further development before it can be utilized. However, based on these typologies, the implications appear to have some promise. For instance, clients who fall within clusters 2 and 5 are assessed to be the lowest-risk client in terms of severity. It could be assumed that this type of client would most likely respond to drinking-and-driving education programs, or psycho-educational modalities. The moderate severity cluster, which is considered to be cluster 3, would appear to require "low intensity" outpatient alcohol treatment and education. The higher-risk client would be represented in clusters 1 and 4, and would require a more intensive form of treatment. The widely accepted assumption in the research community states that the more severe the personality disturbance and drinking behavior, the more intensive the treatment that is required. Matching the characteristics of a client to a specific type of treatment is an attempt to apply research findings to improve treatment outcomes.

This concept, known as Treatment Matching, is gaining acceptance in the DWI field. Treatment-matching theory holds that by identifying the individual characteristics of the DWI client and then referring this client to the most appropriate modality, treatment will be more effective (Wieczorek, 1993; Wells-Parker, Landrum, and Topping, 1990). The criteria developed are differentiated into four groups: severity of alcohol dependence, psychiatric problems, personality, and social stability (for a review of this research, see Donovan and Rosengren, 1992; Miller, 1989; and Miller and Hester, 1986). Although these concepts have been in the DWI literature for some time, they have not been fully developed and more research is needed. Wells-Parker, Landrum, and Topping (1990), Mann (1992), and Donovan and Rosengren (1992) have suggested in their findings that there is a role for treatment matching for DWI offenders. Further research is needed to delineate the types of treatment approaches and modalities that work best with particular subgroups of offenders. Research studies examining typologies conclude that empirical clustering techniques may be the best method to establish subtypes (Wieczorek, 1993). Multivariate typologies show strong promise for identifying relevant treatment-related characteristics in the DWI population (Wieczorek, 1993).

As noted in Chapter 3, gender and ethnic diversity exist within the DWI group. Ethnicity, age, gender, and education all affect treatment outcomes. Christmas (1978) pointed out early in this research process that existing alcoholism services, geared toward white, middle-class males, are not suited to minority populations or females. Therefore, in the alcoholism field, the high drop-out rate of this group from treatment would also seem to affect DWI treatment as well. Research also demonstrates that race and education influence the effectiveness of program modalities. Reis (1983) found home-study courses effective for Caucasian offenders, but not minority groups. Bi-weekly unstructured counseling had more impact on those offenders with a high school education or less, but not with those with some college education. Age also influences treatment outcomes. When comparing contact with a probation officer, short-term counseling, and educational intervention, DWI offenders over age fifty-five with at least twelve years of education had 30 percent less recidivism when given the probation contact. Offenders between thirty and fifty-five, with the same amount of education, showed no reductions in recidivism when given probation contact

(Wells-Parker, Landrum, and Topping, 1990). Under age thirty, African-American offenders with twelve years of education had a 30 percent reduction in recidivism given probation contact. Young minority offenders with less education had better results with a combination of short-term intervention and probation. Caucasian offenders under age thirty with twelve years of education showed no impact with any of the interventions studied. An ever-growing body of research demonstrates that the traditional strategies will not have the same effect on women and different ethnic groups. Increasing numbers of offenders being mandated into treatment will most likely be from these groups. The effectiveness of our intervention strategies will be limited if we do not increase our understanding of the treatment needs of this population.

Nochajski and colleagues (1993) found a differential impact on treatment with offenders who had been arrested for criminal offenses other than DWI. From these studies, and others along similar lines, we can conclude that treatment efficacy can be improved by applying research findings to DWI treatment programs. The application of research conclusions to treatment program designs would also assist in choosing or developing appropriate program content. There have been a number of innovative programs implemented in an effort to improve treatment outcomes. These will be discussed in the next chapter.

Other research studies have been conducted to identify those types of treatment modalities that are the most effective. Studies have compared education groups, individual counseling, psychotherapy groups, and other types of behavior therapies. There are studies comparing single mode and multimodal treatments. Meta-analysis of single and multimodal rehabilitation approaches found validity with programs that utilize several forms of therapy. This analysis shows that when comparing single mode treatment to programs that include several forms of rehabilitation, multimodal programs were 10 percent more effective in reducing recidivism (Wells-Parker, 1994). Those programs utilizing psychotherapy or counseling, education, and follow-up tended to be the most effective. Walsh and colleagues (1991) found that a multimodal approach, with intensive AA involvement upon completion of an inpatient alcohol rehab center, was more effective for reducing subsequent alcohol and other drug abuse than either AA or inpatient treatment alone. Voas and Tippett (1990), in the study of 28-day treatment combined with long-term monitoring for DWI offenders, found a significant reduction in recidivism. In studying interventions, Lipsey (1992) found multimodal interventions were more effective than most other strategies, even when controlling for length and time in treatment.

When beginning to examine treatment programs, a number of questions and methodological issues emerge. If a certain portion of this population have profiles that differentiate them from alcoholics in treatment, then what type of program content is relevant for this population? Clinical practices must use interventions that meet the needs of the client. A wide range of factors must be considered when exploring the questions relevant to improving treatment outcomes. For instance, ethnicity and gender influence treatment outcomes. Therefore, if we are to improve treatment outcomes, we must apply this knowledge to our treatment programs and train our professionals accordingly. Treatment goals must be clearly stated and methods of evaluating program effectiveness must be reliable, sound, and measurable. Empirical evidence will prove invaluable in determining the types of treatment modalities that are effective with each subtype. Establishing clearly defined criteria for treatment matching with regards to characteristics within various subgroups of the DWI population, such as those typologies discussed by Donovan and Marlatt (1983) or based on concurrent criminal history (Nochajski et al., 1993), and also based on alcohol dependence severity (e.g., such as Orford, Oppenheimer and Edwards, 1976 or Litt et al., 1989), would improve the success of treatment.

SUMMARY

Although there were many changes at the community and legislative level, there did not seem to be the same type of innovation occurring within the programs treating the DWI offender. In order to continue to improve our treatment effectiveness, a better understanding of the population being treated is needed. A growing body of literature shows that treatment outcome may be dependent on the characteristics of the individual and the type of treatment received. One of the more important findings includes the understanding that DWI offenders are a diverse group possessing unique characteristics. Much of the research concludes that these characteristics must be considered in treatment program designs if we are to improve our effectiveness in treating the DWI offender. Multimodal programs, rather than education-type programs, seem to be more effective with this diverse group. An important point to make here is that the DWI treatment field currently overutilizes educational-type programs to treat the DWI offender, even though research indicates these are not effective with repeat offenders. It seems that we utilize the least effective form of treatment for a large percentage of DWI offenders in treatment. Therefore, we need to increase the number of programs that utilize a multimodal treatment approach.

Research concludes that the DWI problem must be addressed utilizing both deterrence and treatment programs. There has been controversy over which approach produces the best results, but research and experience indicates that these two approaches are not mutually exclusive. In order to continue reducing alcohol and other drug-related crashes and fatalities, innovations in both deterrence approaches and treatment programs must be a priority. In the next chapter, we will examine program content issues more closely and explore clinical issues within the DWI population.

Chapter 9

Treatment Strategies, Part 2

Our knowledge of the DWI population has changed greatly since the inception of the countermeasure program. However, our treatment models have not kept up with this change in knowledge. The challenge now is to apply that knowledge to our treatment programs, in order to improve treatment outcomes and reduce the incidence of drinking and driving. As we meet this challenge, the result will be more innovative treatment programs. The innovations of today may well be the standards of tomorrow. The purpose of this chapter is to provide an overview of various innovations developed in the United States for the assessment and treatment of the DWI offender. We will also focus on the role that program design and content, counseling techniques, and the delivery of services play in treatment efficacy.

PROGRAM DESIGN ELEMENT

It has been our contention that although education-only programs seem to be effective with first-time offenders, more intensive counseling types of programs need to be provided for first-time offenders who manifest various alcoholism risk factors (e.g., familial alcoholism, sensation-seeking personality traits, other criminal behavior related to alcohol and drugs, etc.). Most of the educational programs we have reviewed are quite similar in content. They will usually provide information about how many drinks it takes to arrive at various blood alcohol levels; how alcohol and drugs affect reaction time, decision-making skills, and driving ability; as well as symptoms of alcoholism and the progression of alcohol and drug dependence. When treating multiple offenders, however, it is noted that no specific treatment modality is designed for the rearrested DWI client (Seigel,

1985; Voas and Tippett, 1990; Walsh et al., 1986). Although education programs are effective with first offenders, it appears that multimodal programs that combine education, psychotherapy or counseling, and follow-up in face-to-face meetings or aftercare were more effective by reducing offender recidivism at least 10 percent (Wells-Parker, 1994). Programs with multiple components may be more successful because they are able to address the complex problems presented by a DWI client. There can be no effective reductions in traffic crashes or improvement in successful treatment outcomes without addressing the "hard core drinking driver" and repeat offenders. When considering the issue of improving treatment modalities, we cannot ignore the significant role repeat offenders play in the still unacceptably high DWI rates and fatalities. It is this population that does not respond to current mainstream treatment methods. As noted in the executive summary of the National Commission Against Drunk Driving Conference Report, December 1996, "Individuals with alcohol problems should not be approached with 'cookie cutter' or 'one size fits all'" treatments (p. 1). Treatment alternatives must be expanded so that a wider variety of offender typologies can be treated more effectively, whether first time or repeat offenders. Miller, Whitney, and Washousky (1984) indicate in their research that the need for "a more complex model for decision making is apparent for clients in the lower ranges of the Mortimer-Filkins Inventory" (p. 457). They found that severe problem drinkers were easily identified when referred to traditional treatment settings. However, the less severe problem drinker often went untreated. They state in the introduction to their paper that by "identifying alcoholism or alcohol abuse in early stages among the drinking drivers may make treatment for alcohol problems more effective" (p. 448). It would also make a significant impact on reducing recidivism if this group were identified and treated appropriately. It appears that many offenders are not going to score as high as alcoholics or drug abusers on standard screening devices and assessment instruments. Research evidence indicates that mismatching the DWI offender with an inappropriate treatment modality produces high drop-out rates or unsuccessful treatment outcomes. Other researchers conclude that recognizing alcoholics and problem drinkers may not be enough. Increasing research shows that we must consider criminal behavior, personality characteristics, and other psychiatric conditions. Treatment matching, as mentioned in

Chapter 8, is seen as one possible way to increase treatment effectiveness. Assessment plays a vital role in determining the best type of treatment for a particular offender.

When discussing the design and content of DWI treatment programs, it is interesting to note approaches utilized in parts of Europe. As stated in Chapter 1, Europe had begun developing education and treatment programs for DWI offenders many years before the United States. We therefore can look at the approaches used in Europe and draw from their experiences. Germany is recognized as a pioneer in developing treatment models for the DWI client (Nickel, 1990). Medical and psychological experts have been utilized to assess the client prior to relicensing since World War II. Germany was the first European country to recognize the need for conducting group discussions for reconvicted drinking drivers. In the early 1970s, three different models for treating repeat offenders were developed that are the cornerstones of the treatment programs in Germany. The first model is based on moderate behavioral techniques, which is seven weeks in length, for a total of twenty-four hours. The second model is based on individual psychological theory, and comprises thirteen two-hour sessions in seven weeks. The third model is called LEER, after the town in which it began. It utilizes group dynamics and consists of fourteen hours in six weekly sessions. This model recognizes different levels of severity and client need, and assigns the client to the appropriate model.

In Germany, the goal of treatment is to produce changes in attitudes, drinking habits, and drinking-driving habits. The purpose of rehabilitation is to produce behavior changes. There appears to be universality among these programs' goals. The education component includes mental and physical effects of alcohol. Germany has long relied on analyses of drinking behavior, self-observation, self-control exercises, behavior modification, and homework. Analyzing drinking-driving behavior is conducted in three parts. The first part is the preparatory phase, which includes keeping a drinking diary. This diary is designed to explore patterns of use. The second part focuses on individual driving habits in typical drinking circumstances in order to formulate strategies to avoid these situations. The last phase reviews drinking history in order to target triggers and other behaviors that are associated with alcohol use. The models include clear goals, and the clinical techniques applied are specifically relevant to achieving those goals. The staffs of these programs are experienced and receive special training.

European and Scandinavian programs have been successful due to several factors. First, in many of these countries, the public support of the anti-drunk-driving movement has been essential in preventing drunk driving. It is considered unacceptable by the general population. One woman from Holland commented that drunk driving is "not something that you do." Even when large public festivals are held, which lend themselves to excessive drinking, most of the townspeople will either ride bicycles or use public transportation. This leads to another important factor. Public transportation in Europe and Scandinavian countries far surpasses that in the United States and is considered more acceptable. In the United States, most teens count the days until they can drive their own car.

Public attitudes often create political will. If we are to move forward, there needs to be joint efforts from many sectors in order to improve interventions. These approaches should not be cookie-cutter types of approaches, but should reflect the demographic make-up of the communities they serve.

The most common recommendations made in the research to consider when designing a DWI treatment program are listed as follows:

1. Referrals should be based on a thorough assessment utilizing valid measurement tools.
2. The results of the assessment should determine the level of care and type of program.
3. The program should be multimodal to provide services to a diverse range of DWI clients.
4. Individualized treatment plans should be developed for each client.
5. Counselors should be provided training in counseling the DWI client.
6. Treatment and program goals should be clear and measurable and include methods for evaluation.
7. Programs should include the development of aftercare plans for each client and provide long-term follow-up.

Due to the emphasis being placed on improving treatment outcomes, there seems to be considerable promise for increasing treatment efficacy by developing multimodal programs with program content matched to type of offender.

INNOVATIONS

Public concern regarding driving under the influence has led to wide support for bolder strategies when dealing with the problem of high recidivism rates. Many community leaders, alarmed by the high rates of rearrest, believed that incarceration and other sanctions as commonly applied did not provide significant enough deterrence. Dr. Voas, Director of Alcohol Programs at Pacific Institute for Research and Evaluation, is considered an expert in evaluating drunk and drugged driving prevention and enforcement programs. In his address at the National Commission Against Drunk Driving conference on the Chronic Drunk Driver, in December 1996, he stated that traditional approaches, such a jail sentences and license sanctions, are limited in their ability to impact recidivism. Dr. Voas stated, " If we could put these individuals in jail for ten years, we would obviously have an impact on their drinking and driving behavior" (Voas, 1996, p. 14). Long-term incarceration as a strategy, he notes, is not supported by the public or law enforcement and would be very expensive. Loss of license is also limited in its impact because it is estimated that 75 percent of those with suspended licenses will drive illegally. Even though treatment is mandatory, offenders did not necessarily complete, or even attend, treatment.

One of the variables affecting treatment success is the completion of treatment. Offenders who do not complete treatment have higher recidivism rates than those offenders who do (Hubbard et al., 1984, McLellan et al., 1982). In order to reduce the impact and incidence of drinking and driving, many communities felt the necessity of taking stronger action to ensure the offender attend and complete treatment. Many communities view deterrence and treatment as two separate approaches. Within that model, offenders are generally responsible for choosing the program they want to attend. These choices are not based on clinical need, but rather on what the offender views as the least costly or closest to home. This model eliminates the possibility of matching the client to the most appropriate type of treatment, which research indicates is another important variable for improving treatment efficacy. Many current models utilize incarceration or treatment, or incarceration followed by treatment. Since there is evidence that a combination of treatment along with sanctions produces the best results, communities looked for ways to combine these strategies.

In recent years more emphasis has been placed on combining intervention strategies, such as sanctions, incarceration, treatment, and follow-up, in order to reduce recidivism. A study funded by the National Highway Traffic Safety Administration, which examined methods to reduce recidivism, recommended sanctions involving personalized assessments and reassessments, individualized treatment regimes, intensive supervision probation, and treatment during confinement for incarcerated offenders (Wiliszowski et al., 1996). More models are being implemented that include the integration of treatment programs with the judicial process. The goal of these types of programs is to provide courts with more sentencing alternatives for those convicted of DWI offenses, based on matching sanctions and type of treatment to the type of offender.

Although this chapter focuses on treatment and program designs, it is important to note that alternatives for sentencing also include other measures, such as those mentioned in Chapter 6. Dr. Voas is a proponent of sentencing approaches utilizing home detention, interlock systems, and smart cards to create a context for changing the behavior of the DWI offender.

We have included in this chapter a few examples of innovative approaches that have been implemented to reduce recidivism and provide more effective treatment for the first-time and rearrested offender. The programs described in the paragraphs below have been developed in an effort to improve interventions. Examples here include innovative judicial approaches, correctional approaches, and treatment approaches. Their inclusion in this book does not reflect the authors' support for one program or modality over another. There are many innovative initiatives throughout the United States. The programs described here, we feel, are representative of the most current trends. These programs have been discussed in the literature or have received some form of national recognition.

Central States Institute of Addiction (CSIA) operates one of the largest DWI programs in the country. It is located in Cook County, Illinois, which includes the city of Chicago. According to the Central States Institute 1998 Program Report, there were 12,903 DWI referrals in Cook County. Central States Institute works in conjunction with the Circuit Court of Cook County and the Department of Human Services Office of Alcoholism and Substance Abuse. They provide intervention services to the local courts in Cook County. Services include a structured, comprehensive, and individualized alcohol and drug evaluation; recommendations to the Court; and monitoring and tracking of the offender. Offenders can volunteer for the assessment or be sent by the court as part of a presentence or pretrial investigation. The assessment is conducted for the court to determine the level of risk to the public, and the possibility of recidivism. The evaluation includes assessment screening, self-administered questionnaires, face-to-face and collateral interviews with the offender and significant others, and objective data, such as previous convictions. A level of risk is assigned as a result of the assessment process. The Level of Risk categories utilized by CSIA are as follows:

- **Minimal:** No prior convictions or court-ordered supervision for DUI; no prior statutory summary suspension; no prior reckless driving invocations reduced from DUI; a BAC of less than .15g/dl at the time of the arrest for DUI; and no symptoms of substance abuse or dependence.
- **Moderate:** No prior conviction or court-ordered supervision for DUI; no prior statutory summary suspension; no prior reckless driving conviction reduced from DUI; a BAC of .15 to .19 or a refusal of chemical testing at the time of the current DUI arrest; and no other symptoms of substance abuse or dependence.
- **Significant:** One prior conviction or court-ordered supervision for DUI, one prior statutory summary suspension, or one prior reckless driving conviction reduced from DUI; and/or a BAC of .20g/dl or higher at the time of the most current arrest for DUI and/or other symptoms of substance abuse.

- **High:** Symptoms of substance dependence, no prior arrest.
- **High +:** Two prior convictions or court-ordered supervisions for DUI, two prior statutory summary suspensions, or two prior reckless driving convictions reduced from DUI within a ten-year period from the date of the most current (third) arrest.
- **High ++:** Symptoms of substance dependence and two prior convictions or court-ordered supervisions for DUI, or two prior statutory summary suspensions, or two prior reckless driving convictions reduced from DUI within a ten-year period from the date of the most current (third) arrest.

The program representative provides assessment results and recommendations as testimony to the court. The judge then decides which combinations of sanctions and treatment match the level of severity. If the court concurs with the recommendations made in the assessment, the offender is then mandated to the program that can provide those comprehensive services.

Upon completion of treatment, a reporting sequence, created as part of a follow-up plan, is established by the treating agency. This follow-up is based on the perceived need of the DWI client. Any violation or noncompliance with the follow-up program is reported and prosecution is immediate. A final report is prepared for the court at termination of the sentence.

This type of approach includes a number of key innovations, which coincide with recommendations being made throughout the literature. An individualized plan is developed based on the severity and characteristics of the offender as a result of a comprehensive assessment. The court plays a key role in this approach, as the assessment is conducted prior to sentencing. The judge then mandates the offender to an appropriate program based on the assessment, in an attempt to match the type of treatment to the type of offender. Long-term follow-up, along with swift and certain prosecution of violators, is considered to be an essential component of any program when attempting to reduce recidivism. Evaluation, as noted in the literature, is another important element of a program, and CSIA has recently begun a research study to measure the impact of this approach.

An interesting feature of this approach is that the assessment is conducted by CSIA prior to the sentencing. Also, offenders have the option of entering this program voluntarily and therefore do not have to wait for adjudication. Even though most courts in the United States have a system for screening, it is not typically as in depth. Offenders are usually divided into two groups, "social drinkers" (or first-time offenders) who are assigned an education program, and those who are problem drinkers, who are assigned three to twelve months of treatment. Some courts screen entirely by offense status, with first offenders receiving educational programs and multiple offenders receiving treatment. Certain courts have screeners on their staff who conduct screening interviews using the short inventories designed to identify problem drinkers. Most courts do not have the resources to go beyond this level of screening. Cook County has made those resources available to its court system. It will be interesting to see the results of this research when it is complete.

Needless to say, in order for these types of approaches to work, comprehensive treatment programs must be available in the community to which the courts can mandate offenders. This type of planning and cooperation between the judicial and treatment communities is essential if the approach is to be effective

An example of one such program is The Haymarket Center, located in Chicago, Illinois. The Haymarket Center is a treatment program that has provided alcohol and drug detox and treatment in the community since 1975 (The Century Council, 1997). Its programs include outpatient services for men and women, services for children, recovery programs for women, and services for the homeless at several locations throughout Chicago. In 1993, it established two Alternative to Incarceration programs by working with prosecutors, probation and social services professionals, the county sheriff, and the Illinois secretary of state. As a result, an intervention program was developed that provides short-term confinement, extensive evaluation, counseling, and treatment. These programs are designed to provide treatment for the high-risk and multiple DUI/DUID, nonviolent, non-felony offenders, where an alternative to incarceration is a better choice. These programs, which are lower in cost than conventional incarceration, provide the court with an alternative sentencing option. The programs are described below.

Rehabilitative Confinement Program (RCP)

Court ordered residential confinement is carried out in increments of seven, fourteen, twenty-one, or twenty-eight days. Program components include twenty-five hours of intensive outpatient substance-abuse treatment per week, attendance at self-help support groups (such as AA, NA, Cocaine Anonymous, Gamblers Anonymous), breathalyzer, and urine drug testing. There is a family component and a family member or significant other is required to participate. Screenings include domestic violence, gambling addiction, and HIV. Offenders can also receive literacy testing. All staff members are trained in criminogenic behaviors, are certified treatment professionals, and design individualized treatment plans. Offenders participate in individual, didactic, and therapeutic group sessions. All programs are offered in English, Spanish, Polish, and American Sign. Community service of forty hours per week is supervised through the Sheriff's Work Alternative Program (SWAP). They are picked up daily by the sheriff's office and taken to their community service.

Work Release Alternative Program (WRAP)

This alternative-sentencing option is similar to the RCP, for offenders who are eighteen years old and older. Confinement is for a minimum of thirty days, but allows for forty hours of approved work release time. Offenders are allowed to leave Haymarket each weekday to work. Instead of performing community service outside the facility under the supervision of the Sheriff's Department, they perform their community service component on premises, under the supervision of the staff. Components of service include those provided in the RCP, except for seventy-five hours of intensive outpatient substance-abuse treatment.

Once remanded to The Haymarket Center, clients are expected to participate in treatment and counselors monitor progress closely. Treatment is a combination of individual and group counseling, education groups, and attendance in self-help groups. Clients complete a log when they attend a self-help meeting. At intake clients complete a computerized, self-administered Drivers Risk Inventory that measures attitudes, risk, and alcohol severity. According to Betty Foley, M.S., Haymarket Center associate director, this instrument has good reliability and is used to evaluate progress in the program. It is an instrument that was designed specifically for the DWI offender. The counselors in the program monitor progress regularly throughout the program, particularly if a client has a high score on the DRI at intake. Prior to completion, the client will take the test again, and the pre- and postscores are compared. This score is used as one measure of progress the client has or has not made. Upon completion of the program, the clients attend an aftercare counseling program. Aftercare programs are established in six, eighteen, or twenty-four month segments. Offenders are required to complete all program components, maintain abstinence, and comply with all court requirements. Upon completion of aftercare, the offender must provide documentation to both the court and the secretary of state that includes not only documentation of successful completion from the program, but also includes letters from a self-help sponsor.

This is an example of a program with clear goals and objectives, working in conjunction with the adjudicating body. It uses in-depth assessment to individualize the treatment plan, with multimodal programmatic elements. Follow-up in an aftercare program provides long-term, face-to-face contact, which has been recognized as a key element in reducing recidivism. The staff receives specialized training on interviewing the DUI offender. Regular onsite training is also conducted on a routine basis. The program does not receive any outside funding and is supported solely by fees set on a sliding scale. In 1998, the program was approved by the Bureau of Justice Assistance in Washington, DC, to be funded for nine indigent beds. Since its inception, it has provided services for approximately 2,800 DWI offenders.

Another program designed to work with the judicial system applies a slightly different approach. It becomes involved after the offender is convicted. This program, called The Weekend Intervention Program (WIP), was developed in 1978 at Wright State University's School of Medicine in Ohio. It is one of the first innovative programs of its kind. It is nationally recognized as an effective program and has been the subject of numerous studies and articles since its inception. It works in tandem with the community's criminal justice and human-service systems. WIP is an intensive, three-day residential program for first and second offenders. It is a component of the interdisciplinary effort to link the court with alcohol and substance abuse treatment services. Offenders receive a comprehensive alcohol and drug assessment. They provide differential diagnostic assessment and treatment program assignment. Offenders are involved with intensive small group and individual counseling emphasizing the necessity of behavioral and cognitive changes. Research shows that WIP exhibited lower recidivism rates than jail or suspended sentences and fines. As a result of the weekend curriculum, 85 percent of participating offenders demonstrated significant attitude changes (Seigel, 1985). An interesting feature of WIP is that offenders are assigned to treatment as a result of an in-depth assessment. It is believed that as result of this process nearly every offender who entered the recommended program completed treatment (Moore, 1989).

Recently, there has been more attention given to an approach known as Alternative Sentencing. This concept, although well accepted within the judicial system, is not widely practiced. Criminal justice experts have endorsed the use of sanctions tailored to the needs of individual offenders. The failure to impose appropriate sanctions results in significant failures in the DWI enforcement systems (Jones,Wiliszowski, and Lacey, 1998). Alternative sentencing programs attempt to utilize a wider variety of sanctions than traditionally used and are individualized to the type of offender. As in the Cook County approach, treatment is a condition of the sentence, with long-term follow-up.

One of the most recognized programs using this approach is called the Todd Program. Judge William F. Todd Jr. of the State Court of Rockdale County, Georgia, first developed this program in 1992 as an individualized alternative sanctioning program. Both first-time and repeat offenders are included in this program. Judge Todd's approach includes several components. First, the range of sentencing options utilized includes a wider range of options than those available in other jurisdictions. In addition to the mandatory jail time, there are fines and other traditional sanctions, house arrest, electronic monitoring, intensive supervision probation, frequent breath-alcohol testing, work release, participation in a wide variety of inpatient or outpatient treatment programs, and involvement in AA.

The second component is a presentence investigation conducted by the judge utilizing a database that he developed. He tailors sanctions based on information elicited from the offender during the sentencing process, on criminal and driving records, and the prosecutor's report. In most cases, the sentences are the result of plea bargain, and less than 5 percent of the offenders elect to go to trial.

The third component includes monitoring and follow-up. Sanctions become a condition of probation, and a private probation company paid for by offender fees conducts the probation. All offenders are required to submit to periodic breath-alcohol tests. Any violations are reported directly to Judge Todd. A failure of a breath alcohol test results in incarceration.

A research study funded by National Highway Traffic Safety Administration concluded that this program had a significantly lower recidivism rate than the control group using minimal sentencing (Jones and Lacey, 1998). Judge Todd adds that although he uses analytically determined relationships, subjective factors play a role. He considers circumstances surrounding the DWI incident, the appearance of the offender in court, the drinking location, and the BAC level in relationship to observed behavior of the driver at the time of arrest (Jones and Lacey, 1998). That is to say, a driver who had a high BAC level that did not appear seriously impaired is viewed as having a possible alcohol problem. Offenders who are deemed to have an alcohol problem will generally receive sentences that include abstinence. Sentences are based on Judge Todd's assessment of the level of severity of the offender. The more severe cases receive stricter sanctions. Close contact with offenders involves reporting on offender compliance and judicial interaction with offenders for a period beyond traditional adjudication and sanctioning. It seems that this program is successful due to the dedication, interest, and personality of Judge Todd. The study concluded that this approach could be used in other jurisdictions, with enough judicial interest in the drinking-driving problem to put such a program in place.

DWI Correctional Treatment Facilities are dedicated detention facilities that offer sentencing alternatives for multiple DWI offenders. These models were developed in order to combine incarceration with treatment. The purpose is to impact the DWI offender population through treatment. Confinement is provided in conjunction with supervised alcohol treatment with long-term follow-up. In-depth diagnostic assessments are provided for all participants. Research has provided some preliminary evidence of reduced recidivism rates with this model. A few examples of this type of facility follow.

In Prince George's County, Maryland, one of the most effective programs in the country was developed in 1985. They constructed a sixty-bed, free-standing facility, providing treatment for the second and third offender. By 1988, this facility treated over 1,000 offenders. Of the offenders who successfully completed the program, only 8 percent were reconvicted (National Commission Against Drunk Driving, 1996).

In 1994, Baltimore County, Maryland, built a 100-bed DWI Correctional Treatment Facility that now serves the entire state of Maryland. A result of a collaboration of public and private efforts, it is operated by a private organization through a contract and monitored by the Bureau of Corrections, with the Bureau of Substance Abuse monitoring the treatment component. It consists of a twenty-eight-day residential treatment program followed by a one-year aftercare program. All residents undergo an intensive drug and alcohol abuse assessment during the initial forty-eight hours. An individualized treatment plan is developed for each offender. It is run like a work-release center. If the residents have jobs, they are allowed to go to their jobs, but undergo an alcohol and drug test upon their return. Treatment activities are conducted from 6:30 p.m. to 10:00 p.m. every night and continued on the weekends. Sundays are family days. Aftercare includes random alcohol and drug tests and participation in self-help support groups. Fees are set on a sliding-scale basis from $0 to $5,000, depending on income. Preliminary statistics show that there has been a significant reduction of recidivism. One year after the first 213 people completed the twenty-eight-day program, only nine had been arrested again.

The Rutland Facility in Massachusetts is a fourteen-day DWI Correction Treatment Facility for second offenders. Offenders have a choice to serve a seven-day jail sentence or enter this fourteen-day program. It combines education, AA meetings, individual counseling, and aftercare plans with incarceration. The counseling staff monitors the clients grasp of information, changes in attitude, and reductions in denial. Long-term follow-up for two years is a condition of probation. Failure to comply with conditions may result in a return to court and the imposition of additional sanctions. According to McCarty and Angeriou (1986), who conducted a study on the effectiveness of this program, offenders admitted to the fourteen-day facility were significantly less likely to be rearrested than the incarcerated offender. Third-time offenders are referred to a ninety-day facility.

In this section, we looked at some of the programs that are taking a more innovative approach to treating the DWI offender. They generally include the elements recommended in the research findings regarding program design. These elements include comprehensive assessment, matching offender type with treatment, individualized treatment planning, clear goals and objectives, evaluation, and long-term aftercare. Research in this area is still sparse. Initial findings show an impact on reducing recidivism, but it is still not clear how this is achieved.

PROGRAM CONTENT

The goal of treatment is to produce behavior change. As indicated in the research, utilizing a variety of modalities to produce change would increase effective program design. There have been numerous studies conducted in order to determine which clinical modalities produce the best results with the DWI population, but very little has been done regarding content. As noted earlier in this chapter, education is the type of treatment that predominates in the United States for the DWI client. Content of education programs provide information mostly on the effects of alcohol and drugs, addiction, effects on family, health, finances, stress management, and so on. Widely accepted among researchers is the belief that education might not be the most potent type of rehabilitation (Miller and Hester, 1986). Fitzpatrick (1988) found that program content in treatment tends to be more didactic than experiential and, therefore, was insufficient to bring about the desired changes in problem drinkers. Information is helpful to understanding, but does not produce the insight necessary to motivate an individual to change. Education certainly is important; however, it should be considered one element of a multimodal program.

Reis (1983) compared re-arrest rates of multiple DWI offenders who underwent eclectic group counseling for one year or brief individual contacts with a no-treatment control group. Over a three-year follow-up, it was found that individual counseling produced a significantly lower recidivism rate. Subgroups exist within the larger cluster of DWI offenders identified as having alcohol-related problems or being at high risk for developing severe alcohol-related problems (Miller and Windle, 1990; Wells-Parker, Crosby, and Landrum, 1986).

It is relevant to question content as it relates to what went right in treatment and what needs improvement. With this in mind, it is appropriate to raise the question as to the type of program content relevant to the treatment needs of this population. Fagan and Fagan (1982) note the importance of examining content from the perspective of keeping the mandated client in treatment. They note that too often the agency and treatment personnel fail to consider the needs of the mandated client. Programs tend to expect the client to fit into the services provided, rather than the agency adapting the programs to the needs of the patient. Programs are often designed based on biases, assumptions, and stereotypes of the population rather than the needs of the individual. In order for this type of intervention to be as effective as possible, the offender must perceive the treatment experiences as relevant. Of course, even if this were somehow accomplished, one could not guarantee that the offender would not drink and drive again. Two essential elements necessary for engaging the coerced client are program content and counseling techniques. Appropriate content and effective counseling techniques support the client in gaining the insight necessary for change. Treatment-productive content would be those areas specific to the DWI population. For instance, focusing on alcohol-related job problems would not be fruitful for most offenders since they do not report having significant job difficulties. The most productive areas would be to demonstrate the progressive nature of alcoholism, family and marital difficulties, and the repetitive nature of alcohol-abusing behavior. Counseling techniques are those techniques designed specifically for the mandated client. Structured therapeutic exercises are useful tools designed to foster participation for the reluctant client.

It is well known that change involves active involvement. Motivating the coerced client to become involved requires clear expectations and active facilitation by the counseling staff. Therefore, even when providing didactic information, it is important to determine how the DWI offender is reacting to what is being presented and encourage him or her to engage the material in some way. The stage must be set for group sessions because participation in these exercises is mandatory. Clear behavioral objectives with the DWI client in mind should be established at the onset of treatment. Appleton, Barkley, and Katz (1986) emphasize this point and state that it is essential to establish guidelines for group members on acceptable and productive behaviors. These behaviors serve as a framework within which the client can collaborate actively in the process of change. The guidelines listed below are adapted from their article. Each participant is expected to:

- *Give feedback.* Provides an opportunity for members to exchange feelings and point out behaviors that other members may want to change without blame or criticism.
- *See yourself as responsible for your own feelings and have a choice in the way you behave.* Learning to identify feelings and associate them with behavior.
- *Demonstrate to others that you understand their feelings.* Clients learn to accept feedback and to listen to the feelings and opinions of others. Participants learn to listen nondefensively to feedback from others, which is an important skill for change.
- *Self-disclose.* The ability to communicate thoughts and feelings to others. This helps the client to bring out feelings and thoughts concerning their alcohol and drug use that have been suppressed or denied. Promotes openness in group.
- *Experiment with new behaviors.* Change requires the willingness to try out other types of behaviors in order to find new ways of managing feelings and situations.
- *Find ways of helping group members who do not meet the competencies.* Through feedback and self-disclosure, members help other members who are struggling with these competencies. Group members are at times more accepting of feedback from other group members than from the group leader.
- *Demonstrate basic assertiveness skills.* Learn and demonstrate that they understand the difference between passive, aggressive, and passive-aggressive behavior.
- *Identify the process you go through and the thoughts you have about yourself when you want to drink (or not drink), and demonstrate behaviors in the group which show that you can change that process and those thoughts.* This is essential to learn if a client is to change behaviors associated with drinking

and also to understand the extent and severity of their problems with alcohol. The more insight a client gains in this area, the more comprehensive the aftercare plan.

- *Make connections and see similarities between your thoughts, feelings, and behavior in the group and outside the group.* Develop insight and understanding into the relationship between thoughts and feelings, and become more aware of how this process creates problems.
- *Having your words and nonverbal behavior say the same thing to others.* Incongruent behaviors are signals of conflict and pointing them out can assist a participant with getting in touch with and expressing true feelings.

These expectations provide therapeutic structure to a program and serve as a set of observable behaviors by which to evaluate a client's level of participation. Generally, we have found beginning DWI groups with some icebreakers to be very helpful. For example, we usually have the group pair off and interview one another, usually giving them specific questions to ask, beyond just name, address, and occupation. In this dyad exercise we also have each offender find out about the other's DWI event. They are instructed to ask about what the person had been drinking, what he or she felt like on the day or evening of the offense, the events leading up to his or her arrest, his or her reactions to the arrest and what it was like to tell friends and family members. We have found that this type of icebreaker helps to get the DWI offender to realize that he or she is not unique in these perceptions or feelings. Program exercises should be designed so as to maximize the opportunity for participants to personalize information. It is critical that the offender be able to put the information into context of his or her own situation and experiences. Program staff needs to encourage self-appraisal of alcohol and drug use. Written exercises, self-reported personal history, and group interactions are techniques designed to bring information out for examination.

Listed below are other types of exercises we have adapted for use with the DWI offender that have proven to be productive. These exercises are designed specifically with the DWI offender in mind. They are useful as a method to initiate discussion and promote self-disclosure. Some of the exercises are for use in small groups, some are used as homework assignments, and others are used to promote discussion along with didactic presentations. Each of the following exercises includes a brief description. The complete exercise appears in Appendix B. These exercises are for anyone to use, as they are simply drawn from established structured exercises found in the clinical literature.

The Abstinence Log. Clients, through this "homework assignment," record triggers and difficulties they experience in socializing, managing stress, and/or going through daily routines without using alcohol. This is designed for outpatient programs. Clients are to complete this assignment and bring it to group each week. You will note that this log also includes an exercise to complete if the participant was not successful in being abstinent that week. Abstinence is framed to the program clients as a necessary goal while in the program because it is difficult to examine drinking issues while drinking. However, in an outpatient setting, we learned that if you make this goal absolute, clients are reluctant to discuss their "lapses" for fear of not being in compliance with the program. When first introducing this homework assignment to the participants, it is preceded with lecture material. During this lecture, clients are asked to discuss their reactions to the goal of abstinence and the type of difficulties they might expect. The lecturer also provides information about what they could experience when they abstain (see lecture outline on symptoms of abstinence in Appendix B). Those that could not abstain are given the opportunity to learn from the experience by receiving feedback from other members, who share strategies the use.

The technique of involving other participants mobilizes group participants through helping one another. If a client is consistently unable to achieve successful abstinence, this information is useful when evaluating the client. Feedback given to us about this exercise is that, though wary at first, clients appreciate being able to talk about their drinking in an open atmosphere. The most frequent comment made by clients is that the only people they have ever talked with about their drinking are drinking right along side of them. This open exploration allows clients to become more aware of their conflicts around their drinking. Without this nonjudgmental atmosphere, clients would not feel comfortable enough to disclose. The group leaders reinforce group norms of self-disclosure and open honest participation.

Sentence Completion. This exercise provides a portion of a sentence for the client to complete. Participants write in their answers and then read the answer to the group. Each person takes a turn reading one answer. This exercise is useful as a warm-up exercise or icebreaker. Each statement is focused on the DWI event. Again, this type of exercise is designed to promote self-disclosure and foster commonalties of experiences and feelings between group members.

Myths Exercise. This is a useful didactic presentation that is followed by group discussion. The information covers the most common myths about DWI events, the effects of alcohol, and symptoms of alcoholism. The lecturer then facilitates a small group discussion about the information, focusing on what each member learned from the exercise. This is in keeping with the idea that the presenter should check to see what the client has taken in as new information.

The Price. This exercise is a structured exercise used in promoting small-group discussion around the financial, family, and social consequences of the DWI arrest. The client is asked to complete all the categories. Each member is then asked to share his or her reactions to the exercise with the group. In motivational theory, this exercise uncovers useful information designed to move the client from the precontemplation stage.

Time Line Exercise. This can be used as an assessment tool or as a structured exercise. Clients mark dates as answers to questions designed to show a pattern of drinking, driving, and alcohol abuse. (Sobell and Sobell, 1992). Clients generally report this to be an extremely powerful exercise. It helps them recognize the recent arrest as not just an isolated event, but as the result of a long-term pattern of drinking, driving, and alcohol abuse.

It is important to note that facilitation of group exercises requires very active participation in the process by the counselor. Counselors must be skilled at working with resistant clients and should be familiar with motivational counseling techniques.

When discussing treatment expectations, it is important to note the use of the Consent Form and the Treatment Contract. These are the most common ways in which treatment expectations are clearly stated. Part of the concern with mandated treatment is the compliance effect. When clients have been mandated into a treatment program, they often are motivated to cooperate solely in order to have their driving licenses returned, rather than as a genuine attempt to change problem behavior. The time necessary to change behavior and the process of change has been the subject of research and discussion. An interesting finding by Argeriou and Manohar (1977), illustrated that those clients with less severe alcohol problems required less time in the program to complete the therapeutic tasks than those with more severe problems related to alcohol. It is interesting to note that clients were measured according to the time it took them to succssfully complete their treatment plan. Many behavioral theorists, who study behavior change, estimate that it takes six to twelve months of practice before new behaviors are integrated. These changes occur in stages, with some clients moving through the change process faster than others.

As noted by Fitzpatrick (1992) in his study on program effectiveness, it is difficult to know which type of content produces the kinds of effects needed. Certainly, the content of programs may affect outcome (Foon, 1988). Foon explains that if information is presented in an ambiguous way it may be misunderstood. We do not seem to know much about how services are delivered or whether they went as planned. This type of evaluation would tell us more about the "black box called treatment" (Fitzpatrick, 1992, p. 160). Longabaugh and Lewis (1988) feel that describing treatment is important if we are to improve outcomes. Foon (1988) also states that programs often lack an exact description of the aim of the course and the methods needed to realize these aims. This contributes to the difficulty of evaluating program effectiveness. In order to assess the programs, evaluation studies must define treatment outcome in terms of measures that can be applied pre- and posttreatment. Holden (1983) looked at whether offenders received the treatment they were assigned by comparing outcomes of those who completed to those who dropped out. Hollister, Kemper, and Wooldridge (1979) point out the necessity of linking the process of treatment to its impact in order to measure treatment effectiveness rather than using recidivism rates. Research is sparse, as of yet, due to the limited range of methodologies available.

Currently, most programs use recidivism as a measure of successful treatment. This data, though concrete, does not tell us about the process of treatment. It is not clear if recidivism is in any way connected to treatment efficacy. It is an assumed relationship. Instead, the data could be measuring changes in law enforcement, changes in host liability laws, or decreased emphasis on arresting DWI offenders. Using this as a measurement of treatment success tells us nothing about the treatment itself and why it worked or did not work. We often judge a successful program by this one measurement. If recidivism rates are not reduced, it is considered to be ineffective. Without examining what happened in the program, we do not learn about what did or did not work. For instance, the program content may have been relevant, but the staff might not have delivered it effectively. Or perhaps the activities occurring in treatment were not the ones that were planned. Perhaps the instructors did not have the expertise, or the offenders were unusually resistant. Without empirical data to guide us in developing appropriate program content and treatment modalities, we will continue to fit the offender into our preconceived programs, rather than designing programs that meet the treatment needs of this population. However, the program is of little use if it cannot meet the treatment needs of the offender. Therefore, it is critical that we expand our programs in order to provide a wider variety of treatment and avoid relying on education as our primary modality.

CLINICAL ISSUES

Engaging the mandated client in counseling is a unique and difficult challenge for the counselor. Although addiction counselors are very familiar with techniques used to manage a resistant or hostile patient, the DWI offender quickly earned a reputation for being unusually resistant and hostile. This population presents distinct and frustrating challenges to the alcoholism treatment community. A number of researchers and authors address this challenge and list many useful clinical strategies to use when treating these clients. This type of client enters a program with a variety of feelings related to being coerced into treatment. The events connected to being arrested, adjudicated, and referred to treatment produce high levels of stress. The financial and emotional strain connected with these events is extreme for most DWI clients. When entering treatment, clients are primarily motivated to do what is necessary to get through the experience. This produces a compliance effect with treatment. Issues around motivation are inherent in this population, due to the nature of countermeasures initiatives. This is key when counseling the DWI offender. Countermeasures strategies are designed to intervene at the secondary and tertiary levels. Then through the use of legal measures, individuals are mandated to treatment. These clients, otherwise, would not be seeking help on their own.

In his research, McGuire (1982) reflected the general view of the day that "very little seems to have an effect" on the repeat offender. Due to the interventive nature of this program, people enter treatment at various levels of severity, with a variety of personal, economic, legal, and social characteristics. The counselor's job is to attempt to increase the DWI client's motivation to engage in the treatment process. Essential to this strategy for the counselor is to start treatment around the precipitating crisis that resulted in the client being in treatment. It seemed to the treating professionals that the DWI offender had not hit bottom yet. Some offenders completing treatment were more convinced that they did not have a problem with alcohol than they did prior to entering treatment. With these cases, treatment had the opposite effect, reinforcing denial rather than reducing it. However, some theories attempt to understand this resistance in terms other than those related to motivation. The hostility exhibited by this population was not viewed so much as denial or resistance, but as a normal reaction to the stresses related to the DWI conviction (Cavaiola, 1984); Garrett, 1980; Panepinto et al., 1982).

Therefore, the following points must serve as the cornerstone of a treatment program:

1. *People come into treatment at various levels of awareness and readiness to change.* Program elements must include modalities that will assist clients in increasing their level of awareness and motivate them to change.
2. *People need to be prepared to change addictive and other dysfunctional behaviors.* Program elements then must include modalities that will assist the client in identifying these behaviors.
3. *Treatment plans address strategies aimed at moving clients through the stages of change.* Program elements must include modalities that will assist the client in developing plans to change these behaviors and ways to maintain them.

It is important that structured group exercises be conducted in a supportive environment. This helps clients feel comfortable when revealing personal information. Therefore, counselors must be skilled in maintaining a therapeutic milieu while exploring this anxiety-producing material. The role of staff in treatment effectiveness cannot be overlooked. If the treatment services are not delivered in a clinically viable manner by an effective staff, content is made irrelevant. In the next section, we will provide case examples illustrating how assessment material, program design, and clinical techniques are used to treat a DWI offender.

Case Example I

The following case example is provided in order to help illustrate some of the clinical issues and concepts that have been discussed within this and previous chapters pertaining to treatment. This first case example is based on an actual person in treatment. Naturally, the name and other information have been changed to protect the identity of this client. The case is presented in a sequence similar to that in which it would normally occur in order to provide an overview of how clinically relevant information is obtained throughout the treatment process.

The program is an outpatient, sixteen-week program that meets for one-and-a-half hours per week. Clients are referred through a county assessment and screening center. Proof of successful completion of the program is required if the offender is to have his or her driving privileges returned.

Information Presented at Intake

Robert J. is a thirty-five-year-old, married, father of two sons ages eight and six, who was referred for DWI treatment after receiving his second DWI conviction approximately six months prior to this referral. His driver's abstract revealed that he had refused a chemical breath test when he was eighteen-years-old. Robert states that he and some friends had been at a Fourth of July barbecue, which they left around 11:00 p.m. to go to another friend's home. Robert recalls that he had "about four beers" over the course of the evening. En route to their friend's home, Robert sideswiped a parked car and left the scene of the accident, only to be apprehended a few miles down the road. He recalls being frightened and, therefore, had refused to take the Breathalyzer test. When asked about his parents' reactions to the drinking and driving incident, Robert recalls that his mother was furious with him at first, however, like his father, she had later adopted a "boys will be boys" approach. He felt that his father was usually more lenient in situations like these because he apparently had been "a heavy hitter" when he was younger.

In describing the events leading up to this most recent offense, Robert states that he and his wife had been at a Christmas party at a co-worker's home. He recalls having had "five or so rum and cokes" over the course of the three hours they were at the party. He also mentioned that he and another co-worker "smoked a joint" on the back porch midway through the party. Robert admits that he "probably should not have gotten behind the wheel" that evening, and he recalls that he and his wife argued about whether he should drive. She, only having had one wine spritzer, apparently pleaded with Robert to let her drive. Robert refused, stating that since it was only a few miles to their home, he felt well enough to drive. Robert came to the attention of the police when he swerved over the center line of the road. He failed the roadside tests and the portable breath test that he was given at the scene. He was then arrested and his blood alcohol levels at the police station were reported to have been .17, .19, and .20, suggesting that Robert probably had his last drink just prior to leaving the party. Robert was not given a urine screen or blood test; therefore, his tetrahydrocannabinol (THC) levels went undetected. Robert was given a Michigan Alcoholism Screening Test (MAST) and the Substance Abuse Subtle Screening Inventory-2 (SASSI-2) at the time of intake. The MAST revealed a score of 2. Here, Robert had only endorsed the item pertaining to his DWI arrest, denying any other problems related to alcohol. On the SASSI-2, Robert similarly had responded to the inventory in a defensive manner, as indicated by an elevated score on the DEF scale.

Assessment

Based upon the intake information presented, Robert had two drinking and driving-related offenses. In the second, more recent offense, Robert admits to being under the influence of alcohol and marijuana. His blood alcohol level was quite elevated. He minimizes his use of both chemicals, as evidenced by his claims to only drink occasionally and that he smokes marijuana "only on weekends, but not all the time." Robert works as a salesman for a sports equipment manufacturer, which involves a lot of travel, mostly by car. He reports that about three times a week, he will stop off at a local tavern where he will have "a couple of beers with the guys at lunch." On the weekends, he reports that he will have "a few beers while watching sports on TV—no big deal." When questioned further about this, Robert indicated that there have been times when he has had to run out to pick his sons up at their friend's houses or run out to the store after he has "had a few beers." He denied having any other alcohol or drug-related arguments with his wife, other than the Christmas party on the night of the DWI. What is also noteworthy in Robert's history is that when he had his first drinking-related incident, his father seemed to take an enabling role. He hired an attorney and would drive him to school, while his mother's reaction was quite the opposite. This area naturally needs to be explored in greater detail. The initial genogram revealed that Robert's maternal grandfather "may have had a drinking problem," which is why Robert feels his mother was so opposed to his drinking. There are also indications of marital conflict, given the argument on the night of the DWI offense, which also needs to be explored further.

Course in Treatment

Robert's initial approach to treatment was that it was nothing to take too seriously. He had a very friendly, affable manner, which probably helped in his sales work. He would often joke with other group members and his counselor and would diffuse any group hostility with jokes or light-hearted comments. Interestingly, Robert complied with all group assignments, such as the mandatory weekly AA meeting attendance. Robert's basic approach to treatment was that the DWI arrests were isolated incidents of excessive drinking and that they were in no way part of any evidence or pattern of abusive drinking. Robert felt that AA was a great organization for "those poor, miserable drunks," but that there was nothing there for him to relate to. Robert vowed that he would "never drink and drive again," that he had "learned his lesson," and that was all that his counselor needed to know. In the third group session, a guest speaker from AA described the program and shared his story. What was interesting was that this AA member had begun his recovery as a result of a death-by-auto arrest in which he killed someone while driving under the influence. This person expressed how he, like many of them, felt that something like this could never happen to him and how drinking and driving was a typical behavior during his active drinking days. What was also noteworthy, and a revelation to the group, was that this person had not been a daily drinker, nor had he lost everything because of his drinking, which helped to dispel some of the common myths surrounding alcoholism. This session seemed to have more of an impact on Robert.

It was not until the fourth session, "Family Night," that things began to change. Each group member was required to bring a family member in with him or her. In some instances, the counselor requests that a specific family member attend, someone who is most knowledgeable about the DWI incident. In this group session, usually the offenders and their significant others meet together for the first part of the session. Then the counselor will meet with significant others alone, while the offenders meet with the cocounselor and talk about the effects of DWI on the family.

Robert's wife, Linda, who had been married to Robert for the past ten years, had unpleasant words for Robert's counselor. She blasted the counselor for "robbing" her husband of his livelihood, given that he did outside sales work and could not drive. She spoke about the financial burdens of his having to "hire a driver" and having to pay fines, insurance surcharges, and attorney's fees. She also spoke of the embarrassment of having to tell their sons why "Daddy is not allowed to drive" and having to tell other extended family members. Linda felt that she and the kids were taking the brunt of the DWI offense. Linda was looking for a target toward which to vent all this rage, since up to this point the police, the courts, the Division of Motor Vehicles were all faceless, inaccessible bureaucrats. Fortunately, the counselor had the patience and fortitude to withstand this barrage. She then asked, in an nonaccusatory way, what happened on the night of the offense; "it sounds like you tried to prevent Robert from driving but he insisted even after you pleaded with him. What were you feeling?" Linda explained how Robert would often get "pig-headed and stubborn" when he drank. She also recounted how she would often have to pick the kids up from soccer practice and games, because she could not trust that he would show up on time or would show up without having been drinking. She also talked about his extreme risk-taking, like the time he went to a regional sales meeting after having quite a few drinks. When the counselor asked whether Linda ever felt that Robert had a drinking problem, her response was typical and mirrored his denial, "No, he doesn't drink every day and he still makes a good living." Linda began to redirect her anger toward Robert and stopped blaming the counselor for Robert's DWI. She had been angry with him for quite some time and there were obviously many other incidents in which Robert's drinking had caused family disruption.

Toward the end of this session, the counselor raised a couple of important questions for the family members to consider. "What do you feel needs to change in order to prevent another drinking and driving offense?" This question helps to convey a common goal of treatment; no one wants to experience a repeat offense. The second question was, "What would you do, or how would you feel, if your significant other had yet another DWI offense?" This question was designed to break through some of the family's denial, which often mirrors that of the DWI offender. Family members are then required to come back within three weeks, and again at the conclusion of treatment. The next question for Linda and Robert was how to present Linda's frustrations in such a way that it could "present reality in a receivable way" to Robert. Linda was agreeable to coming in with Robert for an individual session. It was within that meeting that Linda was able to express her anger, apprehensions, and fears to Robert.

Within the next few group sessions, Robert demonstrated quite a change. He went from being the jokester of the group to someone who seemed rather serious and sullen. When group members commented on this apparent change in behavior and attitude, Robert would reply, "I've got a lot on my mind." Robert seemed rather depressed for a while, and he was still not very forthcoming about what was going on with him emotionally. He did seem to take the group sessions and the AA meetings more seriously. By the ninth session, he began to talk more about what he was feeling. He no longer felt that the DWI was a joke and he admitted that he felt that drinking was a problem for him. Robert was now committed to abstaining. However, as is sometimes common, since he considered his use of marijuana "occasional" and "nonproblematic," he concluded that he could continue to smoke pot without impunity or problems. Despite his counselor's admonitions of the dangers of "substituting one drug for another," or how his use of marijuana could then lower his inhibitions to abstain from alcohol, Robert concluded that he was "right" and his counselor and wife were wrong. Obviously, the counselor could not release him as having "successfully" completed treatment as long as he was continuing to use a mood-altering drug that could jeopardize his progress. It was decided that Robert would continue in treatment, much to his chagrin.

It was approximately five months later that Robert had a "slip" after smoking marijuana at a friend's house. He drank beer that night and continued to drink for about four weeks before Linda called his counselor and asked for a family meeting. It was at this point that Robert finally agreed to abstain from all mood-altering chemicals and was agreeable to attending AA more regularly.

Naturally, not all cases have this type of "closure" or this type of result. It so happens that despite Linda's anger, she was basically supportive of her husband getting help and making changes in his life. Robert initially saw no reason for change and felt that if Linda and the Division of Motor Vehicles would just leave him alone, he would be fine. Obviously, this was not the case, as it was apparent that Robert manifested symptoms of the early stages of alcoholism. He also had many of the personality characteristics of DWI offenders, such as sensation-seeking, immaturity, and willingness to take risks. He was unlike most DWI offenders in that he did not openly display anger, aggressiveness, or hostility. However, this was not to say that Robert was not seething beneath the facade of affability and humor. Hopefully, what this case also illustrates is some of the treatment process.

This case provides a good example of the ways assessment instruments, experiential exercises, and other types of modalities, conducted in a supportive environment, can help a client connect the DWI arrest to the broader issues surrounding his or her alcohol and drug use. Being able to facilitate this type of therapeutic movement in a client not only requires effective content and structure, but also requires good counseling skills. A skilled counselor makes effective therapeutic use of assessment material and keeps a "therapeutic ear" tuned in to opportunities to intervene, such as the events occurring during family night. By addressing the spouse's anger expressed at the counselor in a nondefensive manner, the counselor was able to re-focus her to concerns about the drinking behavior. Counselors, when properly trained to work with DWI offenders and family members, learn to stay grounded in this type of situation by understanding of the source of anger. As noted in Chapter 10, anger is often an indi-cation of a conscious conflict within the family member toward the drinking driver, but the family member cannot as of yet confront the situation (Cavaiola and Wuth, 1987). This case also demonstrates the value of "patience with the process," and the willingness to meet the client and family members "where they are," which is an essential motivational technique. The counseling goal is to assist the family member to direct the anger in an appropriate way at the drinking driver.

This offender was able to verbalize his recognition of having a problem with alcohol. Treatment was effective in moving this client from the precontemplation to the contemplation stage. There is still considerable ambivalence about the problem, evidenced by his re-fusal to give up marijuana. Oftentimes, a client may think that he or she is in the determination stage because he or she "recognizes" the problem and has a plan. When the treatment program does not accept this plan, an offender will often become angry. Clearly stated criteria for successful completion of a program are essential when this situa-tion occurs.

As would be expected with this type of plan, the client eventually re-lapsed. The education, counseling, and support provided the spouse with a way to intervene with the problem effectively. The spouse obvi-ously saw the treatment center as a resource, not as a threat, as many DWI clients and family members do. If the program or spouse were not able to get past this point and "ally" together, the chances are that an-other DWI or some other crisis would have happened. This case dem-onstrates the value of collateral involvement in the treatment process and the creation of a therapeutic alliance with the family of the DWI of-fender.

Case Example II

Sara is a twenty-one-year-old college student who was referred for an evaluation by the court after receiving a DWI, in which she was alleged to have had an extreme blood alcohol level (.22g/dl) and was also reported to have hit a parked car. Sara indicated to the evaluating counselor that she had been out with some of her friends on the evening of the offense and they were celebrating the end of final exams. She stated that she did not have anything to eat that day because of exams and she really didn't realize how much the alcohol would affect her. Sara claims that she had consumed about six Long Island Iced Teas (a drink which contains several types of liquor and liqueurs). She states that she did not drink for the hour just prior to leaving the bar and since she only had a mile or two to drive in order to get back to her off-campus apartment, she felt that she would be okay to drive. Once she got outside the bar, however, she reports that the "alcohol really hit me" while she was driving. Sara claims to have only a partial recollection of what happened from there. She thinks she probably "passed out" at that point, when she sideswiped the parked car. She was frightened and decided to continue driving. Sara made it home, but was only there for about a half hour, when the police came knocking at her door and she was arrested for driving under the influence and leaving the scene of an accident.

In describing her drinking and drug-use history, Sara indicates that she began drinking in high school, occasionally on weekends after football games and perhaps if she went to a school dance or prom. She states that there were no unusual drinking incidents during those years and she characterized her drinking as being "typical teenage drinking." She reports that there may have been one or two instances where she "got drunk," but she would not drink to excess, as her parents would usually check her condition when she got home. Sara recalls being grounded once for coming in drunk, so she claims to have curtailed her drinking after that.

Sara reports that she did well academically and was given an early admission to the state university. Sara states that, in her freshman year, she was in a dorm where most of the freshman would binge drink on Thursdays through Saturdays, depending on whether the football team had a home game or not. Sara recalls that she drank along with her friends, but that she usually would not get as drunk as they did. She was concerned with keeping her grades up, as many of her friends had flunked out of college in their freshman year and ended up having to return home to live with their parents and either working or attending the local community college. Sara claims that her drinking did not have any negative impact on her life until the time of her DWI. She claims that there were no other incidents in which she was pulled over for drinking and driving but not charged. Her driving record indicated she had one speeding offense while she was in high school. Sara claims to have "experimented" with marijuana, and that she used cocaine once with some of her friends; however, she reports that she did not like the effects.

Sara's family history revealed no history of alcohol, drug, or psychiatric problems in either her immediate or extended family. In meeting with Sara's parents as part of this evaluation, Sara's mother described their typical use of alcohol to be confined to holidays or special occasions. Sara's father states that he had a brother-in-law who drank heavily but then went into rehab and has since abstained. When asked how they reacted to learning of the DWI and leaving the scene of an accident, both of Sara's parents indicated that they were shocked and concerned. They were naturally worried at first whether anyone was hurt and were relieved to hear that there were no injuries. They were also angry with Sara for having had too much to drink and then getting behind the wheel of a car. During high school, they tried to impress on Sara that she should not drink or use drugs and, above all, should not drink and drive. They lectured her on never getting in a car with someone who was drinking and to call them if she needed a ride home for "any reason." They indicate that they knew of a couple of instances when Sara drank in high school, but they report that they never had concerns about her drinking on a regular basis. Nor did they ever see any behavioral changes, such as a drop in her school grades, changing friends, or dropping off athletic teams. Sara's parents felt that experimentation with alcohol was something that high school- and college-age people did, and although they did not condone drinking, they had not seen instances in which Sara's occasional drinking was causing any problems in her life. When asked whether their opinion had changed since the DWI, they stated that they see this as an error in Sara's judgment, but they do not feel that Sara necessarily has a drinking problem. They added that they feel that they would restrict Sara's use of the car beyond her suspension period and that she would be made to pay all fines and attorney fees as a way of impressing on her that drinking and driving would not be tolerated. Sara's parents did not feel she needs "alcoholism treatment."

Assessment

As part of the evaluation, Sara was administered the MMPI-2, the MAST, and the SASSI-2. On the MacAndrews Alcohol Scale of the MMPI-2, Sara had received a score of 21, which was below the suggested cutoffs for determining an alcoholism or addiction potential. However, it was also noted on the validity scales of the MMPI-2, that Sara had responded to the inventory in a defensive manner or in such a way as to present herself in a more favorable light. This same pattern of responding was noted on the SASSI-2 as well, which was reflected by a moderately elevated DEF (Defensiveness) score. Sara did not have any other elevations on the face validity alcohol or drug (FVA or FVOD) scales, nor on the obvious attitudes nor subtle attitudes scales. The MAST revealed a score of 2, which is not suggestive of alcoholism. Here, Sara had admitted only to the DWI offense and no other alcoholism symptoms.

Sara presents only one major symptom of alcoholism (i.e., the BAC level of 2.2 percent, which is twice the normal legal limit). This amount of alcohol could be an indication of tolerance to alcohol. What is noteworthy about the DWI is that there was an accident, which Sara fled. However, this may have been out of fear and the fact that her judgment was impaired by alcohol. Sara's high blood alcohol level at the time of her arrest corresponds to the amount she was drinking and the fact that women will have higher blood alcohol levels than men because of differences in metabolism that have been reported in the literature. In fact, binge drinking for men is defined as consuming five or more drinks within a couple of hours, while for women it is consuming four drinks (Wechsler, 1999). Sara has a history of alcohol experimentation in high school and it seems that she drank heavier and more frequently in her freshman year of college. However, neither she nor her parents report any pattern of negative effects. Although Sara denies that drinking and driving was a regular occurrence, it is questionable how many other instances there may have been when Sara drank at these off-campus bars with her friends and drove home.

No reported history exists of alcohol or drug problems within her immediate or extended family that would place Sara at risk for alcoholism. Furthermore, it appears that Sara's parents do not see her as being a frequent or problematic drinker. Are they in denial of Sara's problem or are their perceptions accurate?

Sara's scores on the MMPI-2, MAST and SASSI-2 were not indicative of alcoholism; however, evidence of defensive responding was noted. The question here is whether Sara was indeed trying to hide something or whether she responded defensively in order to present herself in a more favorable light, given that she is being evaluated as a result of the court's recommendation. Sara was referred to a sixteen-week education-type program as a result of the evaluation.

Course in Treatment

Sara participated in all group sessions and was fairly compliant. Throughout the education/treatment process, Sara held to her contention that she did not drink on a regular basis and also did not drink and drive on a regular basis. She continued to claim that the DWI was a result of her own "stupidity" and not part of any pattern of problems related to drinking. Toward the conclusion of the sixteen-week program, in working out a plan to prevent any future drinking and driving offenses, Sara indicated that she would refrain from any instances of drinking and driving in the future. She and her counselor developed a contract stating that she would not drink and drive, which was co-signed by her parents.

The case example is provided as an illustration of instances in which evaluations are not as clear-cut or in which there is only one symptom of alcoholism, i.e., the tolerance indicated by a high BAC level. Although Sara does meet the criteria for a DSM-IV diagnosis of alcohol abuse on the basis of the criteria which cites recurrent use in situations in which use is physically hazardous (e.g., driving while intoxicated), there are no clear-cut indications that a "maladaptive pattern" of alcohol abuse is present, which is suggested in the preface to the diagnostic criteria for substance abuse. A driving while impaired conviction, in and of itself, is not considered a symptom of alcohol dependence or alcoholism (APA, 1994). The main question of whether it represents a singular instance of poor judgment related to drinking or an indication of an increased loss of control over her consumption, and thereby represents a symptom of early stage alcoholism remains unanswered, given the existing information gleaned in the interview.

What is presented by Sara and her parents is that the DWI is representative of poor judgment brought on by excessive drinking; however, they do not present any indications of this being part of a problem drinking pattern. Unfortunately, this perception is based on their subjective report and the inventory/test data does not really refute these claims. In instances such as these, it is important that the counselor trusts gut instincts, yet remains fair and objective in his or her perceptions. The treatment outcome obtained was probably the best that could be obtained in such a situation. Would the counselor have been more comfortable if Sara were to commit to a program of abstinence? Of course. However, this was not going to happen. Another factor that must be taken into account is that the vast majority of college students binge drink and many will drink and drive as Sara did. Although more students are aware of the dangers and perils of drinking and driving and refrain from doing so, if for no other reason than to escape the fines and penalties, there are many more who continue to binge drink, will eventually fail out of college, and will continue to experience major life problems and other symptoms of alcoholism.

Research suggests that the majority of students (in both high school and college) will grow out of these abusive drinking patterns; however, the challenge to the treatment field is to determine which ones will and which will go on to develop alcoholism. Obviously, there are definite risk factors that help to determine those who will go on to develop alcohol dependence (e.g., familial risk factors, history of attention deficit hyperactivity disorder, history of physical or sexual abuse, histories of bipolar depression, and other psychiatric disorders), there are still many individuals, such as Sara, who do not present with such risk factors, and yet may indeed be at risk.

COUNSELOR EFFECTIVENESS

More and more frequently in the research literature, references are made regarding the role counselor effectiveness plays in producing positive treatment interventions. Additional research is needed in order to establish the core counseling competencies necessary to be an effective DWI counselor. Since treatment programs include group modalities, effective group facilitation skills would be an example of a core competency. Another example might be the counselor's ability in managing the client's anxiety, depression, and anger. Some researchers have studied the qualities necessary to be an effective DWI counselor. The qualities a counselor possesses are also an essential part of establishing a helping relationship. In attempting to gain a better understanding of the characteristics DWI clients' value in their counselors, one study listed four main factors (Nickel, 1990). They were:

1. Nondirective behavior
2. Social-integrative behavior
3. Tolerance
4. Competence

Emphasizing the development or enhancement of these qualities in a counselor, through a counseling training program, would seem to be important to the overall impact of treatment. A counselor's reluctance to treat the mandated client can produce negative results. Counselors who are not viewed as competent will have a difficult time establishing the leading (as opposed to directive) role essential for successful structured exercises. A lack of empathy would also create a guarded climate inhibiting client self-disclosure. Garrett (1980) suggests the following to counselors who work with DWI clients:

- Work through the anger and hostility. Long-term stress and frustration contribute greatly to it.
- Intake interviews should include as much written information as possible from the courts, police, BAC, screening tests, and driving abstract. Family assessment is also important.
- Intake information is used to assess the choice of adaptive behavior in dealing with the crisis. The assessment will determine much of the treatment plan.

Programs must include elements which "demonstrate consideration for the patient's lowered self-esteem, reduce his(her) sense of frustration, establish and maintain a pattern of continuity of care, and communicate interest through action. An absence of controls by the therapist is poorly tolerated by and quite threatening to a patient who is leaning towards a loss of ego control" (Panepinto and Higgins,

1969, p. 36). Providing structure to treatment experience is then indicated. Goals and tasks should be made as clear as possible. The use of a treatment contract can be of great value (Seabury, 1976).

For these reasons, it is important then that the DWI counselor have specialized education, training, and credentialing in order to have a well-grounded understanding of these challenges. It is an obvious issue, given what we have learned about the challenges presented when treating this population. Yet, there is little emphasis placed on the training, educating, and credentialing of DWI counselors. This may be due to the fact that the DWI population historically has been viewed as a homogeneous group by the treatment field. Therefore, treatment of the DWI client was subsumed under treatment for the chemically dependent. The standards set would be the same as those for the credentialing of addiction counselors. There is very little mention, if any, of the complicated issues associated with the DWI population—their demographics and characteristics—in the addictions curriculum. The assumption has been made that the skills and knowledge base used to train the certified addictions professional would also be sufficient for treating this population. This challenge to this assumption is becoming more necessary, as our knowledge of the DWI population as a diverse and heterogeneous population increases. The needs of this population differentiate them from the non-DWI population in treatment. As this population changes, our treatment programs will also change in order to meet these needs. With this in mind, we then must say that the staff providing services to this group must be trained in order to understand and appreciate those differences and characteristics. There must be specialized clinical techniques used for this group based on those differences. In other words, without the proper clinical tools, and without a blueprint of clear goals, it is not surprising that we have only achieved 7 to 9 percent reduction in the recidivism rates.

CREDENTIALING ISSUES

Even though almost every state has some type of licensing of DWI programs and an overseeing agency, very little attention is given to the relevance of the program content. A number of states require credentialing and training of DWI staff. Many states require that these approved agencies be reviewed annually or biannually. Many states, however, have no review process. A few states require staff training in DWI assessment and/or training in providing psycho-educational groups. Where training takes place, the curriculum is often provided by the overseeing body. In other states, training is subsumed as part of an agency in-service program. It appears, in reviewing state standards, that even in states that require licensed or credentialed staff in DWI programs, the credential is included under the substance-abuse certification.

No credential is specifically required for the DWI counselor and no established curriculum to train and educate those who treat the DWI client. There would be a number of advantages to considering the establishment of a DWI counselor certification. The first, and most obvious, is that the DWI counselor would be properly trained regarding the nature of the DWI client and the delivery of service to this complicated population. The second point to consider is the issue of staff morale and job satisfaction. Counselors treating this population often feel frustrated when working with this group and do not have a clear idea as to what the treatment goals are. Many counselors treating the DWI client complain about being confused about the goals of treatment. In our working and training within the DWI field, we found what has been reflected by the research. The majority of programs rely primarily on didactic and educational modalities. This may in part be the result of this lack of proper training. The third point to consider is improvement of service delivery to this group, which would result in more successful treatment outcomes. There are currently no national standards for the training of counselors who treat the DWI client. It would seem that the development of a core curriculum for the training of DWI counselors bears further investigation. This would seem to be a critical issue to address as we examine ways to improve our treatment of this difficult population.

SUMMARY

Program content, evaluation methods, and counselor training are issues that require further development in order to improve treatment outcomes and increase the impact of treatment on recidivism rates. Treatment will play a more vital role in addressing the problem of drunk driving as the rates continue to decrease. By examining such issues as treatment matching, drinking-driver subtypes, improved assessment, and treatment referral, it is hoped that more and more programs will utilize multimodal treatment approaches. The challenge to create innovative treatment programs is here as we look for ways to continue the declines we have seen in drunk-driving rates and fatalities.

Treatment is only as good as the clinicians who are providing it. Without a DWI curriculum for training as part of our overall efforts to improve our treatment outcomes, we could be seriously limiting our ability to deliver effective treatment. Treatment is a complicated issue and we have only just begun to understand how complex it is.

Chapter 10

Treating the Family
of the DWI Offender

Larsen (1985) claims that following the founding of Alcoholics Anonymous, there have been three "waves" in the alcoholism recovery movement. The first post-AA wave occurred in the mid-1950s, when the American Medical Association took a position that alcoholism is a disease. The second wave occurred with the advent of an understanding that alcoholism does not just affect the alcoholic, but his or her family as well. The notion that alcoholism was indeed a family disease took shape around forty years ago. The third wave came about within the past fifteen years or so, with the understanding of the dynamics of recovery. Here, the concept that there was "life after alcoholism recovery" and that there were many variations on what constitutes recovery, was developed. It also became understood that just as there was a progression to active addiction, there was also a "progression" to the recovery process. The reason for mentioning all these movements is that the second wave, alcoholism as a family disease, seems to have swept by the DWI treatment delivery system. Yet, at the same time, we have all witnessed a proliferation of inpatient and outpatient chemical dependency treatment programs that offered not just family weekends or once-a-week family recovery meetings, but entire week (or longer) programs for significant others and family members. Also, if one were to search the literature for articles and books on family treatment of addictions there is a plethora of material. So much so, that if one were to read Stanton and Todd (1982) or Bepko and Krestan (1985), one would be thoroughly convinced that to refrain from treating the family constitutes negligence.

When it comes to treating the DWI offender, many of whom we know are alcoholics or perhaps in the early stages of alcoholism, there are only a handful of articles written and even fewer empirical studies that advocate for family involvement. The question that arises is, "Why has family treatment reached overwhelming acceptance in the addiction treatment field and has never attained much acceptance in the DWI treatment field?" We will explore this notion in greater depth later in this chapter.

Prior treatment studies with DWI offenders have investigated several variables such as length of treatment involvement (Reis, 1982; Argeriou and Machar, 1977); treatment of "light" versus "heavy" drinkers (McGuire, 1980, 1982); treatment of resistance as a consequence of the stress caused by the DWI event (Garrett, 1980); short-term education and rehabilitation (Nichols, Ellingstad, and Struckman-Johnson, 1979); short- and long-term effects of behavioral treatment (Conners and Ersner-Hershfield, 1983); and reeducation and rehabilitation programs (Malfetti, 1975). However, none of the aforementioned treatment studies advocate family involvement or had mentioned inclusion of family members in either the assessment or treatment process. Yet, several studies cite family problems as a characteristic of this population. Selzer and Barton (1977), in comparing psychosocial characteristics of DWI offenders, found that alcoholics and drunk drivers were similar in their reports of "family problems distress" when compared to a control group of nonalcoholic licensed drivers. Hyman (1968a, 1968b) found that divorced and separated men were overrepresented in drunk driving incidents. Moskowitz, Walker, and Gomberg (1979) found family problems in 30 percent of DWI offenders, 92 percent of alcoholics, and in only 2 percent of a nonalcoholic control group. They also found that 22 percent to 41 percent of the DWI group was divorced or separated, compared to 50 percent of the alcoholic group and only 5 percent to 7 percent of the control group. The aforementioned studies clearly indicate the presence of family problems within the DWI offender population.

Some DWI profile studies characterize the DWI offender as being primarily male, single, and young (e.g., Donovan and Marlatt, 1982). In those instances, it is not unusual to find these individuals living with their parents and it is therefore not unusual that they will bring a parent with them as their significant other, when required to do so.

Other studies indicate that DWI offenders often come from intact families. For example, a sample of high-risk, problem-drinking, DWI offenders from Arizona, (Sandler et al., 1975) 53 percent were currently married and only 13 percent had never been married. In similar DWI samples from Vermont (Merrill, 1983) and from Mississippi (Weeber, 1981), 58 percent of the DWI offenders were found to be married.

ESTABLISHING THE NEED
FOR FAMILY INVOLVEMENT

The DWI offender presenting for treatment is often very resistant to change and in many instances does not even recognize the necessity of either education or treatment as a means of preventing recidivism. Therefore, the denial structure of the DWI offender appears to be more entrenched than that of most alcoholic clients who present for treatment (Cavaiola, 1984). Keeping this in mind, family members of the DWI offender then can become an integral component in a successful treatment program. Ideally, family members should be involved from the onset of treatment, especially during the initial assessment. Here, it is important to elicit information from the family members regarding their reactions to the DWI event as well as the perception of the events leading up to the DWI incident (see Figure 10.1 for a suggested format for an initial family assessment). For example, the family member or significant other who reacts with shock or surprise to the DWI incident provides much different information than the family member who discloses a feeling of relief because of knowing that the DWI event was bound to occur sooner or later. (In the latter case, there is a recognition that a crisis needed to develop in order to take the drinking/driving family member off the road.) Reactions of family members to the DWI event are not only helpful in the assessment process, but are also useful to determine in what ways he spouse, parent, son, daughter, or significant other may be a part of the problem-drinking system within the family or perhaps ways that they may be part of the solution. Family-systems literature within the field of chemical dependency (Stanton and Todd, 1982; Steiner, 1975) indicates that family members can and do consciously or inadvertently

FIGURE 10.1. Family/Significant Other Assessment Questionnaire

1. Your name and relationship to DWI/DUI offender?

2. How long have you known this person?

3. How many DWI/DUI offenses was your significant other charged with?

_____

4. How many DWI/DUI offenses was your significant other convicted of?

_____

5. From what you were told, or if you were present at the time of the DWI incident, how did the DWI come about? How did the offender come to the attention of the police? Was there an accident? Were there injuries? Loss of life?

6. What was your reaction when you first learned of the DWI incident? check all that apply.

___shock	___surprise	___anger	___guilt	___disbelief
___relief	___fear	___sad	___depressed	___anxiety
___"I told you so"	___rage	___compassion		___other

7. Please explain why you were feeling those items you checked in question #6.

8. Prior to the DWI incident, had you and your family member/significant other ever discussed his or her drinking? Had you ever expressed concerns about his or her drinking?

9. Prior to the DWI incident, did you ever worry that he or she may have a drinking problem? Please explain why or why not.

10. What was your reaction when you learned your family member was referred to an alcohol awareness/treatment program?

11. To the best of your knowledge, is there any history of alcohol or drug use problems within the DWI offender's family (especially among blood relatives: grandparents, aunts, uncles, parents, brothers or sisters)? How about in your family?

12. If you could change anything about your significant other's drinking, what would you change?

13. From what you know today of your significant other's response to having had the DWI/DUI offense, do you think that he or she will continue to drink and drive once his or her license is restored? Do you think he or she will ever have another DWI/DUI? Why or why not?

14. How might you be helpful in preventing your significant other from having another DWI/DUI offense?

collude with the chemically dependent person in order to enable their addiction to continue. Therefore, the reactions of the family members to the DWI event may also coincide with the kind of enabling or collusion that may have occurred prior to the DWI event. For example, it is not unusual for some spouses to react to the DWI incident by calling a moratorium to drinking within the home, with threats to leave if the drinking continues or when the family member enables the drinking to continue by agreeing to drive the DWI offender family member both to work and to his or her favorite tavern or bar. These reactions can be viewed within the context of the classic family study performed by Jackson (1954), in which some alcoholic families were found to "reorganize in spite of the problem" while other families would "attempt to eliminate the problem" by way of marital separation. In most instances, however, the majority of these DWI families appear to be locked into the stage that Jackson characterizes as "attempts to deny the problem."

Also important in the assessment process is the exploration of prior chemical dependency within the family. It is not unusual for the DWI offender to have a history of alcoholism or chemical addiction within the family of origin. It is common, however, for the DWI offender to refrain from disclosing this information or to view his or her parent's drinking as nonproblematic; however, a spouse or significant other may be less defensive in talking about this information. Also, it is not unusual to find that the spouse or significant other has a history of alcoholism within his or her family of origin. One may even view the DWI event as a perfect opportunity for the adult child of an alcoholic (COA) family system to become "responsible" for the drinking-driving spouse or significant other, who then often becomes dependent on this person for transportation. This notion fits well with some of the characteristics of the adult COA, who may need to be "super responsible" in order to maintain loyalty to their family system (Woititz, 1983).

In many instances, it is helpful to bring the family members of the DWI offender into the treatment process merely by letting them know what treatment entails. For example, if an "abstinence contract" is part of the treatment plan or if attendance at AA is required, it is helpful to share that information with the family member. It is also helpful to provide family members with information and education about why education/treatment programs are required for DWI offenders. According to McGrath (1986), there are three goals that DWI offender collateral programs should focus on, "(1) to provide information about alcohol and the disease of alcoholism, (2) to provide an opportunity for collaterals to examine how their or someone else's drinking has affect their life and (3) to introduce collaterals to resources that are available to help persons concerned with their own or someone else's alcohol problems" (p. 146). McGrath emphasizes alcoholism information on the basis of estimates by Selzer (1979) and Yoder and Moore (1973), which suggest that the rates of alcoholism or serious problem drinking among DWI offenders may be as high as 60 percent to 80 percent.

It is idealistic to assume that the family member or significant other will be an ally to the treatment process, and oftentimes the family member may become a willing saboteur to the counseling. This kind of sabotaging often takes place when the family member takes on the same defense system as the DWI offender. Therefore, it is not uncommon to see both the DWI offender and family member projecting blame for the DWI event onto the court system, the police, or the motor vehicle agency. This almost becomes similar to a type of folie-a-deux (Lidz et al., 1970), which has been noted in the family therapy literature. Here, a distorted perception of one spouse or family member is accepted or shared by the other. The goal of treatment, therefore, is to try to confront this denial system or to try to present reality in a receivable way.

REACTIONS OF THE FAMILY TO THE DWI EVENT

Reorganizing Around the Problem

In order to treat the family of the DWI offender, it is important to understand what the family members experience from the moment they learn of the DWI arrest, throughout adjudication, treatment, and then the completion of treatment.

As indicated previously, families have quite varied responses upon learning of the DWI incident. These responses are important reactions to understand in the assessment process because they provide valuable insight into the family's adaptation to the drinking and driving events. For example, drinking and driving may occur on a regular basis. The family's reactions can signal how they may have dealt with these occurrences in the past.

These reactions can be grouped into broad categories. Based upon our clinical experience working with DWI family members and significant others over several years, as well as the self-report of the DWI offenders, the following categories of family response are most often seen:

Shock and Surprise. Family members appear to be truly surprised by the DWI arrest and cannot figure out how such a thing could have happened. This is a common reaction among families of first offenders who may not have much of a prior pattern of problematic drinking or drinking driving.

When this response does occur with a multiple DWI offender family, then it usually signals a strong denial pattern and a family member who may have minimized the arrest in order to protect the denial system. With a first offender a similar denial pattern may be evident, especially if the DWI is accompanied by other instances of drinking- or drug-related problems. Shock and surprise can also suggest that this may be an individual for whom drinking and driving is not a regular occurrence but was perhaps an error in judgment, as would be the case with someone who had been at a wedding or other celebration, had too much to drink, and decided to drive when it would have been more prudent to have asked for a ride home. This individual may fall within the approximate 40 percent or so of first offenders who probably do not manifest a drinking problem or alcoholism.

Anger. This is the most common reaction, demonstrating a lot of frustration within the family concerning the arrest. The family will often be angry at the DWI offender, but may also collude with him or her and, in doing so, will evidence denial of the DWI being a drinking-related event. Here, the family member may be more interested in punishing the offender and will often resist treatment.

It should be noted that anger may serve as a defense against feelings of guilt. Family counselors working in inpatient chemical dependency centers will often report that it is difficult to motivate families to come in for family counseling, as many family members will initially report feeling angry, "It's his or her problem. He or she is the drunk, let him or her deal with it; leave me alone," is often the message that family counselors will hear. Beneath this anger, however, are often feelings of guilt, based on the "responsibility trap" (Bepko and Krestan, 1985) that family members/significant others often find themselves in. Here, family members may be saying, "If I come in, you'll blame me for the DWI. It is my fault; I should have prevented it somehow."

Counselors often find that anger is a "surface emotion" and can be the outward expression of many internal feeling states. For example, the parents who become angry that their teenager has missed curfew may be inwardly fearful that something happened to him or her. The DWI family member who is outwardly angry may also harbor intense fears and apprehensions, "Will my significant other lose his or her job?" "How will we survive financially if he or she does?" "Will he or she ever get a driver's license again?" "How much will our car insurance rates go up, providing that we're not dropped by our insurance company?" These are just a few of the fears that often underlie the anger reaction.

"I Told You So." This reaction often reflects an awareness within the family that drinking has been problematic in the past and that drinking and driving behavior is probably a relatively frequent occurrence. Comments may have been made to the offender by the family urging him or her to cease drinking and driving, but have not met with much success up to this point. Therefore, when the inevitable happens, the family responds with, "See, I told you so!"

This reaction is illustrative of a family who has been trying to confront the drinking issue. However, it has not been in formalized manner, but usually in the wake of a drinking episode, when the spouse or family member reacts in anger at yet another drinking episode or crisis. This family member usually recognizes the seriousness of the problem and can therefore often provide valuable clinical information that can be brought out in the treatment process. Therefore, this individual also may be invested in preventing another DWI and will often be an ally in the treatment process.

Relief. This reaction seems to be almost a cry for help from family members. They often will express this sense of relief to convey their hope that finally something will be done and now the offender can get some help. They may view the treatment agency or counselors as saviors, and though this may look like an easy family to work with they can often be quite difficult.

Here, the counselor is looked upon as the person who is going to solve all the problems that the drinking has caused within the family. When the family begins to discover, however, that much more may be involved (such as their participation in treatment or Al-Anon or Nar-Anon), they may become resistant to treatment. Or the family may become disillusioned when they find that the counselor is not omnipotent and will not be able to "fix" the DWI offender and break through all of his or her denial. It is important, however, for the counselor to keep aligned with the family and to emphasize the importance of their continued involvement in the treatment process. These families, for example, can sometimes be motivated to do a formal intervention with the DWI offender (Johnson, 1985). This does not happen in all situations however, as there are some families who have actively sought help for themselves prior to the DWI event taking place. These families are usually quite willing to work with the counselor on bringing about effective change.

Reorganization Concerning the DWI Event

Once the family has responded to the news of the arrest, they usually become task-oriented in dealing with immediate issues such as hiring a lawyer, preparing for the court date, and the eventual loss of license. These are overwhelming tasks for the average family. Most families are unfamiliar with the workings of the judicial system and feel very much out of place with legal strategies and legal jargon. The financial burden of lawyer's fees, court fines, insurance surcharges, and the possible loss of income all place the family under tremendous stress. The DWI offender also experiences a loss of status within the family, within the community (most municipalities report DWI arrests in local newspapers), and perhaps on the job as well. This especially would be the case where driving is an integral part of one's job. One municipal yard worker, who drove snowplows, dump trucks and so on, naturally had to maintain a CDL (commercial drivers license) in order to perform his job responsibilities. When he lost his license for a DWI, he was demoted and lost his place in the promotion hierarchy. One DWI offender admitted that the toughest part of being arrested for a DWI was telling his eleven-year-old son why he was not allowed to drive. These pressures place tension and strain on the family. Normal routines are disrupted as the focus is shifted to handling the stress of the DWI arrest (Garrett, 1980).

According to Jackson (1954) families impacted by alcoholism strive to maintain homeostasis or balance. Family members will react to whatever is going on within the family so as to reduce discord, with the goal of returning to "normal" functioning as quickly as possible. Equilibrium must be maintained at all costs. Here, equilibrium is defined as the "permissible" range of variations that may occur within a system without the loss of its identity and organization (Lennard and Berstein, 1969). A similar conceptualization was later echoed by Rapaport (1965), who writes about crisis theory. The DWI is viewed, naturally, as a crisis event, which results in two possible outcomes. The first is a return to the individual's previous level of functioning prior to the crisis. The second is a change in awareness, which results in a higher level of functioning. For this second resolution to happen, three conditions must be met: (1) there is a new perception of the problem or crisis brought about by the assimilation of new information, (2) there is a resolution of emotions brought about by this new awareness and by catharsis, and (3) help is sought and new resources are utilized. The goal, therefore, of most DWI treatment programs is to turn the DWI crisis into an opportunity for positive change.

Families as well as the DWI offender, therefore, usually want to "get through" the legal process and subsequent punishments as quickly as possible, as a means of maintaining homeostasis or equilibrium. It is not unusual, therefore, for the offender and his or her family to view the education/treatment program as just another punishment and another roadblock preventing them from putting the DWI event behind them, allowing them to get back to "normal," everyday functioning. Offenders and their families or significant others rarely, if ever, see the necessity for education/treatment programs and resent these programs as intrusions. In their eyes, treatment produces feelings of stigma and is a threat to the identity of the family.

The aforementioned stress model and crisis theory also helps to justify why it is important to include families in the treatment process. For example, if the increase in stress is accompanied by resistance within the family, then the DWI offender will be less likely to change. Therefore, if the offender is struggling with an emerging awareness of his or her drinking or drug use as problematic, the family's willingness to support this change becomes a crucial issue. Likewise, the family can motivate change and be the impetus for growth, even if the DWI offender is resistant to such changes.

Family reactions also vary according to who the offender is within the family unit—his or her status and importance to the family. For example, the spouse who may be dependent on the DWI offender as the breadwinner may feel trapped and will be less likely to break from the collusion and may support the problem drinking.

FAMILY MEMBERS IN TREATMENT

As was alluded to earlier, when family members are first requested to come into the treatment agency, their reactions are usually angry and defensive. It is not unusual for the significant other to take on the same defensive structure of the DWI offender. Therefore, it is common for family members to express anger and hostility toward the courts, police, motor vehicle laws, and so on. Some of this anger will often refer to the sacrifices that the family has had to endure as a result of the DWI event. For example, the expense of the DWI, i.e., fines, court fees, insurance costs, attorney's fees; or the fact that the significant other has had to take over transportation needs. Therefore, it is not unlikely that the spouse or significant other will feel that he or she too is being punished, and will see the treatment provider as a mere extension of the authorities dealt with previously.

Through continued contact with the family members, one may be able to peel off the outer layers of anger and hostile defensiveness. As indicated earlier, the counselor needs to be able to look for what lies beneath the surface of this anger. Therefore, counselors need to ask themselves, "What is being defended?" Certainly, no family member is advocating that everyone, including the offender, has the inalienable right to drink and drive. Therefore, is that family member protecting an alcoholic family system or is he or she protecting the co-alcoholic self from feelings of guilt, responsibility, or shame? Or is the anger really a reaction to the stress that the family is experiencing in trying to survive the DWI arrest/conviction?

The role of the counselor in working with family members in treatment is usually to educate with the hope of trying to create a new awareness and, in doing so, to try to break through some of the aforementioned defenses or denial issues. Sometimes this can be accomplished by creating cognitive dissonance. According to Dissonance Theory (Festinger, 1957), there is a natural tendency to resolve inconsistent notions or feelings that create disequilibrium by negating one of the ideas in order to restore balance. For example, cigarette smokers who read a report that cigarette smoking is dangerous to their health might rationalize that smoking is not truly dangerous or that their health will ultimately not be effected. By accepting this, they have restored balance. Similarly, with the DWI offender who may come to know of the DWI event as a symptom of alcoholism or through court fines, license suspensions, and so on, comes to know the DWI event as a criminal act, may reduce his or her dissonance by either giving up drinking or by refuting the notion that he or she may be an alcoholic or a criminal. In fact, many DWI offenders rationalize their DWI by stating that they have "cut down" on their drinking for a period after the DWI arrest perhaps to "prove" that they are not alcoholics. Or they may emphasize their history of civic or community work and other good deeds, also as a means of reducing dissonance.

Family members will often engage in a similar kind of dissonance reduction or denial. Therefore, one of the goals of treatment is to create dissonance by getting the family to focus in on the DWI arrest as being the result of problematic drinking or alcoholism, rather than focusing on all the stress that has taken place as result of the DWI . One practical way of creating this dissonance is to raise the question, "What if a subsequent DWI were to take place?" Many family members would respond that a subsequent DWI would convince them that there is a drinking problem or that the spouse or significant other is an alcoholic. The next question is whether the family wants to sanction another DWI, via condoning continued drinking and driving? In many instances, this will motivate family members to take a stand regarding the offender's drinking behavior and sometimes to take a stand on abstinence. According to Yoder (1975), "Three fourths of (DWI) convictions would have been prevented if friends and relatives had dissuaded the person who had been drinking from driving, and 40 percent would have been prevented if the host had provided alternate means of transportation and his guests had used them . . ." (p. 1575).

VARIATIONS ON A THEME

Thus far, we have been discussing the DWI offender and his or her family as if they are a homogeneous group; however, many variations in both offenders and family members need to be taken into account. For example, hopefully, the reactions of family members to a first offense will be much different from reactions to a multiple-offense situation. Do not be surprised, however, when they are not. Just as the multiple DWI offender may rationalize that the first offense was really not an offense because he or she refused the Breathalyzer or his or her blood alcohol was "just over the limit," so too will family members often feed into these rationalizations. First-offender families will usually be more resistant to the treatment referral than the multiple-offender family, who may realize that something needs to be done. Here, for example, spouses of multiple offenders may be more willing to take a stand regarding abstinence and the need for ongoing treatment of some sort. However, this is not always the case. As odd as it sounds, many of these multiple-offender family members remain in as much denial as the DWI offender. Alcohol and drug counselors can accept this denial as part of the disease process, and know that addictions are not based on logical thought.

Another variation occurs when a young DWI offender, who is living on his or her own, brings as collateral a girlfriend or boyfriend. This presents a special difficulty, in that the girlfriend or boyfriend may not be as invested in the relationship as perhaps a spouse or parent would be, therefore, she or he may not see the need to support the treatment process. Oftentimes this individual may be the drinking companion, and therefore may see nothing unusual about the drinking pattern of the DWI offender, as if to say, "I drink the same way she or he does, and I don't have a problem, therefore, he or she doesn't have a problem." Whenever possible, it is better to specify and require that the most "invested" or concerned family member accompany the offender into treatment.

Prior research indicates that most DWI offenders are likely to be young males. Many will fall between the nineteen- to twenty-five-year-old age category and it is not unusual for young DWI offenders to be living at home and to bring their mother or father in as their collateral contact. What is often found in situations such as this is that the DWI offender appears to be in a state of "prolonged adolescence," essentially, functioning more in the role of an adolescent than they are as a mature adult. This sometimes can be a function of the developmental lag often found in chemically dependent teenagers (Cavaiola and Kane-Cavaiola, 1989) and should be explored as a possibility. These angry young DWI offenders are often characterized by impulsiveness, hostility, irritability, and low frustration tolerance (Donovan and Marlatt, 1982). In these instances, parents often come in feeling exasperated over the DWI offense and the consequences that both their son or daughter and they have been forced to endure. The DWI may also bring to light a prolonged state of dependence on the parent, which has just been made longer by the license suspension. In many instances the parents may be giving a message to their son or daughter, "See, you can't take care of yourself [as demonstrated by the DWI]; therefore, I need to continue to take care of you." Oftentimes, these youthful offenders are characterized not only by a heavy and frequent drinking history, but also by a general lack of direction in their lives. Therefore, it is not unusual for these offenders to be unemployed or employed in menial, directionless types of jobs. Cases like this usually require more lengthy, intensive treatment.

Another variation occurs where the DWI offender has an active alcoholic or addicted family member at home, who may or may not be involved as a collateral. In most instances, the active alcoholic usually wants no part of any kind of treatment, not even as a collateral contact, so usually a nonalcoholic family member will come in for the family session. In instances such as this, the DWI offender often feels singled out or scapegoated by the system, as if to say, "Why are you picking on me, when I have an alcoholic father, (or mother, brother, sister) at home." The coalcoholic family member who does come into treatment as a collateral often will feel helpless and exasperated. He or she feels surrounded by alcoholism and frustrated in being able to effect any change within the family. Often it is helpful to get these coalcoholic family members into Al-Anon as quickly as possible, as an adjunct to treatment.

A final consideration occurs depending on the gender of the DWI offender. Males still outnumber females in nationwide DWI statistics. In those cases, however, in which the DWI offender is female, her collateral contact (e.g., boyfriend, fiancé, husband, or father) often comes into treatment being very protective and often colluding in the denial of the female DWI offender, sometimes rationalizing that she was singled out because of being a woman. In the majority of cases, in which the DWI offender is male, he will bring his girlfriend, fiancé, wife, mother, or an adult daughter as his collateral contact. His selection is usually based upon who will remain most loyal to him and perhaps least likely to disclose information to the counselor.

PRACTICAL TREATMENT SUGGESTIONS

The value of family involvement is probably most evident in the assessment process. Information provided by family members can be useful in confronting the DWI offender. However, involving family in other facets of treatment is also indicated. Educating family about symptoms of alcoholism can help the entire family to recognize the offense as perhaps more than just an isolated instance of abusive drinking. In helping the family to learn about the progression of alcoholism, they can be helpful in distinguishing whether the offender may be on his or her way to alcoholism or in early, middle, or late stages of the disease. Also, if indeed a diagnosis of alcoholism is made, then the family can be mobilized to come up with effective intervention strategies.

As indicated throughout this chapter, however, the family's denial may prevent them from seeing the DWI offense as being an indication of a problem. If there has been an increase in loss of control over drinking, then it is important to determine how this may have been incorporated into the family's belief system. This would also include whether drinking and driving has been a chronically occurring situation. Most studies suggest that the majority of convicted DWI offenders will drink and drive on a repetitive basis. Therefore, it is important to explore how family members have responded to this. If it is possible to break through the denial of the family member regarding the seriousness of the DWI incident, and not just continue to focus on the ramifications of it, then there is a possibility that progress can be made.

In order to successfully include the family into a DWI education/ treatment program, consideration should be given to the needs of the family members. Families feel intruded upon when asked to attend such a program. Attending the program may also mean being made to deal with their angry feelings or confronting uncomfortable realities. Therefore, the counselor needs to make a special effort to address these feelings and to allow the family members to vent their feelings about attending such a program. Counselors should be noncritical and nonjudgmental. Oftentimes the best response to this onslaught of angry feelings is "I hear you." To try to get into the importance of DWI awareness programs as a means of helping to reduce DWI recidivism will be a waste of time and will fall on deaf ears. It is also better to just continue stressing the importance of the family members' input. After all, if they are invested in their significant other, they and the counselor have a similar goal, i.e., preventing recidivism. Therefore, it is then important for the counselor to stress this notion at a point in which it is more likely to be heard. In addition, the point should be made that the family members know the DWI offender far better than any counselor will probably ever know this person; therefore, the input from the family members again becomes vital to providing effective solutions to the DWI recidivism problem. The main message that the counselor gives the family is "I need your help if I'm going to be helpful to your DWI offender."

Up to this point, the focus has been so directed to the offender that family members are often taken aback when asked to attend the program also or they may feel that treatment agencies have no right to expect them to come. Basically, we are aware of two approaches to deal with this issue. First, some programs make it known from the onset that family involvement is required and that this is a nonnegotiable requirement. Sometimes it is best to do the intake assessment first, and find out who the significant others are in the DWI offender's life, so that those family members most invested in the DWI offender can be asked to attend the program. The offender can refuse to participate in the program, which in most states will result in ending up back in court. The obvious disadvantage to this approach is that it may bring about more resistance to treatment. The second approach taken is one advocated by McGrath and Pandiani (1987). They used financial rebates as a means of increasing participation among family members. One group of DWI offenders were offered a $25 rebate if their family member successfully completed the family program, and another group was offered a $50 rebate. They found that higher rebates resulted in increased percentages of participating family members, regardless of the severity of the offender's drinking problem. This approach has the advantage of encouraging participation while decreasing resistance. The disadvantage is that not all agencies can afford rebates, nor can they be built into all fee structures. The second disadvantage is that even with a larger financial incentive, less than half of the families completed the family program.

Certain issues need to be addressed when designing a program. From a practical standpoint, ideally, separate groups for DWI offenders and their family members should be provided. Family members may feel too inhibited to express their feelings with the offender present in the same group. The goal of the family group will also be different, as will the focus of the offender group; therefore, it is best to offer separate groups and perhaps to comingle the groups at a later point in the treatment process. Comingled groups offered too early in the treatment process are more likely to become gripe sessions that can easily get out of the counselor's control, whereas a comingled group later on in treatment that focuses on a specific agenda (e.g., coming up with ways to prevent another DWI) may lend to more effective work being done. Programs will differ in the number of sessions required for families to attend; however, there should be a minimum of three to four sessions, not including an individual wrap-up session.

At some point, toward the later stage of treatment, the counselor should meet with the DWI offender and family member(s) to discuss what they have gotten out of the program and also to discuss solutions or ways that they plan to avoid another DWI offense. It is recommended that the counselor write this plan out in a written contract form (see Appendix B) along with a plan for what will take place if the DWI offender relapses to abusive drinking or drinking and driving. Here again, it is important for the spouse, parent, or significant other to be aware of the services available to them as well as for their offender in the event that such a relapse occurs.

CONCLUDING REMARKS

In taking all of the aforementioned information into consideration, it is clear that all DWI treatment programs need to include family members and/or significant others to one degree or another. Based upon our clinical experience, we have found that family members need to be included on a regular basis throughout the duration that the DWI offender is participating in education or treatment. A one-time family session will not accomplish the goals that need to be addressed. We also need to emphasize that we are not advocating that the family member or significant other become responsible for policing the DWI offender. That would be counter to all that has been written on codependency treatment and certainly counter to Al-Anon philosophy; however, family members can perhaps become a positive influence in the prevention of a subsequent DWI offense.

Since many of the hypotheses and recommendations presented in this chapter have been derived from several years of clinical observation and years of work with DWI offenders and their families, a definite need exists for further research in order to empirically validate these impressions. It is optimistically speculated that as we learn more about the DWI offender and more about effective treatment approaches, there will also be a greater focus on understanding the family of the DWI offender and the expansion of family treatment programs to coincide with DWI offender treatment.

Chapter 11

Where We Are—Where We Are Going

The purpose of this chapter is to provide an overview of the research and developments presented in this book and also to look at some of the areas that need to be addressed in future research and treatment. Obviously, there have been several important developments in the assessment and treatment of DWI offenders over the past quarter of a century, since the inception of the ASAP programs in the mid-1970s. However, as long as drinking drivers continue to plague our nation's highways, there will be a need for better assessment and treatment techniques in order to help prevent recidivism. The National Highway Traffic Safety Administration has targeted 2005 as the date by which time they hope to reduce alcohol-related traffic fatalities to less than 11,000 annualy (NHTSA, 1999). Several efforts by NHTSA are being implemented in order to address these goals; however, as with any major social problem there is a need for new, varied, and innovative approaches. The purpose and focus of this book is not to address all of these DWI reduction methods, but rather to focus on those assessment and treatment methods that would apply to the convicted DWI offender and recidivist who is referred to a treatment program as a means of preventing future drinking-and-driving offenses.

First, the good news. As reported by the National Highway Traffic Safety Administration, the toll of alcohol-related fatalities had dropped to less than 40 percent in 1997, for the first time since 1977 (NHTSA, 1998). This statistic is certainly encouraging to all who work in prevention, law enforcement, and treatment of DWI offenders, as it suggests that something is working. What is difficult, however, to assess empirically is exactly what might account for this dramatic decline. Is it greater public awareness of the dangers of drinking and driving? Could it be that people have become more health conscious in general and are drinking less? Could it be that the notion of the "designated driver" has become acceptable and somewhat more ingrained in our culture? Are tougher laws, with fewer chances to plea bargain, responsible for the reduction in alcohol-related fatalities? Are some of the innovations in DWI laws, such as vehicle impoundment or interlock ignition devices responsible for this change? Are DWI treatment programs rendering more effective assessment and treatment strategies that are better able to target those individuals who are at higher risk for subsequent DWI offenses? Or could it be that a combination of the aforementioned factors is responsible for the decline in DWI related fatalities?

NHTSA is currently conducting research in five of the states that have witnessed the most dramatic decline in order to determine reasons for this decline. At this time, however, it is clear that there is not a simple way to answer these questions. What is known is that it takes a team approach to bring about these changes and it will continue to take a team effort to bring about even more positive and lasting changes. This team naturally includes legislators; judges; attorneys; state and municipal police and other law enforcement personnel; citizen awareness groups such as MADD and SADD; both federal and state governmental efforts, such as those sponsored by the NHTSA and state countermeasures programs; researchers both in university settings as well as private institutes, such as the Research Institute on Addictions; prevention specialists; teachers; students; and addiction counselors and other counselors/therapists. All of these individuals need to be included in the team effort to prevent DWI, enforce DWI laws, and treat DWI offenders in order to stem the tide of DWI offenses and DWI recidivism.

It is also important to take into account that we cannot emphasize one approach at the expense of another. Such is the case currently in our national policies with regard to the alcoholism and drug crisis. Instead of making treatment available to more addicts and alcoholics, our government continues to build more prisons; therefore, punitive measures are being emphasized at the expense of treatment opportunities. Unfortunately, alcohol and drug treatment programs are closing at an alarming rate. Those programs that continue to survive usually have lengthy waiting lists. In New Jersey alone, some twenty-two programs (outpatient and inpatient) have closed in the past five years, mostly under the weight of restrictive managed-care policies and funding cutbacks. What we know from behavioral psychology is that punishment merely tells a person *what not to do;* it does not instruct the person about *what to do.* In other words, treatment becomes the place to explore alternatives to drinking or alternatives to drinking and driving. Therefore, we cannot sacrifice any one element or team member if we are going to continue to make strides in reducing the rates of DWI and rates of drinking-driving fatalities.

A case in point: several years ago, we happened to be working with an alcoholism counselor who had been in recovery for about eight years. One day, we happened to be talking about our early days in the treatment field and she shared that she had begun her recovery in a DWI treatment program. We were somewhat surprised to hear this, at first, since many DWI offenders often go through treatment and may be compliant but nothing more. We need to remember that there are DWI treatment success stories such as these, as well as many more instances in which first-time DWI offenders do not repeat the DWI offense—and in doing so, become responsible drivers. One of the problems in the treatment field is that we often do not see the fruits of our labor. Following a regular interval of aftercare phone contacts, we have fortunately often run into some of our clients in malls or supermarkets. It is good to hear of their successes and the changes they have made as a result of treatment. Although reluctantly, some will tell us that being forced into treatment was the best thing that ever happened to them, as it saved their marriage, their job, or their lives (or the lives of others). Many have become active members of AA or NA and have been helpful in working with DWI offenders who have been mandated into treatment, just as they once were. These recovering individuals are very effective in breaking through the denial of repeat offenders, because they too once manifested the same denial.

The bad news is that, even as this is being written, someone is being killed in a DWI-related accident, someone is getting behind the wheel of a vehicle drunk or stoned. In 1997, someone was killed in an alcohol-related crash every thirty-two minutes. The DWI problem continues to exist even if one person dies in an alcohol- or drug-related crash. Even with improvement in statistics noted, there are still 1.4 million DWI offenses being committed each year (NHTSA, 1999).

What is unfortunate is that many of the innovations that have taken place in the last ten years or so have taken place in the legislative and enforcement areas. Examples of this include vehicle impoundment statutes, interlock ignition devices, community service obligations and mandatory jail time, and electronic monitoring of DWI offenders. Some of these innovations were discussed in Chapter 6 on countermeasures and again in Chapter 9 on treatment approaches. It appears that both individualized sanctions such as those being implemented in Judge Todd's court in Rockland County, Georgia, or individualized treatment approaches such as those presented in Cook County, Illinois, are probably suggestive of the trends that are taking place in the DWI field.

Even with many of the innovative legal sanctions, DWI offenders continue to drive while their driver's licenses are revoked. According to the National Commission Against Drunk Driving (1999), " It is estimated that up to 80 percent of chronic drinking drivers continue to drink and drive after license suspension, and the probability of being caught doing so is low. . . . There is virtually no difference in recidivism rates between those who receive jail time or public service only and those who do not." Although the problem of drunk drivers who continue to drive while on the revoked list has been partially addressed by ignition interlock devices, zebra sticker laws, and vehicle impoundment, this would not prevent a DWI offender from using someone else's vehicle. Donald Feeney (2000) who is the Director of the Monmouth County (New Jersey) Intoxicated Driver Resource Center advocates for a Megan's Law for DWI offenders. Megan's Law was created in response to the brutal rape/murder of a New Jersey girl by a known sex offender. Under Megan's Law, convicted sex offenders who are released from prison are made known to police, neighbors, parents, school officials, teachers, and other adults responsible for caring for children in that town or neighborhood. As Mr. Feeney suggests, perhaps a similar law is needed for DWI offenders to make those within that neighborhood aware that a convicted DWI offender is in their midst and should not be behind the wheel of a car.

Unfortunately, it seems that for those of us in the DWI treatment field not as many innovations have occurred as in the area of adjudication and sanctions. Instead, some DWI treatment programs continue year after year to show the same films, or continue to have the same AA speakers, or will continue to deliver the same lecture on the medical horrors of alcohol and drugs, with little forethought as to whether these techniques really work and, if they do, how they change the thinking and behavior of the DWI offender. Our main contention is that we get nowhere by "talking at" people; rather, we must "talk with" them. Many programs have instituted Victim Impact Panels as a means of breaking through denial. These panels were first instituted by MADD in Clackamas County, Oregon, in 1987, and were designed to confront DWI offenders with the devasting impact of their drinking and driving behavior on those who have been victimized by drinking drivers. Family members who have lost a loved one in a drunk driving crash or survivors of alcohol-related crashes volunteer their time to confront DWI offenders who are participating in education programs (Foley, 1997).

Chapter 7 provides insight in ways in which counselors need to better assess the level of motivation of the DWI offender using the Prochaska-DiClemente Transtheoretical Model. This allows for more individualized treatment planning and individualized treatment techniques. Given the heterogeneity of the DWI offender population, it is imperative that we look toward more individualized approaches. In addition, more research is required on the length of treatment needed to achieve impact on preventing recidivism as well as the types of treatment techniques that are the most effective in bringing about change. For example, what type of DWI offender will respond best to a "skills training approach," what type will respond to relapse prevention approaches, and what type will respond to a more behavioral approach? Perhaps this is where the innovations in assessment discussed in Chapters 4 and 5 come into play. Assessment strategies have improved beyond the mere direct question measures techniques of the 1970s. Here, the marriage of research and applied practice can best be realized, as there are several measures currently available that have incorporated the enormous research literature on DWI offenders in order to more accurately assess those DWI offenders who are at greater risk for recidivism.

Alcohol and drug counselors are now able to gain better insight into the character of each DWI offender they are working with. In being able to better assess each offender, it is then possible to come up with more individualized treatment plans in order to work more effectively with these offenders. This would especially be true with re-peat offenders, who are probably the most difficult to treat. Again, not all repeat offenders are alike, as there is certainly heterogeneity within this population as well. The challenge to the treatment field, as well as for researchers, is how to best treat the variety of repeat offenders that may enter our treatment programs. One method may be to mandate a period of inpatient treatment, such as those being offered in Maryland and Massachusetts, as was discussed in Chapter 9. Another approach would be to include long-term follow-up beyond an initial intensive treatment program, with regular court contact, such as that described above in Judge Todd's Rockland County, Georgia, court.

With regard to other treatment issues, it is also imperative that the substance abuse treatment field begin to take a look at offering special-ized training programs that would lead to a specialized counselor cer-tification specifically for treating DWI offenders. As was indicated in Chapter 9, there are already some states that are offering just such a certification. Although many states offer specialized certifications for those with expertise in prevention programs or for those counselors working with MICA clients (mentally ill chemical abusers), there is a need to recognize DWI treatment as a specialized treatment that re-quires specialized training in assessment and treatment techniques. Many treatment agencies have a client base made up of 25 to 40 per-cent DWI offenders. With so much time, effort, and resources being devoted to treating this population, it seems to make sense that the treatment field would address DWI offenders in a more concerted way, especially given the public safety aspect of this work.

The idea of being granted a driver's license by the state one lives in is an accepted concept. Being granted this license carries an implica-tion that the licensed driver is expected to drive in accordance with state and local laws regarding speed limits, rules of the road, and, nat-urally, to laws pertaining to alcohol and drug use. Several years ago, we came across an editorial in *The New York Times* suggesting that perhaps people should be required to have a license in order to drink alcohol. In other words, just as one is issued a license to drive once certain requirements are met, so too, one would ostensibly be issued a license to drink, which would then also carry with it certain responsi-bilities and adherence to rules governing the responsible use of alco-hol. If one were to abuse this right, the license to drink would be taken away. This is certainly an interesting concept, although one that would be impossible to enforce. If such licensure were enforceable, however, it would have far-reaching implications—it would not only reduce drunk driving, it also would reduce alcoholism as a major public health issue.

At this point in time, it seems that although we have come a long way toward being able to more effectively assess and treat DWI offenders, we still have a long way to go before being able to eradicate the intensity and scope of this problem.

Appendix A

Traffic Safety Facts 1998— State Alcohol Estimates

TABLE A.1. Fatalities by Highest Blood Alcohol Concentration in the Crash, 1982

State	Total Fatalities	No Alcohol (BAC = 0.00 g/dl)		Low Alcohol (BAC = 0.01-0.09 g/dl)		High Alcohol (BAC ≥ 0.10 g/dl)		Any Alcohol (BAC ≥ 0.01 g/dl)	
		Number	Percent	Number	Percent	Number	Percent	Number	Percent
Alabama	839	372	44	89	11	379	45	467	56
Alaska	105	48	45	3	3	54	52	57	55
Arizona	724	317	44	73	10	334	46	407	56
Arkansas	550	214	39	66	12	270	49	336	61
California	4,615	1,894	41	498	11	2,223	48	2,721	59
Colorado	668	242	38	75	11	342	51	416	62
Connecticut	515	163	32	66	13	286	56	352	68
Delaware	122	42	34	11	9	70	57	80	66
District of Columbia	35	14	40	6	17	15	43	21	60
Florida	2,653	1,418	53	252	10	983	37	1,235	47
Georgia	1,229	509	41	145	12	575	47	720	59
Hawaii	163	63	39	18	11	82	50	100	61
Idaho	256	143	56	26	10	87	34	113	44
Illinois	1,651	683	41	202	12	766	46	968	59
Indiana	961	495	52	91	9	375	39	466	48
Iowa	480	255	53	47	10	179	37	225	47
Kansas	498	274	55	41	8	183	37	224	45
Kentucky	822	379	46	99	12	344	42	443	54
Louisiana	1,091	496	45	139	13	457	42	595	55
Maine	166	84	50	18	11	64	39	82	50
Maryland	640	292	46	61	10	288	45	348	54
Massachusetts	659	266	40	79	12	314	48	393	60
Michigan	1,392	562	40	136	10	693	50	830	60
Minnesota	571	260	46	47	8	265	46	311	55
Mississippi	730	319	44	79	11	332	46	411	56
Missouri	890	444	50	96	11	350	39	446	50
Montana	254	87	34	32	13	135	53	167	66
Nebraska	261	136	52	24	9	101	39	125	48
Nevada	280	93	33	34	12	152	55	187	67
New Hampshire	173	72	42	20	12	81	47	101	58

TABLE A.1 *(continued)*

State	Total Fatalities	No Alcohol (BAC = 0.00 g/dl) Number	Percent	Low Alcohol (BAC = 0.01-0.09 g/dl) Number	Percent	High Alcohol (BAC ≥ 0.10 g/dl) Number	Percent	Any Alcohol (BAC ≥ 0.01 g/dl Number	Percent
New Jersey	1,061	467	44	145	14	449	42	594	56
New Mexico	577	210	36	67	12	300	52	367	64
New York	2,162	1,143	53	241	11	777	36	1,019	47
North Carolina	1,303	520	40	137	11	646	50	783	60
North Dakota	148	53	36	15	10	80	54	95	64
Ohio	1,607	699	44	159	10	749	47	908	56
Oklahoma	1,054	463	44	121	11	471	45	591	56
Oregon	518	193	37	55	11	270	52	325	63
Pennsylvania	1,819	756	42	219	12	845	46	1,063	58
Rhode Island	105	36	34	20	19	49	47	69	66
South Carolina	730	300	41	69	9	361	50	430	59
South Dakota	148	59	40	11	7	78	53	89	60
Tennessee	1,055	397	38	112	11	546	52	658	62
Texas	4,213	1,325	32	553	13	2,335	55	2,888	69
Utah	295	182	62	18	6	95	32	113	38
Vermont	107	38	36	20	19	48	45	69	64
Virginia	881	416	47	87	10	378	43	465	53
Washington	748	273	37	73	10	402	54	475	63
West Virginia	450	221	49	33	7	196	44	229	51
Wisconsin	770	295	38	67	9	408	53	475	62
Wyoming	201	90	45	17	8	95	47	111	55
U.S. Total	43,945	18,780	43	4,809	11	20,356	46	25,165	57
Puerto Rico	480	245	51	40	8	195	41	235	49

Source: National Center for Statistics and Analysis, Washington, DC.

TABLE A.2. Fatalities by Highest Blood Alcohol Concentration in the Crash, 1998

State	Total Fatalities	No Alcohol (BAC = 0.00 g/dl) Number	Percent	Low Alcohol (BAC = 0.01-0.09 g/dl) Number	Percent	High Alcohol (BAC ≥ 0.10 g/dl) Number	Percent	Any Alcohol (BAC ≥ 0.01 g/dl) Number	Percent
Alabama	1,071	665	62	77	7	329	31	406	38
Alaska	71	40	56	3	4	28	39	31	44
Arizona	980	557	57	89	9	334	34	423	43
Arkansas	625	432	69	48	8	146	23	193	31
California	3,494	2,170	62	315	9	1,009	29	1,324	38
Colorado	628	396	63	43	7	189	30	232	37
Connecticut	329	187	57	29	9	112	34	142	43
Delaware	115	70	61	7	6	37	33	45	39
District of Columbia	54	27	49	8	16	19	35	27	51
Florida	2,824	1,899	67	210	7	715	25	925	33
Georgia	1,569	1,060	68	130	8	380	24	509	32
Hawaii	120	64	53	14	12	42	35	56	47
Idaho	265	175	66	15	6	75	28	90	34

State	Total Fatalities	No Alcohol (BAC = 0.00 g/dl)		Low Alcohol (BAC = 0.01-0.09 g/dl)		High Alcohol (BAC ≥ 0.10 g/dl)		Any Alcohol (BAC ≥ 0.01 g/dl)	
		Number	Percent	Number	Percent	Number	Percent	Number	Percent
Illinois	1,393	794	57	122	9	477	34	599	43
Indiana	978	599	61	72	7	307	31	379	39
Iowa	449	285	64	43	9	121	27	164	36
Kansas	493	319	65	42	8	132	27	174	35
Kentucky	858	573	67	80	7	225	26	285	33
Louisiana	922	496	54	103	11	323	35	426	46
Maine	192	138	72	8	4	45	24	54	28
Maryland	606	403	66	59	10	144	24	203	34
Massachusetts	406	214	53	59	15	134	33	192	47
Michigan	1,367	831	61	120	9	416	30	536	39
Minnesota	650	370	57	64	10	216	33	280	43
Mississippi	948	597	63	57	6	294	31	351	37
Missouri	1,169	644	55	139	12	386	33	525	45
Montana	237	133	56	23	10	81	34	104	44
Nebraska	315	196	62	31	10	88	28	119	38
Nevada	361	184	51	49	14	127	35	177	49
New Hampshire	128	67	53	25	20	36	28	61	47
New Jersey	743	472	64	77	10	194	26	271	36
New Mexico	424	231	55	41	10	152	36	193	45
New York	1,498	1,133	76	115	8	250	17	365	24
North Carolina	1,596	1,083	68	91	6	422	26	513	32
North Dakota	92	48	53	4	4	40	43	44	47
Ohio	1,422	958	67	83	6	381	27	464	33
Oklahoma	755	503	67	44	6	208	28	252	33
Oregon	538	305	57	50	9	183	34	233	43
Pennsylvania	1,481	862	58	103	7	516	35	619	42
Rhode Island	74	39	52	9	13	26	35	35	48
South Carolina	1,002	698	70	50	5	254	25	304	30
South Dakota	165	98	59	13	8	54	33	67	41
Tennessee	1,216	717	59	105	9	394	32	499	41
Texas	3,577	1,785	50	383	11	1,408	39	1,792	50
Utah	350	300	86	12	3	39	11	50	14
Vermont	104	66	63	7	7	31	30	38	37
Virginia	935	592	63	76	8	267	29	343	37
Washington	660	353	54	62	9	244	37	307	46
West Virginia	354	209	59	17	5	128	36	145	41
Wisconsin	714	412	58	58	8	244	34	302	42
Wyoming	154	86	56	13	8	55	36	68	44
U.S. Total	41,471	25,536	62	3,479	8	12,456	30	15,935	38
Puerto Rico	558	271	49	78	14	209	37	287	51

Source: National Center for Statistics and Analysis, Washington, DC. National Highway Traffic Safety Agency.

Appendix B

Samples of Forms and Contracts Adapted for the DWI Offender

AFTERCARE PREP EXERCISE

Here are examples of aftercare contracts that outline the steps clients will take to avoid another DWI. The contract identifies behavior change and issues of responsibility and allows the counselor and client to focus on those key changes identified in treatment. Through the follow-up process, clients can also identify modifications to the contract as they become necessary.

Sample Aftercare Contracts

(This aftercare contract would be utilized in instances in which the DWI offender clearly meets the criteria for alcohol dependency, alcohol abuse, and/or when the client has a genetic vulnerability for substance dependency; there is a past history of loss of control over alcohol or substance use; other alcoholism symptoms; or a past history of substance abuse treatment. In other words, the counselor concludes that this offender is unable to use alcohol without risking future problems and a future DWI offense.)

I, [DWI offender's name], agree to adhere to the following contract in order to avoid a future DWI offense and to avoid future problems related to drinking or mood-altering chemical use.

- I will continue to abstain from alcohol and all other mood-altering chemicals.
- Under no circumstances will I drink and drive.
- I will continue to avoid people, places, and situations that are conducive to drinking or drug use.
- I will continue to attend AA or NA as specified (x# of meetings per week); I will continue to attend my home group regularly and will have regular contact with my sponsor.

- I agree that if I break this contract in any way (e.g., I resume drinking, I stop going to AA or NA meetings) that I will contact my counselor immediately and will let my significant other know immediately.
- I agree to have regular monthly phone contact with my counselor on the first day of each month for the next twelve months.

I am aware that in signing this contract I am responsible for maintaining the progress that I have made in this program and that I will adhere to the stipulations and spirit of this contract to the best of my ability. I am also aware that if I break this contract that I am solely responsible for the potential damage that I might cause to others or myself or property, as well as placing myself at risk for a future DWI offense.

_____   _____
DWI offender's signature   Date

_____   _____
Significant other's signature   Date

_____   _____
Counselor's signature   Date

(This is a sample of an aftercare contract that would be developed for a client who has not met the criteria for an alcohol dependence diagnosis, nor have they demonstrated any other symptoms of alcoholism, or a genetic vulnerability for alcoholism that would suggest that abstinence would be the more viable treatment goal.)

I, [DWI offender's name], having completed this phase of my treatment, do hereby agree to adhere to the following:

- Under NO circumstances will I drive a motor vehicle or water vehicle if I have been drinking alcohol or using any mood-altering medicine or drug.
- If I do consume any alcohol or use any mood-altering medicine, I agree to find an alternate means of transportation to my destination, such as a taxi or a designated sober driver.
- If I break this contract, I agree to call my counselor within twenty-four hours of the incident in order to set up a meeting with him or her. I also agree to make my significant other aware of this event immediately.
- I will continue to utilize refusal skills, and other skills and techniques that I have learned in this program in order to avoid having a future DWI offense. I will avoid situations, places, and people that encourage abusive drinking or drug use.
- I agree to have regular monthly phone contact with my counselor on the first day of each month for the next twelve months.

I agree to adhere to the contract as specified above and am aware that if I break this contract I am solely responsible for placing myself in jeopardy for being rearrested for a subsequent DWI offense, incurring injury to others or myself, or damage to property.

_____   _____
DWI offender's signature   Date

_____   _____
Significant other's signature   Date

_____   _____
Counselor's signature   Date

ABSTINENCE LECTURE

Abstinence is a requirement of any DWI program. This lecture discusses what offenders could experience if they abstain. It also serves as a trigger for further discussion on the resistance most offenders experience when the goal of abstinence is introduced. This exercise is used prior to introducing the Abstinence Log.

Key points to address in the Symptoms of Abstinence presentation:

1. Mood swings may occur
2. May experience forgetfulness, sleep disturbances, trouble with concentration.
3. Coffee intake may increase, sugar intake may increase.
4. Increased irritability
5. Sleep difficulties
6. Boredom
7. Managing thoughts, urges, and cravings

Discussion questions:

1. What do you think you will miss the most about alcohol and/or other drugs?
2. When do you think you will experience the most difficulty in not drinking?
3. If you cannot adhere to abstinence, what do you think it means?
4. How do you think your family will react to your being abstinent?

ABSTINENCE LOG

NAME _____   DATE _____

If you completely abstained from using alcohol and/or drugs during the week, please answer the following:

1. Describe a time during the week when you were doing something, were out, or with friends when you would normally have consumed alcohol or used drugs, but chose not to instead.

2. Describe the feelings you experienced during this time when you would normally have consumed alcohol.

3. If there were others around, did they notice that you were not drinking? If so, what comments did they make and how did you handle them?

4. How do you feel about not drinking and/or using drugs during the circumstance you described?

ABSTINENCE LOG

NAME _____   DATE _____

If you drank, used drugs, or both during the past week, please answer the following:

1. Describe the circumstances surrounding the incident(s) of use.

2. Was it a situation in which you would usually drink and/or use drugs?

3. How much did you use?

4. What were your feelings just prior to your use?

5. What was the effect of your use on you, physically and emotionally?

DISCUSSION EXERCISE

The Economic and Social Cost of Alcohol and Drug Abuse

(This exercise provides the group participants with concrete examples the impact alcohol and or drug abuse has had on them financially, socially, and how it has impacted the family.)

1. What economic price have you paid for your DWI arrest? Fill in the appropriate amounts in the space provided. Complete total at the bottom of the page.

   a. Attorney fees $ _____._____

   b. Court fine and fees $ _____._____

   c. Increased insurance $ _____._____

   d. Assessment and treatment fees $ _____._____

   e. License restoration fees $ _____._____

   f. Auto repairs (if accident) $ _____._____

   g. Transportation costs $ _____._____
      (Cabs, buses, trains)
                  TOTAL $ _____._____

1. What price has your family paid? Check the statements below that are true for you.

   _____ Significant Other is now responsible to provide the transportation.
   _____ Significant Other must drive to social events and gatherings.
   _____ Others must drive or run the errands.
   _____ Extra transport demands puts strain on Significant Other.
   _____ Tension and arguments have increased as a result of license loss.
   _____ Transport to work puts extra strain on Significant Other.
   _____ Economic sacrifices

2. How has the DWI affected your social life? Circle the statement(s) that are true for you.

   a. Spend more time at home and less time socializing
   b. Less money for vacations and leisure activities due to extra financial burdens.
   c. Inhibits/prevents previous level of activities in leisure-time activities, interests, and hobbies.
   d. Not able to spend as much time with friends, co-workers.

GROUP PROCESS SHEET

(Completed at the end of group, this allows members to anonymously record thoughts and feelings about what they are learning. In the early stages of group, or when groups are open-ended, in an outpatient setting, this allows the facilitator to get feedback about the individual's experiences in group, when members may not be cohesive enough for this type of sharing.)

_____   _____
Date   Title of group exercise

1. Describe one thing you learned in this group that was helpful to you.

2. Was there anything presented or discussed in this group that you would like brought up again for further discussion?

3. What was the least helpful part of the group?

4. If there was anything you would like to have said in group, but did not get the chance, please describe it below.

SENTENCE COMPLETION

(The focal point of these questions is to probe for more about feelings related to alcohol use, and about the DWI. It also helps to build some cohesion in group through a sharing of mutual feelings about a common event. This type of exercise can be easily modified by adding, changing, or modifying questions as situations require.)

1. The most difficult part of not having a license is _____.
2. When I see a person driving under the influence I feel _____.
3. When I have to tell someone I don't have a license I feel _____.
4. A benefit I would like to get by being in treatment is _____.
5. When I think about the consequences of my DWI arrest, I feel _____.
6. When I think about the effect on my family I feel _____.
7. The best part of being here in treatment is _____.
8. The worst part of being in treatment is _____.

GROUP GROUND RULES

In order to obtain the maximum benefits from attending this group, the following ground rules must be followed:

1. You are required to attend all group sessions and to show up on time. Missing a group session for any reason will merely result in your treatment being extended until you complete the specified number of group sessions. If you miss more than two group meetings, you will be referred back to the court. This can result in an extension of your driving suspension.
2. You must show up on time for group. If you are more than five minutes late, you will not be given credit for that group session and this too will extend your treatment.
3. Any person showing up under the influence of alcohol or drugs will not be permitted to participate in group. Instead, you will be escorted to an emergency room in order to determine if detoxification services are required. You may be referred to a more intensive level of treatment, such as an inpatient program, if this were to happen.
4. You must participate in group discussion and group exercises. In order to gain the maximum benefit from group, you must participate in the group process. This means that you are expected to talk honestly about yourself and to give feedback to other group members. Part of the group process is that group members can learn from one another, therefore, it is important to be an active participant in group. At the end of the specified number of group sessions, your primary counselor and you will determine whether you have completed the group successfully or not. In order to make this determination, your counselor will need to know something about you and how you have resolved to prevent any future drinking and driving offense. Therefore, it is important that you participate actively in group.
5. Everything that is said in group remains in group. You are not to discuss anything said in group with ANYONE. This includes revealing the identity of anyone in the group to ANYONE outside of the group. If something in group upsets you, you are to bring these issues up only with your counselor.
6. All fees (if applicable) must be paid according to the fee schedule you have been given.

_____   _____

Client signature   Date

_____   _____

Counselor signature   Date

Glossary

ADS (Alcohol Dependence Scale): Twenty-five item scale developed by the Addiction Research Foundation.

ASAP (Alcohol Safety Action Project): Thirty-nine pilot programs funded by NIAAA to promote treatment for alcoholics and DWI offenders.

ASI (Addiction Severity Index): A structured clinical interview for assessing substance abuse disorders.

AUI (Alcohol Use Inventory): 228 multiple-choice items with 24 scales measuring several aspects of alcohol use and alcohol problems.

BAC (Blood or Breath Alcohol Concentration): The usual ratio standards are the number of grams of alcohol either per 100 milliliters of blood, or per 210 liters of breath.

BAL (Blood Alcohol Level): The usual ratio standards are the number of grams of alcohol either per 100 milliliters of blood, or per 210 liters of breath.

Biopsychosocial assessment: Part of the intake procedure in treatment programs that gathers information on areas of dysfunction caused by alcohol and other drugs.

BrAC: Breath alcohol concentration. The usual ratio standards are the number of grams of alcohol per 210 liters of breath.

CDP (Comprehensive Drinker Profile): A structured interview utilizing a card sort technique.

Countermeasures: Measures, strategies, programs, and methods used to reduce, prevent, or intervene with a targeted problem.

DAST (Drug Abuse Screening Test): A twenty-eight item self-report questionnaire that is based on the MAST, is self-administered, and takes about 15 to 20 minutes to complete.

Deterrence: The use of fear and legal punishment to deter individuals from engaging in the proscribed activity.

DRI (Driver Risk Inventory): Considered very reliable with a well-established validity, the DRI consists of 131 questions about alcohol and drug use and driving practices. It is normed for both men and women, and is available in a Spanish version. The results yield risk levels on four scales.

DSM-III: American Psychiatric Association's *Diagnostic and Statistical Manual of Mental Disorders,* a multiple criteria-based diagnostics system (Third Edition).

DSM-III-R and DSM-IV: American Psychiatric Association's Diagnostic and Statistical Manual of Mental Disorders, (Third Revision and Fourth Edition) The fourth edition is currently in use and includes specific criteria for each disorder, along with a demographic descriptor for each disorder. The criteria also allows for the possibility that individuals with the same disorder (e.g., alcohol dependence) can manifest that disorder in different ways and yet still meet the diagnostic criteria for that disorder.

DUI (Driving Under the Influence): General term used to describe the criminal action of operating a vehicle while under the influence of alcohol or other drugs.

DUSI (Drug Use Screening Inventory): Consists of 149 "Yes-No" items and takes about twenty minutes to administer in either a structured interview or self-administered questionnaire format.

DWI (Driving while intoxicated, or driving while impaired): General term used to describe the criminal action of operating a vehicle while intoxicated, impaired, or under the influence of alcohol or other drugs.

European Model: Established the basis used today of requiring proof of the effectiveness of treatment, not just compliance with treatment, by the offender prior to license restoration.

fake bad: Someone who is trying to present themselves as being more pathological or distressed by endorsing a variety of test items.

fake good: Someone who is trying to portray themselves in a more favorable light, usually by means of nonself-disclosure and/or defensive responding.

false negative: When a test fails to correctly identify the presence of a problem.

false positive: When a test incorrectly identifies an individual as having manifesting a problem when they do not.

FARS (Fatality Analysis Reporting System): (Formerly Fatal Accident Reporting System.) A NHTSA system that has collected information on fatal crashes since 1975 in all states, including data on alcohol involvement.

general deterrence: Aims at changing the general behavior of the population regarding drinking and driving whether they drink and drive or not.

GES: The National Highway Traffic Safety Administration's General Estimates System, which uses data from many sources including police reported crashes and the National Automobile (formerly Accident) sampling system to generate national estimates of all types of crashes including all types of vehicles.

MAC-R (MacAndrews Alcoholism Scale-Revised): Of the Minnesota Multiphasic Personality Inventory-2. Contains 567 items that measure alcohol problems or alcohol vulnerability. It is designed to be subtle.

MAST (Michigan Alcohol Screening Test): A ten to fifteen minute, twenty-four item (Yes-No) test; self or counselor administrated resulting in one of three categories: no drinking problem, possible problem, alcoholism.

MCMI-III (Million Clinical Multiaxial Inventory): A pencil-and-paper measure of psychopathology that also contains scales which determine test-taking attitudes (faking). It is an excellent tool for detecting Axis II (Personality Disorder) diagnoses.

Mortimer-Filkins: A fifty-eight (True-False, Yes-No, and short answer) questionnaire plus a structured interview resulting in one of three categories: social drinker, presumptive problem drinker, problem drinker. Specifically designed for court assessment of DWI/DUI offenders.

N or n: Mathematical term denoting sample size.

NIAAA (National Institute on Alcohol Abuse and Alcoholism): One of seventeen institutes that comprise the National Institutes of Health. NIAAA supports and conducts biomedical and behavioral research on the causes, consequences, treatment, and prevention of alcoholism and alcohol-related problems.

per se: Legal term used to mean that there is a presumption of a relationship between the level of alcohol in a driver's blood stream, and impairment that is used as evidence for conviction.

RBT (Roadside Breath Test): Usually conducted at highway checkpoints and a very effective countermeasure intervention used internationally.

recidivism: A term derived from the criminal justice system used to mean that a person repeats a criminal act.

reliability: When a test consistently measures what it is designed to measure.

RIASI (Research Institute on Addictions Screening Instrument): A self-administered inventory designed to be used with the DWI population, consisting of fifty-two items that yield various subscales. Also can detect defensive responding.

SALCE (Substance Abuse Life Circumstances Evaluation): Based upon the Criteria for Diagnosis of Alcoholism developed by the Criteria Committee of the National Council on Alcoholism.

SASSI (Substance Abuse Subtle Screening Inventory-II): A screening tool to assess individuals with chemical dependency consisting of two major scales.

Scandinavian Model: Developed in Scandinavia and Norway prior to WWII, establishing the basis for DWI laws and countermeasures still in use today.

SCID: A structured clinical interview devised by Spitzer and Williams to diagnose mental disorders, including substance abuse disorders, as directed by revised diagnostic criteria of the American Psychiatric Association.

specific deterrence: Aims at changing the behavior of the drinking-driver offender.

TLFB (Timeline Follow Back): Can be used as a self-administered questionnaire, and can be completed in 30 minutes. It is a method of drinking estimation that attempts to gain information regarding the client's daily drinking behavior by the use of various memory aids.

treatment: The application of clinical and therapeutic methods to produce behavior change.

validity: When a test is able to consistently detect what it is designed to detect.

Bibliography

Foreword

Levy, P., Voas, R. B., Johnson, P., and Klein, T. (1977). Evaluation of the ASAPs. *Journal of Safety Research* 10:162-176.

Marques, P. R., Tippetts, A. S., Voas, R. B., and Beirness, D. J. (2001). Predicting repeat DUI offenses with the alcohol interlock recorder. *Accident Analysis and Prevention.*

Marques, P. R., Voas, R. B., Tippetts, A. S., and Beirness, D. J. (1999). Behavioral monitoring of DUI offenders with the alcohol ignition interlock recorder. *Addiction, 94*(12): 1861-1870.

McKnight, A. J., Langston, E. A., McKnight, A. S., Resnick, J. A., and Lange, J. E. (1995). *Why people drink and drive: The basis of drinking-and-driving decisions* (DOT HS 808 251). Washington, DC: U.S. Department of Transportation, National Highway Traffice Safety Administration.

McKnight, A. J. and Voas, R. B. (1982). *A guide to self-sufficient funding of alcohol traffic safety programs* (Report under NHTSA Contract No. DTNH22-81-C-05180). Washington, DC: U.S. Department of Transportation, National Highway Traffic Safety Administration.

NHTSA and FHWA (1998). *Repeat intoxicated driver laws* ([Docket No. NHTSA-98-4537] RIN 2127-AH47). Washington, DC: Department of Transportation, National Highway Traffic Safety Administration (NHTSA) and Federal Highway Administration (FHWA).

Nichols, J. L. and Ross, H. L. (1990). The effectiveness of legal sanctions in dealing with drinking drivers. *Alcohol, Drugs, and Driving, 6*(2), 33-55.

Nichols, J. L., Weinstein, E. B., Ellingstad, V. S., and Struckman-Johnson, D. L. (1978). The specific deterrent effectiveness of ASAP education and rehabilitation programs. *Journal of Safety Research, 10*(4): 177-187.

Project MATCH Research Group. (1997). Matching alcoholism treatments to client heterogeneity: Project MATCH posttreatment drinking outcomes. *Journal of Studies on Alcohol, 58*(1): 7-29.

Ross, H. L. (1981). *Deterring the drinking driver: Legal policy and social control.* (Second edition). Lexington, MA: Lexington Books.

Ross, H. and Gonzales, P. (1988). The effect of license revocation on drunk-driving offenders. *Accident Analysis and Prevention, 20*(5): 379-391.

Shinar, D. and Compton, R. (1995). Victim impact panels: Their impact on DWI recidivism. *Alcohol, Drugs and Driving, 11*(1), 73-87.

Simpson, H. M., Mayhew, D. R., and Beirness, D. J. (1996). *Dealing with hard-core drinking drivers* (107 pp.). Ottawa, Canada: Traffic Injury Research Foundation.

Single, E. (1996). Harm reduction as an alcohol-prevention strategy. *Alcohol Health & Research World, 20*(4): 239-243.

Stewart, E. I. and Malfetti, J. L. (1970). Rehabilitation of the drunken driver: A corrective course in Phoenix, Arizona, for persons convicted of driving under the influence of alcohol. New York: Teachers College Press.

U.S. Department of Justice (USDOJ) (1984). *Crime victim compensation: Program models.* Washington, DC: National Institute of Justice.

U.S. Department of Transportation (1968). *1968 Alcohol and highway safety. Report to the U.S. Congress.* Washington, DC: U.S. Government Printing Office.

Voas, R. B. (1999a). The NHTSA rules on repeat intoxicated driver laws: An important fist step to control high-risk drivers. *Impaired Driving Update, Spring 1999,* 27-30.

Voas, R. B. (1999b). The three Rs for controlling the hard-core drinking driver: MADD's program for the repeat DWI offender. *The Prevention Pipline, 12*(3): 1-6.

Voas, R. B. (2001, in press). Controlling the hard-core drunk driver: Deterrence or incapacitation. *Addiction.*

Voas, R. and DeYoung, D. J. (2001, in press). Vehicle action: Effective policy for controlling drunk and other high-risk drivers? *Accident Analysis and Prevention.*

Voas, R. B., Marques, P. R., Tippetts, A. S. and Beirness, D. J. (1999). The Alberta Interlock Program: The evaluation of a province-wide program on DUI recidivism. *Addiction, 94*(12): 1857-1867.

Voas, R. B. and Williams, A. F. (1986). Age differences of arrested and crash involved drinking drivers. *Journal of Studies on Alcohol, 47*(3): 244-248.

Waller, J. A. and Turkel, H. W. (1966). Alcoholism and traffic deaths. *New England Journal of Medicine:* 275, 532.

Widmark, E. M. P. (1932). Die theoretischen grundlagen und die praktsch verwendbarkeit der gerichlich-medizinischen alkoholbetimmung. Berlin: Urban und Schwarzenberg.

Chapter 1

Alcohol and Health (1974). Alcohol and Highway Safety.

Alcohol Health and Research World, Volume 14, Number 1, Fall 1990. Highlights of the Proceedings of the Surgeon General's Workshop on Drunk Driving (pp. 5-8). National Institute on Alcohol Abuse and Alcoholism.

Andenaes, J. (1978). The effects of Scandinavia's drinking-driving laws: Facts and hypotheses. *Scandinavian Studies in Criminology* 6:65-53.

Andenaes, J. (1988). The Scandinavian experience. In M.D. Laurence, J.R. Snortum, and F.E. Zimring (Eds.), *Social control of the drinking driver,* pp. 43-63. Chicago: University of Chicago Press.

Argeriou, M., McCarty, D., and Blacker, E. (1985). Criminality among individuals arraigned for drinking and driving in Massachusetts. *Journal of Studies on Alcohol,* 46, 525-530.

Borkenstein, R. F., Crowther, R. F., Shumate, R. P., Zeil, W. B., and Zylman, R. (1964). *The role of the drinking driver in traffic accidents.* Department of Police Administration, Indiana University.

Cruze, A. M., Harwood, H. J., Kristiansen, P. L., Collins, J.J ., and Jones, D. C. (1981). *Economic costs to society of alcohol and drug abuse and mental illness.* Volume 1. Rockville, MD: Alcohol, Drug Abuse, and Mental Health Administration.

Donovan, J. E. (1993). Young adult drinking-driving—behavioral and psychosocial correlates. *Journal of Studies on Alcohol 54*(5): 600-613.

Ellinsgstad, V. S. and Springer, T. J. (1976). Program level Evaluation of ASAP Diagnosis, Referral and Rehabilitation Efforts. Volume III: Evaluation of Rehabilitation Effectiveness. Contract No. DOT HS 191 3 759. Washington, DC: National Highway Traffic Safety Administration.

Federal Bureau of Investigation (1988). *Crime in the United States: Uniform crime reports.* Washington, DC: Department of Justice.

Fell, J. C. (1993). Repeat DWI offenders: Their involvement in fatal crashes. In H. D. Utzelmann, G. Berhaus, and G. Kroj (Eds.), *Alcohol, drugs, and traffic safety, 92,* (pp. 1044-1049). Cologne, Germany: Verlag TUV Rheinland GmbH.

Fischer, E. and Reeder, R. (1974). *Vehicle traffic law.* Evanston, IL: Traffic Institute of Northwestern University.

Greene, R. (1985). Personal communication. New Jersey Division of Motor Vehicles, Bureau of Alcohol Countermeasures.

Hingson, R. and Howland, J. (1990). *Use of laws to deter drinking and driving. Alcohol Health & Research World, 14*(1): 36-43. National Institute on Alcohol Abuse and Alcoholism.

Homel, R., Carseldine, D., and Kearns, I. (1988). Drink-driving countermeasures in Australia. *Alcohol, Drugs, and Driving 4*(2): 113-144.

Insurance Institute for Highway Safety (1995). *I. I.H.S. Facts: DUI/DWI Laws.* Washington, DC.

James, W. H. (1990.) A report on driving while intoxicated (DWI) among Asian-Americans, African-Americans, Hispanic-Americans, and Native Americans for the Washington traffic safety commission. Seattle, Washington: Center for the Study and Teaching of At-Risk Students, University of Washington.

Johnson, N. (1982). Drinking and driving. *Alcohol Health and Research World 7*(1): 2-3. National Institute on Alcohol Abuse and Alcoholism.

Jones, R.K. and Joscelyn, K. B. (1978). *Alcohol and highway safety 1978: A review of the State-of-knowledge.* Washington, DC: National Highway Traffic Safety Administration.

Jones, R. K. and Lacey, J. H. (1998). *Final report alcohol highway safety: Problem update.* Washington, DC: National Highway Traffic Safety Administration, April.

Laurell, H. (1991). The Impact of low BACs in legislation. Paper presented at the 36th International Institute on the Prevention of Treatment of alcoholism, Stockholm, Sweden, June 2-7.

Lund, A. K. and Wolfe, A. C. (1991). Changes in the Incidence of Alcohol-Impaired Driving in the United States, 1973-1986. *Journal of Studies on Alcoholism 52*(4): 293-301.

Maisto, S. A., Sobell, C., Zellhart, P. F. (1979). Driving records of persons convicted of driving under the influence of alcohol. *Journal of Studies on Alcohol 40:* 70-77.

Miller, W. R. and Hester, R. K. (1986). Matching problem drinkers with optimal treatments. In W. R. Miller and N. Heather (Eds.), *Treating Addictive Disorders: Processes of Change,* (pp. 175-203). New York: Plenum Press.

Mounce, N. H. and Pendleton, O. J. (1992). The relationship between blood alcohol concentration and crash responsibility for fatally injured drivers. *Accident Analysis and Prevention 24*(2): 201-210.

National Drug Safety Network (1995). One in Six Workers Involved in Fatal Accidents Tests Positive for Alcohol or Drugs, *News Briefs,* Washington, DC: U.S. Department of Transportation.

National Highway Traffic Safety Administration (1974). *Alcohol safety action projects: Evaluation of operations,* Volume 2. Detailed Analysis. Publication No. DOT-HS-801-709. Washington, DC: U.S. Department of Transportation.

National Highway Traffic Safety Administration (1996). *Alcohol Traffic Safety Facts 1995.* Washington, DC: U.S. Department of Transportation.

National Highway Traffic Safety Administration (1997). *Young Drivers Traffic Safety Facts 1997.* Washington, DC: U.S. Department of Transportation.

National Highway Traffic Safety Administration (1998). *Alcohol Traffic Safety Facts 1997.* Washington, DC: U.S. Department of Transportation.

National Highway Traffic Safety Administration (1998). Final Report: Alcohol Highway Safety Problem Update, April, p. 7a. US. Department of Transportation.

National Highway Traffic Safety Administration (1999). *Impaired Driving Program.* Washington, DC: U.S. Department of Transportation.

National Highway Traffic Safety Administration Technology Transfer Series (1999). *National Survey of Drinking and Driving Documents Attitudes and Behaviors in 1997.* Traffic Tech Number 12, February. Washington, DC: U.S. Department of Transportation.

National Institute on Alcohol Abuse and Alcoholism. (1978). Third special report to the U.S. Congress on alcohol and health from the Secretary of Health, Education and Welfare. Noble, E., P. (Ed.). DHEW Publication No. (ADM) 78-569. Washington, DC: Superintendent of Documents, U.S. Government Printing Office.

Nichols, J. L. (1990). Treatment versus deterrence. *Alcohol Health & Research World 14*(1): 44-51.

Nichols, J. L. and Dickman, F. B. (1989). Effectiveness of roadside sobriety checkpoint operations. Unpublished paper. National Highway Traffic Safety Administration, Washington, DC.

Nichols, J. L. and Ross, H. L. (1989). The effectiveness of legal sanctions in dealing with drinking drivers. In *Surgeon General's workshop on drunk driving. Background papers* (pp. 93-112). Rockville, MD: Office of the Surgeon General, U. S. Department of Health and Human Services.

Perrine, M. W. (1990). Who are the drinking drivers? A spectrum of drinking drivers revisited. *Alcohol and Research World 14*(1): 26-35.

Robbins, L. (1988). Driving under the influence of alcohol and drugs: The judge's role. National Commission Against Drunk Driving Conference on Recidivism, A Summary of the Proceedings.

Ross, H. L. (1982a). *Deterence of the drinking driver: Legal policy and social control.* Lexington, MA: Lexington Books.

Ross, H. L. (1982b). Prevention and deterrence: The international experience. *Alcohol Health and Research World 7:* 26-32.

Ross, H. L. (1992). *Confronting drunk driving: Social policy for saving lives.* New Haven, CT: Yale University Press.

Selzer, M. L., Vinokur, A., and Wilson, T. D. (1997). A psychosocial comparison of drunken drivers and alcoholics. *Journal of Studies on Alcohol, 38:* 1294-1312.

Simpson, H. M. (1990). Importing and exporting countermeasures: Cultural determents of success. In Perrine, M.W. (Ed.), *Alcohol, drugs, and traffic safety.* Proceedings of the 11th International Conference T'89, Cologne, Germany, October 24-27, 1989 (pp. 22-31). Chicago: National Safety Council, 1990.

Simpson, H. M. (1995). Who is the persistent drinking driver? Part II: Canada and elsewhere. In *Strategies for dealing with the persistent drinking driver, Transportation Research Circular 437:* 21-25.

Simpson, H. M. and Mayhew, D. R. (1992). *The hard-core drinking driver. Update.* Ottawa, Ontario: Traffic Injury Research Foundation of Canada.

Vingilis, E. (1983). Drinking drivers and alcoholics: Are they from the same population? In R. G. Smart, F. B. Glaser, Y. Israel, H. Kant, R. E. Popham, and W. Schmidt (Eds.), *Research Advances in Alcohol and Drug Problems,* Volume 7 (pp. 229-342). New York: Plenum Press.

Voas, R. B. (1982). *Drinking and driving: Scandinavian laws, tough penalties, and United States alternatives.* National Highway Traffic Safety Administration Report No. DOT-HS-806-240. Springfield, Virginia: National Technical Information Center.

Voas, R. B. and Lacey, J. H. (1989). Issues in the enforcement of impaired driving laws in the United States. In *Surgeon General's workshop on drunk driving. Background papers* (pp. 136-156). Rockville, MD: Office of the Surgeon General, U.S. Department of Health and Human Services.

Volpe, J. et al. (1983). *Final Report of the Presidential Commission Against Drunk Driving.* Washington, DC: The White House.

Wieczorek, W. F., Miller, B. A., and Nochajski, T. H. (1990). Alcohol diagnoses among DWI offenders. In *The Problem-Drinking Driver Project Research Note* 90-6, 1-2.

Wieczorek,W. F., Miller, B. A., and Nochajski, T. H. (1991). Multiple location drinking and problem behavior among DWI offenders: A replication. In *The problem-drinker driver project.* Research note 91. Albany, NY: New York State Division of Alcoholism and Alcohol Abuse.

Chapter 2

American Psychiatric Association (APA) (1994). *Diagnostic and statistical manual of mental disorders,* Fourth edition. Washington, DC: American Psychiatric Press.

Babiak, P. (1995). When psychopaths go to work: A case study of an industrial psychopath. *Applied Psychology: An International Review 44:* 171-188.

Cavaiola, A. A. (1984). Resistance issues in the treatment of DWI offenders. *Alcoholism Treatment Quarterly 1:* 79-100.

Cavaiola, A. A. and DeSordi, E. (1999). Locus of control in a group of DWI offenders versus non-offenders. Paper presented at the 74th Annual Meeting of the Eastern Psychological Association, April, Providence, Rhode Island.

Cavaiola, A. A., Wolf, J. M., and Lavender, N. J. (1999). Comparison of DWI offenders and non-offenders on the MMPI-2 and MAST. Paper presented at the 34th Annual Conference on Recent Advances on the MMPI-2 and MMPI-A. April, Huntington Beach, CA.

Clay, M. L. (1972). Which drunks shall we dodge? In *Alcohol and Drug Problems Association of North America.* Selected papers presented at the General Sessions, 23rd Annual Meeting, September, Atlanta, GA.

Cleckley, H. (1976). *The mask of sanity,* Fifth edition. St. Louis, MO: Mosby.

Derogotis, L. R. (1983). *SCL-90-R Administration, Scoring and Procedures Manual-II,* Towson, MD: Clinical Psychometric Research.

Donovan, D. M. (1980). Drinking behavior, personality factors, and high-risk driving. PhD Dissertation, University of Washington.

Donovan, D. M. and Marlatt, G. A. (1982). Personality subtypes among driving-while-intoxicated offenders: Relationships to drinking behavior and driving risk. *Journal of Consulting and Clinical Psychology 50:* 241-249.

Donovan, D. M., Marlatt, G. A., and Salzburg, P. M. (1983). Drinking behavior, personality factors and high risk driving: A review and theoretical formulation. *Journal of Studies on Alcohol 44:* 395-428.

Donovan, D. M., Queisser, H. R., Salzberg, P. M., and Umlauf, R. L. (1985). Intoxicated and bad drivers: Subgroups within the same population of high risk men drivers. *Journal of Studies on Alcohol 46:* 375-382.

Donovan, D. M., Umlauf, R. L., and Salzberg, P. M. (1990). Bad drivers: Identification of a target group for alcohol-related prevention and early intervention. *Journal of Studies on Alcohol 51:* 136-141.

Finch, J. R. and Smith, J. P. (1970). *Psychiatric and Legal Aspects of Automobile Fatalities.* Springfield, IL: Charles C Thomas Publishers.

Fine, E. W., Scoles, P., and Mulligan, M. (1975). Under the influence: Characteristics and drinking practices of persons arrested for the first time for drunk driving, with treatment implications. *Public Health Reports 90:* 424-429.

Fischer, M., Barkley, R. A., Edelbrock, C. S., and Smallish, L. (1990). The adolescent outcome of hyperactive children diagnosed by research criteria: Academic, attentional and neuropsychological status. *Journal of Consulting and Clinical Psychology 58:* 580-588.

Gittleman, R., Mannuzza, S., Shenker, R., and Bonagura, N. (1985). Hyperactive boys almost grown up. *Archives of General Psychiatry 42:* 937-947.

Hare, R. D. (1993). *Without conscience: The disturbing world of the psychopath among us.* New York: Simon and Schuster, Inc.

Helzer, J. E. and Pryzbeck, T. R. (1988). The co-occurrence of alcoholism with other psychiatric disorders in the general population and its impact on treatment. *Journal of Studies on Alcohol 49:* 219-224.

Herz, L. R., Volicer, L., D'Angelo, N., and Gadish, D. (1990). Additional psychiatric illness by Diagnostic Interview Schedule in male alcoholics. *Comparative Psychiatry 30:* 72-79.

Jessor, R. (1987). Problem behavior theory, psychosocial development and adolescent problem drinking. *British Journal of Addiction 82:* 331-342.

Jonah, B. A. and Wilson, R. J. (1986). Impaired drivers who have never been caught: Are they different from convicted impaired drivers? In *Alcohol, Accidents and Injuries,* (P-173), SAE Technical Paper. Series 860195. Warrendale, PA: Society of Automotive Engineers.

McCord, J. (1984). Drunken drivers in longitudinal perspective. *Journal of Studies on Alcohol 45:* 316-320.

McDonald, S. and Pederson, L. L. (1990). The characteristics of alcoholics in treatment arrested for driving while impaired. *British Journal of Addictions 85:* 97-105.

McMillen, D. L., Pang, M. G., Wells-Parker, E., and Anderson, B. J. (1992). Alcohol, personality traits and high risk driving: A comparison of young, drinking drivers. *Addictive Behaviors 17:* 525-532.

Miller, B. A. and Windle, M. (1990). Alcoholism, problem drinking and driving while impaired. In R. J. Wilson and R. E. Mann (Eds.), *Drinking and Driving* (pp. 68-95). New York: Guilford Press.

Murty, K. S. and Roebuck, J. B. (1991). The DUI offender as a social type. *Deviant Behavior 12:* 451-470.

Nakken, C. (1997). *The addictive personality: Roots, rituals and recovery* (revised). Center City, MN: Hazelden Publications.

Nochajski, T. H., Leonard, K. E., Blane, H. T., and Wieczorek, W. F. (1991). Comparison of problem-drinking young men with and without a DWI arrest. Paper presented at Research Society on Alcoholism Conference, June, Marco Island, FL.

Nochajski, T. H., Miller, B. A., and Parks, K. A. (1994). Comparison of first-time and repeat DWI offenders. Paper presented at the Annual Meeting of the Research Society on Alcoholism, June, Maui.

Nochajski, T. H., Wieczorek, W. F., and Miller, B. A. (1996). Factors associated with high risk of rapid DWI recidivism for first time offenders. Paper presented at the Annual Meeting of the Research Society on Alcoholism, June, Washington, DC.

Nolan, Y., Johnson, J. A., and Pincus, A. L. (1994). Personality and drunk driving: Identification of DUI types using the Hogan Personality Inventory. *Psychological Assessment 6:* 33-40.

Pelz, D. C. and Schuman, S. H. (1974). Drinking, hostility and alienation in driving of young men. In *Proceedings of the Third Annual Alcoholism Conference of the National Institute of Alcohol Abuse and Alcoholism.* June, Washington, DC.

Penick, E. C., Powell, B. J., Liskow, B. I., Jackson, J. O., and Nickel, E. J. (1988). The stability of coexisting psychiatric syndromes in alcoholic men after one year. *Journal of Studies on Alcohol 49:* 395-405.

Perrine, M. W. (1970). Identification of personality, attitudinal and biographical characteristics of drinking drivers. *Behavioral Research on Highway Safety 2:* 207-225.

Perrine, M. W. (1990). Who are the drinking drivers? *Alcohol Health and Research World 14:* 26-35.

Perrine, M. W., Peck, R. C., and Fell, J. C. (1989). Epidemiologic perspectives on drunk driving. In *Surgeon General's workshop on drunk driving. Background papers* (pp. 35-76). Rockville, MD: Office of the Surgeon General, U.S. Department of Health and Human Services.

Pristach, E. A., Nochajski, T. H., Wieczorek, W. F., Miller, B. A., and Greene, B. (1991). Psychiatric symptoms and DWI offenders. *Alcohol and Alcoholism, Supplement 1:* 493-496.

Reynolds, J. R. (1988). Repeat DWI offenders: Variables associated with the pursuit of treatment. Unpublished manuscript. University of Missouri, Columbia, MO.

Reynolds, J. R., Kunce, J. T., and Cope, C. S. (1991). Personality differences of first-time and repeat offenders arrested for driving while intoxicated. *Journal of Counseling Psychology 38:* 289-295.

Selzer, M. L. and Barton, E. (1977). The drunken driver: A psychosocial study. *Drug and Alcohol Dependence 2:* 239-253.

Selzer, M. L., Vinokur, A., and Wilson, T. D. (1977). A psychosocial comparison of drunken drivers and alcoholics. *Journal of Studies on Alcohol 38:* 1294-1312.

Soltenberg, S. F., Hill, E. M., Mudd, S. A., Blow, F. C., and Zucker, R. A. (1999). Birth cohort differences in features of antisocial alcoholism among men and women. *Alcoholism: Clinical & Experimental Research 23:* 1884-1891.

Steer, R. A. and Fine, E. W. (1978). Mood differences of men arrested once and men arrested twice for driving while intoxicated. *Journal of Studies on Alcohol 39:* 922-925.

Steer, R. A., Fine, E., and Scoles, P. E. (1979). Classification of men arrested for driving while intoxicated and treatment implications: A cluster analysis study. *Journal of Studies on Alcohol 40:* 222-229.

Sutker, P. B., Brantley, P. J., and Allain, A. N. (1980). MMPI response patterns and alcohol consumption in DUI offenders. *Journal of Consulting and Clincial Psychology 48*: 350-355.

Tarter, R., McBride, H., Buonpane, H., and Schneider, D. (1977). Differentiation of alcoholics: Childhood history of minimal brain dysfunction, family history, and drinking pattern. *Archives of General Psychiatry 34:* 761-768.

Vingilis, E., Stoduto, G., Macartney-Filgate, M. S., Liban, C. B., and McLellan, B.A. (1994). Psychosocial characteristics of alcohol-involved and nonalcohol-involved seriously injured drivers. *Accident Analysis and Prevention 26:* 1-12.

Walter, D., Nogoshi, C., Muntaner, C., and Haertzen, C. (1990). The prediction of drug dependence from expectancy for hostility while intoxicated. *International Journal of Addictions 25:* 1151-1168.

Weiss, G. and Hechtman, L. (1986). *Hyperactive children grown up.* New York: Guilford Press.

Wieczorek, W. F., Miller, B. A., and Nochajski, T. H. (1990). Alcohol diagnoses among DWI offenders. *The Problem-Drinker Driver Project Research Note, 90-6,* Research Institute on Addictions: Buffalo, NY, August: 1-2.

Wieczorek, W. F., Miller, B. A., and Nochajski, T. H. (1991). The relationship of sensation seeking, hostility, and childhood hyperactivity to multiple location drinking among DWI offenders. Paper presented at the Research Society on Alcoholism Annual Meeting, June, Marco Island, FL.

Wilson, R. J. (1991). Subtypes of DWIs and high risk drivers: Implications for differential intervention. *Alcohol, Drugs and Driving 7:* 1-12.

Wilson, R. J. (1992). Convicted impaired drivers and high-risk drivers: How similar are they? *Journal of Studies on Alcohol 53:* 335-344.

Wilson, R. J. and Jonah, B. A. (1985). Identifying impaired drivers among the general driving population. *Journal of Studies on Alcohol 46:* 531-537.

Windle, M. and Miller, B. A. (1989). Alcoholism and depressive symptomatology among convicted DWI men and women. *Journal of Studies on Alcohol 50:* 406-413.

Windle, M. and Miller, B. A. (1990). Problem drinking and depression among DWI offenders: A three-wave longitudinal study. *Journal of Consulting & Clinical Psychology 58:* 166-174.

Zelhart, P. F. Jr., Schurr, B. C., and Brown, P. A. (1975). The drinking driver: Identification of high risk alcoholics. In S. Israelstam and S. Lambert (Eds.), *Alcohol, Drugs and Traffic Safety: Proceedings of the Sixth International Conference on Alcohol, Drugs and Traffic Safety.* Toronto, Canada: Addiction Research Foundation.

Zuckerman, M. (1990). The psychophysiology of sensation seeking. *Journal of Personality 58:* 313-345.

Zylman, R. (1976). All alcoholics are high risk drivers: A myth. *Journal of Traffic Safety Education 23:* 7-10.

Chapter 3

Argeriou, M., McCarty, D., and Blacker, E. (1985). Criminality among individuals arraigned for drinking and driving in Massachusetts. *Journal of Studies on Alcohol 46:* 525-529.

Beerman, K. A., Smith, M. M., and Hall, R. L. (1988). Predictors of recidivism in DUIs. *Journal of Studies on Alcohol 49:* 443-449.

Beitel, G. A., Sharp, M. C., and Glauz, W. D. (1975). Probability of arrest while driving under the influence of alcohol. _Journal of Studies on Alcohol 36:_ 109-116.

Bell, R. A., Warheit, G. J., Bell, R. A., and Sanders, G. (1978). An analytic comparison of persons arrested for driving while intoxicated and alcohol detoxification patients. _Alcoholism: Clinical and Experimental Research 2:_ 241-243.

Borkenstein, R. F. (1974). Problems of enforcement, adjudication and sanctioning. In S. Israelstam and S. Lambert (Eds.), _Alcohol, Drugs and Traffic Safety: Proceedings of the Sixth International Conference on Alcohol, Drugs, and Traffic Safety._ Toronto, Canada: Addiction Research Foundation.

Callahan, D., Cisin, I. H., and Crossley, H. M. (1969). _American drinking practices: A national survey of drinking behavior and attitudes._ New Brunswick, NJ: Rutgers Center of Alcohol Studies.

Cavaiola, A. A. (1984). Resistance issues in the treatment of DWI offenders. _Alcoholism Treatment Quarterly 1:_ 79-100.

Cavaiola, A. A., Wolf, J. M., and Lavender, N. J. (1999). Comparison of DWI offenders and non-offenders on the MMPI-2 and MAST. Paper presented at the 34th Annual Conference on Recent Advances on the MMPI-2 and MMPI-A. Huntington Beach, CA, April.

Donelson, A. C. (1985). _Alcohol and road accidents in Canada: Issues related to future strategies and priorities._ Ottawa: Ottawa Traffic Injury Research Foundation of Canada.

Donovan, D. M. (1980). Drinking behavior, personality factors and high risk driving, PhD Dissertation, University of Washington.

Donovan, D. M. and Marlatt, G. A. (1983). Personality subtypes among driving-while-intoxicated offenders: Relationships to drinking behavior and driving risk. _Journal of Consulting and Clinical Psychology 50:_ 241-249.

Donovan, D. M., Marlatt, G. A., and Salzburg, P. M. (1983). Drinking behavior, personality factors and high risk driving: A review and theoretical formulation. _Journal of Studies on Alcohol 44:_ 395-428.

Donovan, D. M., Queisser, H. R., Salzberg, P. M., and Umlauf, R. L. (1985). Intoxicated and bad drivers: Subgroups within the same population of high risk men drivers. _Journal of Studies on Alcohol 46:_ 375-382.

Dowling, A. M. and McCartt, A. T. (1990). _Evaluation of the New York State drinking driver program._ Albany, NY: State University of New York.

Filkins, L. D., Mortimer, R. G., Post, D. V., and Chapman, M. W. (1973). _Field evaluation of court procedures for identifying problem drinkers: Final report._ Ann Arbor, MI: Highway Safety Research Institute: University of Michigan.

Fine, E. W., Scoles, P., and Mulligan, M. (1975). Under the influence. Characteristics and drinking practices of persons arrested for the first time for drunk driving with treatment implications. _Public Health Reports 90:_ 424-429.

Franklin, S. (1989). Demographic and diagnostic characteristics of 108 women convicted of DWI in Allen County, Indiana. In _Women, Alcohol, Drugs and Traffic,_ Proceedings of the International Workshop. Stockholm, Sweden, ICADTS.

Hyman, M. M. (1968). The social characteristics of persons arrested for driving while intoxicated. _Quarterly Journal of Studies on Alcohol, Supplement #4,_ 138-177.

James, W. H. (1990). _A report on driving while intoxicated (DWI) among Asian Americans, Hispanic Americans and Native Americans for the Washington Traffic Safety Commission._ Seattle, Washington: Center for the Study and Teaching of At-Risk Students, University of Washington.

Jones, R. K. and Lacey, J. H. (1998). *Final report alcohol and highway safety: problem update.* Washington, DC: National Highway Traffic Safety Administration.

Kelleher, E. J. (1971). A diagnostic evaluation of 400 drinking drivers. *Journal of Safety Research 3:* 52-55.

Lund, A. K. and Wolfe, A. C. (1991). Changes in the incidence of alcohol-impaired driving in the United States, 1973-1986. *Journal of Studies on Alcohol 52:* 293-301.

Maguire, K. and Flanagan, T. J. (Eds.) (1991). *Sourcebook of criminal justice statistics 1990.* Washington, DC: U.S. Department of Justice, Bureau of Justice Statistics, U.S. Government Printing Office.

McCormack, A. (1985). Risk for alcohol-related accidents in divorced and separated women. *Journal of Studies on Alcohol 46:* 240-243.

McGuire, F. L. (1980). "Heavy" and "light" drinking drivers as separate target groups for treatment. *American Journal of Drug and Alcohol Abuse 7:* 101-107.

McMillen, D. L., Pang, M. G., Wells-Parker, E., and Anderson, B. J. (1992). Alcohol, personality traits and high-risk driving: A comparison of young, drinking drivers. *Addictive Behaviors 17:* 525-532.

Mercer, G. W. (1986, February). *Counterattack Traffic Research Papers, 1985.* Victoria, Canada: Ministry of the Attorney General.

Miller, W. R. and Rollnick, S. (1991). Motivational interviewing: Preparing people to change. *Addictive Behaviors.* New York: Guilford Press.

Mortimer, R. G., Filkins, L. D., Lower, J. S., Kerlan, M. W., Post, D. V., Mudge, B., and Rosenblatt, C. (1971). *Court procedures for identifying problem drinkers: Report on Phase I.* DOT HS-800 630. Washington, DC: Department of Transportation.

Moskowitz, H., Walker, J., and Gomberg, C. (1979). Characteristics of DWIs, alcoholics and controls. In *Proceedings of the 1979 NCA Alcohol and Traffic Safety Session* (pp. 9-79). Washington, DC: National Highway Traffic Safety Administration.

Nochajski, T. H., Augustino, D. K., and Wieczorek, W. F. (1997). Treatment outcome and drinking driving recidivism. Paper presented at the Research Society on Alcoholism Annual Meeting, July, San Francisco, CA.

Nochajski, T. H., Leonard, K. E., Blane, H. T., and Wieczorek, W. F. (1991). Comparison of problem-drinking young men with and without a DWI arrest. Paper presented at Research Society on Alcoholism Conference, June, Marco Island, FL.

Nochajski, T. H., Miller, B. A., and Parks, K. A. (1994). Comparison of first-time and repeat DWI offenders. Paper presented at the Annual Meeting of the Research Society on Alcoholism, June, Maui, HI.

Nochajski, T. H., Miller, B. A., Wieczorek, W. F., and Whitney, R. (1993). The effects of a drinker-driver treatment program: Does criminal history make a difference? *Criminal Justice and Behavior 20:* 174-189.

Nochajski, T. H., Wieczorek, W. F., and Miller, B. A. (1996). Factors associated with high risk of rapid DWI recidivism for first time offenders. Paper presented at the Annual Meeting of the Research Society on Alcoholism. June, Washington, DC.

Norstrom, T. (1978). Drunken driving: A tentative causal model. In R. Hauge (Ed.), *Drinking and Driving in Scandanavia.* Oslo, Norway: Scandanavian University Books.

Packard, M. A. (1987). DUI/DWAI offenders compared to clients seen in an outpatient alcohol-treatment facility. *Journal of Alcohol and Drug Education 32:* 1-6.

Panepinto, W., Garrett, J. A., Williford, A., and Priebe, J. (1982). A short term group treatment model. In M. Altman and R. Crocker (Eds.), *Social Work Group and Alcoholism* (pp. 33-41). Binghamton, NY: The Haworth Press, Inc.

Parks, K. A., Nochajski, T. H., Wieczorek, W. F., and Miller, B. A. (1996). Assessing alcohol problems in female DWI offenders. In H. Kalant, J. M. Khana, and Y. Israel (Eds.), *Advances in Biomedical Alcohol Research* (pp. 493-496). Oxford, England: Pergamon Press.

Perrine, M. W. (1990). Who are the drinking drivers? *Alcohol Health and Research World 14:* 26-35.

Perrine, M. W., Peck, R. C., and Fell, J. C. (1989). Epidemiologic perspectives on drunk driving. In *Surgeon General's workshop on drunk driving. Background papers* (pp. 35-76). Rockville, MD: Office of the Surgeon General, U.S. Department of Health and Human Services.

Pokorny, A D., Miller, B. A. and Kaplan, H. B. (1972). The brief MAST: A shortened version of the Michigan Alcoholism Screening Test. *American Journal of Psychiatry 129:* 342-343.

Popkin, C. L. and Council, F. M. (1993). A comparison of alcohol-related driving behavior of white and non-white North Carolina drivers. *Accident Analysis and Prevention 25:* 355-364.

Popkin, C. L., Rudisill, L. C., Waller, P. F., and Geissinger, S. B. (1988). Female drinking and driving: Recent trends in North Carolina. *Accident Analysis and Prevention 20:* 219-225.

Reynolds, J. R., Kunce, J. T., and Cope, C. S. (1991). Personality differences of first-time and repeat offenders arrested for driving while intoxicated. *Journal of Counseling Psychology 38:* 289-295.

Ross, H. L., Howard, J. M., Ganikos, M. L., and Taylor, E. D. (1991). Drunk driving among American Blacks and Hispanics. *Accident Analysis and Prevention 23:* 1-11.

Saltstone, R. (1989). Distinguishing driving while impaired offenders from among alcoholics, criminals and drunk drivers: A preliminary study. *Criminal Justice and Behavior 16:* 211-222.

Selzer, M. L. (1969). Alcoholism, mental illness and stress in 96 drivers causing fatal accidents. *Behavioral Science 14:* 1-10.

Selzer, M. L. (1971). The Michigan Alcoholism Screening Test: In search for a new diagnostic instrument. *American Journal of Psychiatry 127:* 1653-1658.

Selzer, M. L. and Barton, E. (1977). The drunken driver: A psychosocial study. *Drug and Alcohol Dependence 2:* 239-253.

Selzer, M. L. and Vinokur, A. (1974). Life events, subjective stress and traffic accidents. *American Journal of Psychiatry 131:* 903-906.

Selzer, M. L., Vinokur, A., and Wilson, T. D. (1977). A psychosocial comparison of drunken drivers and alcoholics. *Journal of Studies on Alcohol 38:* 1294-1312.

Shore, E. R. and McCoy, M. L. (1987). Recidivism among female DUI offenders in a Midwestern American city. *Journal of Criminal Justice 15:* 369-374.

Shore, E. R., McCoy, M. L., Toonen, L. A., and Kuntz, E. J. (1988). Arrests of women for driving under the influence. *Journal of Studies on Alcohol 49:* 7-10.

Simpson, H. M. and Mayhew, D. R. (1992). *The hard core drinking driver. Update.* Ottawa, Ontario: Traffic Injury Research Foundation of Canada.

Sutton, L. R. (1993). Assessment of the female impaired driver: Implications for treatment. In H.D. Utzelman, G. Berghaus, and G. Kroj (Eds.), *Alcohol, Drugs and Traffic Safety.* Cologne, Germany: Verlag Tuv Rheinland.

Valerius, M. R. (Ed.) (1989). Women, alcohol, drugs and traffic. In Proceedings of the International Workshop. Stockholm, Sweden: ICADTS.

Vingilis, E. (1983). Drinking drivers and alcoholics: Are they from the same population? In R. G. Smart, F. B. Glaser, Y. Israel, H. Kalant, R. E. Popham, and W. Schmidt (Eds.), *Research Advances in Alcohol and Drug Problems.* New York: Plenum Press.

Waller, J. A. (1967). Identification of problem drinking among drunken drivers. *Journal of the American Medical Association 200:* 114-120.

Weeber, S. (1981). DWI repeaters and non-repeaters: A comparison. *Journal of Alcohol and Drug Education 26:* 1-9.

Wells-Parker, E., Cosby, P. J., and Landrum, J. W. (1986). A typology for drinking driving offenders: Methods for classification and policy implications. *Accident Analysis and Prevention 18:* 443-453.

Wells-Parker, E., Pang, M. G., Anderson, B. J., McMillen, D. L., and Miller, D. I. (1991). Female DUI offenders: A comparison to male counterparts and an examination of the effects of intervention on women's recidivism rates. *Journal of Studies on Alcohol 52:* 142-147.

Wieczorek, W. F., Miller, B. A., and Nochajski, T. H. (1989). DSM-III and DSM-III-R alcohol diagnoses for problem drinking drivers. Paper presented at the American Psychological Association Convention, New Orleans, LA.

Wieczorek, W. F., Miller, B. A., and Nochajski, T. H. (1990). Alcohol diagnoses among DWI offenders. *Problem-Drinking Driver Project Research Note 90:* 6. Research Institute on Addictions, Buffalo, NY.

Wieczorek, W. F., Miller, B. A., and Nochajski, T. H. (1992). The limited utility of BAC for identifying alcohol-related problems among DWI offenders. *Journal of Studies on Alcohol 53:* 415-419.

Wilson, R. J. and Jonah, B. A. (1985). Identifying impaired drivers among the general driving population. *Journal of Studies on Alcohol 46:* 531-537.

Yoder, R. D. and Moore, R. A. (1973). Characteristics of convicted drunken drivers. *Quarterly Journal of Studies on Alcohol 34:* 927-936.

Zador, P. L. (1991). Alcohol-related relative risk of fatal driver injuries in relation to driver age and sex. *Journal of Studies on Alcohol 52:* 302-310.

Chapter 4

Babor, T. F., Kranzler, H. R., and Lauerman, R. J. (1989). Early detection of harmful alcohol consumption: Comparison of clinical, laboratory, and self-report screening procedures. *Addictive Behaviors, 14:* 139-157.

Brown, R. A. (1980). Knowledge about responsible drinking in drinking drivers and social drinkers. *International Journal of Addictions 15:* 1213-1218.

Campbell, D. T. and Fiske, D. W. (1959). Convergent and discriminant validation by the multitrait-multimethod matrix. *Psychological Bulletin 56:* 81-105.

Cavaiola, A., Wolf, J., and Lavender, N. (1999). Comparison of DWI offenders with a non-DWI offender group using the MMPI-2 and the MASAT. Paper presented at the Thirty-Fourth Annual Symposium on Recent Developments in the Use of the MMPI-2 and MMPI-A. Huntington Beach, CA: April

Dowling, A. M. and McCartt, A. T. (1990). *Evaluation of the New York State drinking driver program.* Albany, NY: State University of New York.

Dunham, R. G. and Mauss, A. L. (1982). Reluctant referrals: The effectiveness of legal coercion in outpatient treatment for problem drinkers. _Journal of Drug Issues 12:_ 4-20.

Fagan, R. W. and Fagan, N. M. (1982). Impact of legal coercion on the treatment of alcoholism. _Journal of Drug Issues 12:_ 103-114.

Fine, E. W., Scoles, P., and Mulligan, M. (1975). Under the influence: Characteristics and drinking practices of persons arrested for the first time for drunk driving, with treatment implications. _Public Health Reports 90:_ 424-429.

Fitzpatrick, J. L. (1992). Problems in the evaluation of treatment programs for drunk drivers: Goals and outcomes. _Journal of Drug Issues 22:_ 155-167.

Kruzich, D. J., Silsby, H. D., and Gold, J. D. (1986). An evaluation of education program for driving while intoxicated offenders. _Journal of Substance Abuse Treatment, 3:_ 263-270.

Miller, B. A., Whitney, R., and Washousky, R. (1984). The decision to recommend alcoholism treatment for DWI offenders. _American Journal of Drug and Alcohol Abuse, 10:_ 447-459.

Miller, G. A. (1994). _The Substance Abuse Subtle Screening Inventory._ Bloomington, IN: The SASSI Institute.

Mortimer, R. G., Filkins, L. D., Lower, J. S., Kerlan, M. W., Post, D. V., Mudge, B., and Rosenblatt, C. (1971). _Court procedures for identifying problem drinkers: Report on Phase I._ DOT HS-800 630. Washington, DC: Department of Transportation.

Nochajski, T. H. and Miller, B. A. (1995). _Training Manual for the Research Institute on Addictions Self-Inventory (RIASI)._ Buffalo, NY: Research Institute on Addictions.

Nochajski, T. H., Miller, B. A., Wieczorek, W. F., and Parks, K. A. (1993). The utility of non-obvious indicators for screening DWI offenders. Paper presented at the Research Society on Alcoholism Annual Meeting, June, San Antonio, TX.

Otto, R. K., Lang, A. R., and Megargee, E. I. (1988). Ability of alcoholics to escape detection by the MMPI. _Journal of Consulting and Clinical Psychology 56:_ 452-457.

Popkin, C. L., Stewart, J. R., and Lacey, J. H. (1988). A follow-up evaluation of North Carolina's alcohol and drug education traffic schools and mandatory substance abuse assessments: Final report. Chapel Hill: Highway Safety Research Center, University of North Carolina.

Selzer, M. L. (1971). The Michigan Alcoholism Screening Test: A quest for a new diagnostic instrument. _American Journal of Psychiatry 127:_ 89-94.

Vingilis, E. (1983). Drinking drivers and alcoholics: Are they from the same population? In R. G. Smart, F. B. Glaser, Y. Israel, H. Kalant, R. E. Popham, and W. Schmidt (Eds.), _Research Advances in Alcohol and Drug Problems: Vol. 7_ (pp. 299-342). New York: Plenum Press.

Wieczorek, W. F., Miller, B. A., and Nochajski, T. H. (1992). The limited utility of BAC for identifying alcohol-related problems among DWI offenders. _Journal of Studies on Alcohol 53:_ 415-419.

Zung, B. J. and Ross, M. (1980). Factor structure of the Michigan Alcoholism Screening Test (MAST) among acutely disturbed psychiatric patients. _Journal of Clinical Psychology 36:_ 806-812.

Chapter 5

ADE (1986). _Substance abuse life circumstances evaluation manual._ Clarkston, MI: ADE, Inc.

Anderson, B. J., Snow, R. W., and Wells-Parker, E. (2000). Comparing the predictive validity of DUI risk screening instruments: Development of validation standards. *Addiction 95:* 915-929.

Buros, O. K. (1988). *The supplement to the mental measurements yearbook* (Ninth edition). Lincoln, NE: The Buros Institute of Mental Measurements.

Cavaiola, A. A., Wolf, J. M., and Lavender, N. J. (1999). Comparison of DWI offenders and non-offenders on the MMPI-2 and MAST. Paper presented at the 34th Annual Conference on Recent Advances on the MMPI-2 and MMPI-A, April, Huntington Beach, CA.

Chan, A. W. K. (1987). Factors affecting the drinking driver. *Drug and Alcohol Dependency 19:* 99-119.

Dodgen, C. E. and Shea, W. M. (1997). *Psychoactive substance use disorders: A comprehensive resource for clinicians and researchers.* Florham Park, NJ: C and D Publications.

Dowling, A. M. and McCartt, A. T. (1990). *Evaluation of the New York State drinking driver program.* Albany, NY: State University of New York.

Fowler, R. D. (1975). A method for the evaluation of the abuse prone patient. Paper presented at the Annual Meeting of the American Academy of Family Physicians, Chicago, IL.

Gavin, D. R., Ross, H., and Skinner, H. (1989). Diagnostic validity of the Drug Abuse Screening Inventory. *British Journal of Addictions 84:* 301-307.

Graham, J. R. (1978). A review of some important MMPI special scales. In P. McReynolds (Ed.), *Advances in psychological assessment,* Volume IV (pp. 311-331). San Francisco, CA: Jossey-Bass.

Graham, J. R. (1990). *MMPI-2: Assessing personality and psychopathology.* Oxford, England: Oxford University Press.

Graham, J. R. and Mayo, M. A. (1985). A comparison of MMPI strategies for identifying black and white male alcoholics. Paper presented at the 20th Annual Symposium on Recent Developments in the Use of the MMPI, Honolulu, HI, March.

Hathaway, S. R. and McKinley, J. C. (1989). *The Minnesota Multiphasic Personality Inventory-2.* Minneapolis, MN: Regents of the University of Minnesota.

Hoffman, H., Loper, R. G., and Kammeier, M.L. (1974). Identifying future alcoholics with the MMPI alcoholism scales. *Quarterly Journal of Studies on Alcohol 35:* 490-498.

Horn, J. L., Wanberg, K. W., and Foster, F. M. (1987). *Guide to the alcohol use inventory.* Minneapolis, MN: National Computer Systems.

Jacobson, G. R. (1983). Detection, assessment, and diagnosis of alcoholism: Current techniques. In M. Galanter (Ed.), *Recent developments in alcoholism, Volume 1* (pp. 377-413). New York: Plenum Press.

Kranitz, L. (1972). Alcoholics, heroin addicts and non-addicts: Comparisons on the MacAndrew Alcoholism scale on the MMPI. *Quarterly Journal of Studies on Alcohol 33:* 807-809.

Lacey, J. H., Jones, R. K., and Wilisnowski, C. H. (1999). Validation of problem drinking screening instruments for DWI offenders. Technical Report prepared for National Highway Traffic Safety Administration (DTNH22-90-C-07287).

Lanyon, R. I. (1968). *Psychological Screening Inventory: Manual.* Goshen, NY: Research Psychologists Press.

Lapham, S. C., Skipper, B. J., Owen, J. P., Kleyboecker, K., Teaf, D., Thompson, B., and Simpson, G. (1995). Alcohol abuse screening instruments: Normative test data collected from a first DWI offender screening program. *Journal of Studies on Alcohol 56:* 51-59.

Lapham, S. C., Skipper, B. J., and Simpson, G. L. (1997). A prospective study of the utility of standardized instruments in predicting recidivism among first DWI offenders. *Journal of Studies on Alcohol 58:* 524-530.

Levenson, M. R., Aldwin, C. M., Butcher, J. N., De Labry, L., Workman-Daniels, K., and Bosse, R. (1990). The MAC scale in a normal population: The meaning of "false positives." *Journal of Studies on Alcohol 51:* 457-462.

Lindeman, H. and Scrimgeour, W. G. (1999). *Driver risk inventory (DRI): An inventory of scientific findings.* Phoenix, AZ: Behavior Data Systems, Ltd.

MacAndrew, C. (1965). The differentiation of male alcoholic out-patients from nonalcoholic psychiatric patients by means of the MMPI. *Quarterly Journal of Studies on Alcohol 26:* 238-246.

MacAndrew, C. (1981). What the MAC scale tells us about men alcoholics: An interpretative review. *Journal of Studies on Alcohol 42:* 604-623.

Marion, L., Fuller, S., Johnson, P., Michels, P., and Diniz, C. (1996). Drinking problems in nursing students. *Journal of Nursing Education 35:* 196-203.

Marlatt, G. A. and Miller, W. R. (1984). *Comprehensive drinker profile.* Odessa, FL: Psychological Assessment Resources, Inc.

McLellan, A. T., Kushner, H., Metzger, D., Peters, R., Smith, I., Grissom, G., Pettinati, H., and Argeriou, G. (1992). The fifth edition of the Addiction Severity Index. *Journal of Substance Abuse Treatment 9:* 199-213.

Miller, B. A., Whitney, R., and Washousky, R. (1984). The decision to recommend alcoholism treatment for DWI offenders. *American Journal of Drug and Alcohol Abuse 10:* 447-459.

Miller, B. A., Whitney, R., and Washousky, R. (1986). Alcoholism diagnoses for convicted drinking drivers referred for alcoholism evaluation. *Alcoholism: Clinical and Experimental Research 10:* 651-656.

Miller, B. A. and Windle, M. (1990). Alcoholism, problem drinking and driving while impaired. In R. J. Wilson and R. E. Mann (Eds.), *Drinking and Driving: Advances in Research and Prevention,* (pp. 68-95). New York: Guilford Press.

Miller, G. A. (1994a). *The Substance Abuse Subtle Screening Inventory Manual,* Bloomington, IN: The SASSI Institute.

Miller, G. A. (1994b). SASSI scales: Clinical feedback. *News and reports: Closer look.* Bloomington, IN:The SASSI Institute.

Moore, R. A. (1972). The diagnosis of alcoholism in a psychiatric hospital: A trial of the Michigan Alcoholism Screening Test (MAST). *American Journal of Psychiatry 128:* 1565-1569.

Mortimer, R. G. and Filkins, L. D. (1970). Procedures for identifying problem drinkers (PIPD): A screening and assessment package for courts and treatment agencies: A Self-Instructional Guide. Department of Transportation, National Highway Traffic Safety Administration, (DOT HS 806-988).

Mortimer, R. G. and Filkins, L. D. (1986). Procedures for identifying problem drinkers: A screening and assessment package for courts and treatment agencies. National Highway Traffic Safety Administration, (DOT HS 806-999).

Mortimer, R. G., Filkins, L. D., and Lower, J. S. (1971). *Court procedures for identifying problem drinkers: Final report.* DOT Contract FH-11-7615. Ann Arbor, MI: Highway Safety Research Institute, University of Michigan.

Myerholtz, L. E. and Rosenberg, H. (1997). Screening DUI offenders for alcohol problems: Psychometric assessment of the Substance Abuse Subtle Screening Inventory. *Psychology of Addictive Behaviors 11:* 155-165.

Nochajski, T. H. and Miller, B. A. (1995). *Training Manual for the Research Institute on Addictions Self-Inventory (RIASI).* Buffalo, NY: Research Institute on Addictions.

Nochajski, T. H., Miller, B. A., Augustino, D. K., and Kramer, R. J. (1995). Use of non-obvious indicators for screening of DWI offenders. *Alcohol, Drugs and Traffic Safety,* Proceedings of the 13th International Conference on Alcohol Drugs and Traffic Safety, August, Adelaide, Australia.

Nochajski, T. H., Miller, B. A., and Parks, K. A. (1994). Effectiveness of the RIASI for screening of convicted DWI offenders. Paper presented at the Annual Meeting of the Research Society on Alcoholism, June, Maui, Hawaii.

Nochajski, T. H., Miller, B. A., and Wieczorek, W. F. (1992). Non-obvious indicators of alcohol/drug problems among DWI offenders. Paper presented at the Research Society on Alcoholism Annual Meeting, June, San Diego, CA.

Nochajski, T. H., Miller, B. A., Wieczorek, W. F., and Parks, K. A. (1993). The utility of non-obvious indicators for screening DWI offenders. Paper presented at the Research Society on Alcoholism Annual Meeting, June, San Antonio, TX.

Nochajski, T. H., Walter, J. M., and Wieczorek, W. F. (1997). Identification of drinker-driver recidivists. Paper presented at the 14th International Conference on Alcohol, Drugs and Traffic Safety, September, Annecy, France.

Otto, R. K., Lang, A. R., Megargee, E. I., and Rosenblatt, A. I. (1988). Ability of alcoholics to escape detection by the MMPI. *Journal of Consulting and Clinical Psychology 56:* 452-457.

Robins, L. N., Helzer, J. E., Ratcliff, K., and Seyfried, W. (1982). Validity of the Diagnostic Interview Schedule, Version II: DSM-III diagnoses. *Psychological Medicine 12:* 855-870.

Rouse, S. V., Butcher, J. N., and Miller, K. B. (1999). Assessment of substance abuse in psychotherapy clients: The effectiveness of the MMPI-2 substance abuse scales. *Psychological Assessment 11:* 101-107.

Selzer, M. L. (1971). The Michigan Alcoholism Screening Test: The quest for a new diagnostic instrument. *American Journal of Psychiatry 127:* 1653-1658.

Selzer, M. L., Vinokur, A., and van Rooijen, L. (1975). A self-administered short Michigan Alcoholism Screening Test (SMAST). *Journal of Studies on Alcohol 36:* 117-126.

Skinner, H. A. (1982). The Drug Abuse Screening Test. *Addictive Behaviors 7:* 363-371.

Sobell, L. C. and Sobell, M. B. (1992). Timeline Follow-Back: A technique for assessing self-reported alcohol consumption. In *Measuring Alcohol Consumption: Psychosocial and Biomedical Methods.* Totowa, NJ: Humana Press.

Sobell, L. C., Toneatto, T., and Sobell, M. B. (1994). Behavioral assessment and treatment planning for alcohol, tobacco, and other drug problems: Current status with an emphasis on clinical applications. *Behavior Therapy 25:* 533-580.

Spitzer, R. L., Williams, J. B. W., Gibbon, M., and First, M. B. (1990). *Structured clinical interview for DSM-III-R.* Washington, DC: American Psychiatric Press.

Staley, D. and El-Geubaly, N. (1990). Psychometric properties of the Drug Abuse Screenng Test in a psychiatric patient population. *Addictive Behaviors 15:* 257-264.

Sutker, P. B., Brantley, P. J., and Allain, A. N. (1980). MMPI response patterns and alcohol consumption in DWI offenders. *Journal of Consulting and Clinical Psychology 48:* 350-355.

Tarter, R. E. and Hegedus, A. M. (1991). The Drug Use Screening Inventory. *Alcohol Health and Research World 15:* 65-75.

Vingilis, E. (1983). Drinking drivers and alcoholics: Are they from the same population? In R. G. Smart, F. B. Glaser, Y. Israel, H. Kalant, R. E. Popham, and W. Schmidt (Eds.), *Research Advances in Alcohol and Drug Problems*, Volume 7, (pp. 299-342), New York: Plenum Press.

Walters, G. D., Greene, R. L., and Jeffrey, T. B. (1984). Discriminating between alcoholic and nonalcoholic blacks and whites on the MMPI. *Journal of Personality Assessment 51:* 140-150.

Walters, G. D., Greene, R. L., Jeffrey, T. B., Kruzich, D. J., and Haskin, J. J. (1983). Racial variations on the MacAndrew Alcoholism scale of the MMPI. *Journal of Consulting and Clinical Psychology 51:* 947-948.

Wanberg, K. W. and Horn, J. L. (1983). Assessment of alcohol use with multidimensional concepts and measures. *American Psychologist 38:* 1055-1069.

Wanberg, K. W. and Horn, J. L. (1987). The assessment of multiple conditions in persons with alcohol problems. In W. M. Cox (Ed.), *Treatment and prevention of alcohol problems: A resource manual* (pp. 27-55). Orlando, FL: Academic Press.

Wanberg, K. W., Horn, J. L., and Foster, F. M. (1990). *Alcohol Use Inventory: Interpretive Report User's Guide.* Minneapolis, MN: National Computer Service.

Wendling, A. and Kolody, B. (1992). An evaluation of the Mortimer-Filkins Test as a predictor of alcohol-impaired driver recidivism. *Journal of Studies on Alcohol 43:* 751-766.

Wieczorek, W. F., Miller, B. A., and Nochajski, T. H. (1992). The limited utility of BAC for identifying alcohol-related problems among DWI offenders. *Journal of Studies on Alcohol 53:* 415-419.

Wisniewski, N. M., Glenwick, D. S., and Graham, J. R. (1985). MacAndrew scale and sociodemographic correlates of adolescent alcohol and drug use. *Addictive Behaviors 10:* 55-67.

Wolfson, K. P. and Erbaugh, S. E. (1984). Adolescent responses to the MacAndrew Alcoholism scale. *Journal of Consulting and Clinical Psychology 52:* 625-630.

Chapter 6

American Psychiatric Association (APA) (1994). *Diagnostic and statistical manual of mental disorders* (Fourth edition). Washington, DC: Author.

American Society of Addiction Medicine (ASAM) (1998). Patient placement criteria for the treatment of substance-related disorders (Second edition). Mee-Lee, D., Miller, M., Gartner, L., Shulman, G., and Wilford, B. B. (Eds.). Annapolis Junction, MD: ASAM.

Beals, G. (1999). Rudy takes the keys. *Newsweek,* March 8, *133* (10): 28.

Bureau of Driver Education and DUI Programs, Florida Department of Highway Safety and Motor Vehicles. (1999). National Compendium - Southeastern DUI Offender Systems Conference Private Questionnaire.

Century Council, The (1997). National hardcore drunk driver project. <http://www.dwidata.org>

Coben, J. H. and Larkin, G. L. (1999). Effectiveness of ignition interlock devices in reducing drunk driving recidivism. *American Journal of Preventive Medicine 16:* 81-87.

Courtright, K. E., Berg, B. L., and Mutchnick, R. J. (1997). The cost effectiveness of using house arrest with electronic monitoring for drunk drivers. *Federal Probation 61:* 19-22.

DeYoung, D. J. (1997). An evaluation of the effectiveness of alcohol treatment, driver license actions and jail terms in reducing drunk driving recidivism in California. *Addiction 92:* 989-997.

Highlights of the proceedings of the Surgeon General's workshop on drunk driving (1990). *Alcohol Health and Research World 14*(1): 5-11.

Hingson, R., Heeren, T., and Winter, M. (1998). Effects of Maine's 0.05% legal blood alcohol level for drivers with DWI convictions. *Public Health Reports 113*(5): 440-446.

Incentive grants encourage states to enact 0.08 BAC laws (1998). *Nation's Health,* October 28(9): 4.

Liddle, A. (1999). 23 states consider tighter DWI limits. *Nation's Restaurant News,* March 22, 33(12): 4-5.

National Commission Against Drunk Driving (1999). What the research says about treatment effectiveness and ways to apply this research. <http://www.ncadd.com/tsra/abstracts/treatment.html>.

NHTSA (1998). Highway office identifies loopholes in DWI enforcement. *Alcoholism and Drug Abuse Weekly,* April 13, 10(15): 7.

Nichols, J. L. (1990). Treatment versus deterrence. *Alcohol Health and Research World 14*(1): 44-50.

Senate passes 0.08 plan, but House bottles it up. (1998). *Alcoholism Report 26*(4): 1.

Voas, R. B. and Tippetts, A. S. (1994). *Assessment of Impoundment and Forfeiture Laws for Drivers Convicted of DWI, Phase II Report: Evaluation of Oregon and Washington Vehicle Plate Zebra Sticker Laws.* Washington, DC: National Highway Traffic Safety Administration.

Chapter 7

Cavaiola, A. A. and DeSordi, E. (1999). Locus of control in a group of DWI offenders versus non-offenders. Paper presented at the Seventy-fourth Annual Meeting of the Eastern Psychological Association, April, Providence, RI.

Cavaiola, A., Wolf, J., and Lavender, N. (1999). Comparison of DWI offenders with a non-DWI comparison group on the MMPI-2 and Michigan Alcoholism Screening Test. Paper presented at the 34th Annual Symposium on Recent Development in the Use of the MMPI-2 and MMPI-A, April 18, 1999, Huntington Beach, CA.

Davidson, P. O. (1976). Therapeutic compliance. Paper presented at the Canadian Psychological Association, Toronto, Canada.

Donovan, D. M. (1980). Drinking behavior, personality factors, and high risk during, PhD Dissertation, University of Washington.

Forest, G. G. (1982). *Confrontation in psychotherapy with the alcoholic.* Holmes Beach, FL: Learning Publications, Inc.

Garrett, J. A. (1980). Adjustment demand: Resistance to alcoholism treatment with a DWI population. In L. Godberg (Ed.), *Alcohol, Drugs and Traffic Safety.* Stockholm, Sweden: Almquist and Wiskell International.

Gilliland, B. E. and James, R. K. (1997). *Crisis intervention strategies,* Third edition, Pacific Grove, CA: Brooks/Cole Printing.

Hathaway, S. R. and McKinley, J. C. (1989). *Minnesota Multiphasic Personality Inventory-2 (MMPI-2).* Minneapolis, MN: National Computer Systems, Inc.

Lazarus, A. A. and Fay, A. (1982). Resistance or rationalization? A cognitive-behavioral perspective. In P. L. Wachtel (Ed.), *Resistance: Psychodynamic and Behavioral Approaches* (pp. 115-132). New York: Plenum.

MacAndrews, C. (1965). The differentiation of male alcoholic outpatients from nonalcoholic psychiatric outpatients by means of the MMPI. *Quarterly Journal of Studies on Alcohol 26:* 238-246.

Marlatt, G. A. and Gordon, J. R. (1985). *Relapse prevention: Maintenance strategies in the treatment of addictive behaviors.* New York: Guilford Press.

Miller, G. A. (1994). *The Substance Abuse Subtle Screening Inventory Manual.* Bloomington, IN: The SASSI Institute.

Miller, W. R. and Rollnick, S. (1991). *Motivational interviewing: Preparing people to change addictive behaviors.* New York: Guilford Press.

Mortimer, R. G., Filkins, L. D., and Lower, J. S. (1971). *Court procedures for identifying problem drinkers: Final Report.* DOT Contract FH-11-7615. Ann Arbor, MI: Highway Safety Research Institute, University of Michigan.

Nichols, J. L. (1990). Treatment versus deterrence. *Alcohol Health and Research World 14:* 44-51.

Prochaska, J. O. and DiClemente, C. C. (1982). Transtheoretical therapy: Toward a more integrative model of change. *Psychotherapy: Theory, Research, and Practice 19:* 276-288.

Rollnick, S., Heather, N., Gold, R., and Hall, W. (1992). Development of a short "readiness to change" questionnaire for use in brief, opportunistic interventions among excessive drinkers. *British Journal of Addictions 87:* 743-754.

Selzer, M. L. (1971). The Michigan Alcohol Screening Test: The quest for a new diagnostic instrument. *American Journal of Psychiatry 127:* 1653-1658.

Small, J. (1981). Becoming naturally therapeutic. Austin, TX: Eupsychian Press.

Turkat, T. D. and Meyer, V. (1982). The behavioral-analytic approach. In P. L. Wachtel (Ed.), *Resistance: Psychodynamic and Behavioral Approaches* (pp. 251-259). New York: Plenum.

Wachtel, P. L. (1982). *Resistance: Psychodynamic and Behavioral Approaches.* New York: Plenum.

Wells-Parker, E., Kenne, D. R., Spratke, K. L., and Williams, M. T. (2000). Self-efficacy and motivation for controlling drinking and drinking/driving: An investigation of changes across a driving under the influence (DUI) intervention program and of recidivism prediction. *Addictive Behaviors 25:* 229-238.

Whitehead, P. C. (1975). DWI programs: Doing what's in or dodging what's indicated. *Journal of Safety Research 7:* 127-133.

Wieczorek, W. F. (1993). The role of treatment in reducing alcohol-related accidents involving DWI offenders. Unpublished manuscript, Research Institute on Addictions, Buffalo, NY.

Yoder, R. D. and Moore, R. A. (1973). Characteristics of convicted drunken drivers. *Quarterly Journal of Studies on Alcohol 34:* 927-936.

Zelhart, P. F. and Schurr, B. C. (1977). People who drive while impaired: Issues in treating the drinking driver. In N. J. Estes and M. E. Heinemann (Eds.), *Alcoholism: Development, consequences and interventions* (pp. 204-216). St. Louis, MO: Mosby Publishers.

Chapter 8

Angeriou, M. and Manohar, V. (1977). Treating the problem drinking driver: Some notes on the time required to achieve impact. *British Journal of Addiction 72:* 331-338.

Annis, H.M. (1982). Treatment in corrections: Hoax or salvation. *Canadian Psychology 22*(4): 321-326.

Annis, H. M. and Chan, D. (1983). The differential treatment model: Empirical evidence from a personality typology of adult offenders. *Criminal Justice and Behavior 10*(2): 159-173.

Beerman, K. A., Smith, M. M., and Hall, R. L. (1988). Predictors of recidivism in DUIs. *Journal of Studies on Alcohol 49:* 443-449.

Bloomberg, R. O., Preusser, D. F., and Ulmer, R. O. (1987). Deterrent effects of mandatory license suspension for DWI convictions. DOT HS 807 138. Washington, DC: National Highway Traffic Safety Administration.

Brown, R. A. (1980a). Conventional education and controlled drinking education courses with convicted drunken drivers. *Behavior Therapy 11*(5): 62-642.

Brown, R. A. (1980b). Knowledge about responsible drinking in drinking drivers and social drinkers. *International Journal of Addiction 15:* 1213-1218.

Cavaiola, A. A. (1986). Resistance issues in the treatment of DWI offenders. *Alcoholism Treatment Quarterly 1:* 87-100.

Christmas, J. J. (1978). Alcoholism services for minorities: Training issues and concerns. *Alcohol Health and Research World 2*(3): 20-27.

Donovan, D. M. and Marlatt, G. A. (1983). Personality subtypes among driving while intoxicated offenders: Relationship to drinking behavior and driving risk. *Journal of Consulting and Clinical Psychology 50*(2): 241-249.

Donovan, D. M. and Rosengren, D. (1992). Effectiveness of alcohol treatment and treatment matching: How DUI treatment may be improved by insights from the alcoholism treatment field. In *Drinking and Driving Prevention Symposium* (pp. 129-145). Ontario, CA: Automobile Club of Southern California.

Federal Bureau of Investigation (1988). *Crime in the United States: Uniform Crime Reports.* Washington, DC: U.S. Department of Justice.

Fillmore, K. M. and Kelso, D. (1987). Coercion into alcoholism treatment: Meanings for the disease concept of alcoholism. *Journal of Drug Issues 17*(3): 301-319.

Fitzpatrick, J. L. (1992). Problems in the evaluation of treatment programs for drunk drivers: Goals and objectives. *Journal of Drug Issues 22*(1): 155-167.

Frawley, P. J. (1988). Defining desirable treatment outcomes. *Alcohol Health and Research World 12:* 210-213.

Garrett, J. A. (1980). Adjustment demand: Resistance to alcoholism treatment with a DWI population. In Goldberg, L. (Ed.), *Alcohol, drugs and traffic safety.* Stockholm: Almquist and Wiskell International.

Gurnak, A. M. (1989). Rehabilitation outcomes for alcohol impaired drivers referred for assessment in two Wisconsin counties. *Journal of Alcohol and Drug Education 35:* 45-59.

Hagen, R. E. (1977). Effectiveness of license suspension or revocation for drivers convicted of multiple driving-under-the-influence offenses (Report No. 59). Sacramento, CA: Department of Motor Vehicles.

Hoffman, N. G., Ninonuevo, F., Mozey, J., and Luxenberg, M.G. (1987). Comparison of court-referred DWI arrestees with other outpatients in substance abuse treatment. *Journal of Studies on Alcohol 48:* 591-594.

Holden, R. T. (1983). Rehabilitative sanctions for drunk driving: An experimental evaluation. *Journal of Research in Crime and Delinquency 20:* 55-72.

Klein, T. (1989). Changes in alcohol-involved fatal crashes associated with tougher state alcohol legislation. (Contract No. DTNH 22 88 C 07045.) Washington, DC: National Highway Traffic Safety Administration.

Lewis, R. R. (1985). Estimates of DWI recidivism in Minnesota fatal crashes. Unublished report, Minnesota Criminal Justice System Task Force, St. Paul, MN.

Lipsey, M. W. (1992). Juvenile delinquency treatment. A meta-analytic inquiry to variability of effects. In T. D. Cook (Ed.), *Meta Analysis for Explanation* (pp. 83-128). Beverley Hills, CA: Sage Publications.

Litt, M. D., Del Boca, F., Cooney, N. L., Kadden, R. M., and Babor, T. (1989). Matching alcoholics to aftercare treatment by empirical clustering: Predicting relapse. *Alcohol Clinical Experimentation 13:* 350.

Longabaugh, R. and Lewis, D. C. (1988). Key issues in treatment outcome studies. *Alcohol Health and Research World 12*(3): 168-175.

Mann, R .E., (1992). Effectiveness of DUI treatment and the importance of screening and matching clients to appropriate treatment. In *Drinking and Driving Prevention Symposium* (pp. 129-145). Ontario, CA: Automobile Club of Southern California.

Mann, R. E., Anglin, L., Wilkins, K., Viniglis E. R., MacDonald, S., and Sheu, W. (1994). Rehabilitation for convicted drinking drivers (second offenders): Effects on mortality. *Journal of Studies on Alcohol 55:* 372-374.

Mann, R. E., Leigh, G. Vingilis, E. R., and deGenova, K. (1983). A critical review on the effectiveness of drinking-driving rehabilitation programs. *Accident Analysis and Prevention 15:* 441-461.

McCarty, D. and Argeriou, M. (1986). Rearrest following residential treatment for repeat offender drunken drivers. *Journal of Studies on Alcohol 49*(1): 1-4.

McGuire, F. L. (1980). "Heavy" and "light" drinking drivers as separate target groups for treatment. *American Journal of Drug and Alcohol Abuse 7:* 101-107.

McGuire, F. L. (1982). Treatment of the drinking driver, *Health Psychology 1:* 137-152.

Miller, B. A. and Hester, R. K. (1986). Treating alcohol problems: Toward an informed eclecticism. In R. K. and W. R. Miller (Eds.), *Handbook of Alcoholism Treatment Approaches* (pp. 3-13). New York: Pergamon.

Miller, W. R. (1989). Matching individuals with interventions. In R. K. Hester and W. R. Miller (Eds.), *Handbook of Alcoholism Treatment Approaches* (pp. 261-277). New York: Pergamon.

Nichols, J. L. (1979). The effectiveness of ASAP education and rehabilitation programs. In I. R. Johnson (Ed.), *Proceedings: Seventh International Conference on Alcohol, Drugs and Traffic Safety.* Canberra, Australia: Australian Government Publishing Service.

Nichols, J. L. (1990). Treatment versus deterrence. *Alcohol Health and Research World 14*(1): 48-51.

Nichols, J. L. and Dickman, F. B. (1989). Effectiveness of roadside sobriety checkpoint operations. Unpublished paper. National Highway Traffic Safety Administration, Washington, DC.

Nichols, J. L., Ellingstad, V. S., and Struckman-Johnson, D. L. (1979). An experimental evaluation of the effectiveness of short-term education and rehabilitation programs for convicted drinking drivers. In M. Gallanter (Ed.), *Currents in Alcoholism: Treatment and Rehabilitation and Epidemiology* (pp. 157-177). New York: Grune and Stratton.

Nichols, J. L. and Ross, H. L. (1989). The effectiveness of legal sanctions in dealing with drinking drivers. In *Surgeon General's workshop on drunk driving: Background papers* (pp. 93-112). Rockville, MD: Office of the Surgeon General, U.S. Department of Health and Human Services.

Nichols, J. L., Weinstein, E. B., Ellingstad, V. S., and Reis, R. E. (1981). The effectiveness of education and treatment programs for drinking drivers: A decade of evaluation. In L. Goldberg (Ed.), *Alcohol, Drugs and Traffic Safety, Vol. III* (pp. 1298-1328). Stockholm: Almqvist and Witsell International.

Nochajski, T. H., Miller, B. A., Wieczorek, W. F., and Whitney, R. (1993). The effects of a drinker-driver treatment program: Does criminal history make a difference? *Criminal Justice and Behavior 20:* 174-189.

Nunnally, J. C. and Durham, R. L. (1975). Validity, reliability, and special problems of measurement in evaluation research. In E. L. Struening and M. Guttentag (Eds.), *Handbook of Evaluation Research* (pp. 289-352). Beverly Hills, CA: Sage Publications.

Orford, J., Oppenheimer, E., and Edwards, G. (1976). Abstinence or control: The outcome for excessive drinkers two years after consultation. *Behaviour Research and Therapy 14:* 409-418.

Packard, M. A. (1987). DUI/DWAI offenders compared to clients seen in an outpatient alcohol-treatment facility. *Journal of Alcohol and Drug Education 32*(2): 1-6.

Panepinto, W. C., Garrett, J. A., Williford, W. R., and Prince, J. A. (1982). Short term group treatment model for problem-drinking drivers. *Social Work with Groups 5*(1): 33-40.

Panepinto, W. and Higgins, M. (1969). Keeping alcoholics in treatment. *Quarterly Journal of Alcohol Studies 38*(2): 414-419.

Peck, R. C., Sadler, D. D., and Perrine, M. W. (1985). The comparative effectiveness of alcohol rehabilitation and licensing control actions for drunk driving offenders: A review of the literature. *Alcohol, Drugs and Driving: Abstracts and Reviews 1:* 15-39.

Popkin, C. L., Li, L. K., Lacey, J. H., Stewart, J. R., and Waller, P. F., (1983). *An initial evaluation of the North Carolina Alcohol and Drug Education Traffic Schools* (Volume I). Chapel Hill, NC: Highway Safety Research Center, University of North Carolina.

Reis, R. E. (1983). The traffic safety impact of DWI education and counseling programs. In *DWI reeducation and rehabilitation programs* (pp. 38-61). Falls Church, VA: AAA Foundation for Traffic Safety.

Ross, H. L. (1984). *Deterring the drinking driver.* Lexington, MA: Lexington Books.

Rossi, P. H. (1978). Issues in the evaluation of human services delivery. *Evaluation Quarterly 2:* 573-599.

Sadler, D. D. and Perrine, M. W. (1984). An evaluation of the California Drunk Driving Countermeasures system: Volume II. The long-term traffic safety impact of a pilot alcohol abuse treatment as an alternative to license suspensions. Report No. 90. Sacramento, CA: Department of Motor Vehicles.

Scoles, P. and Fine, E. W. (1977). Short-term effects of an educational program for drinking drivers. *Journal of Studies on Alcohol 38:* 633-637.

Selzer, M. L., Vinokur, A., and Wilson, T. D. (1977). A psychosocial comparison of drunken drivers and alcoholics. *Journal of Studies on Alcohol 38:* 1294-1312.

Simpson, H. M. (1986). Epidemiology of road accidents involving marijuana. *Alcohol, Drugs and Driving 2:* 15-30.

Simpson, H. M. (1995). Who is the persistent drinking driver? Part II: Canada and elsewhere. In *Strategies for dealing with the persistent drinking driver, Transportation Research Circular, 437,* February: 21-25.

Simpson, H. M. and Mayhew, D. R. (1991). _The hard core drinking driver._ Ottawa, Canada: Traffic Injury Research Foundation of Canada.

Smiley, A., Ziedman, K., and Moskowits, H. (1981). _Pharmacokinetics of drug effects on driving performance: Driving simulator tests of marijuana alone and in combination with alcohol_ (Contract 271-76-3316). Washington, DC: National Institute of Drug Abuse and National Highway Traffic Safety Administration.

Smith, M. M. and Hall, R. L. (1988). Predictors of recidivism in DUIs. _Journal of Studies on Alcohol 49:_ 443-449.

Steer, R. A., Fine, E. W., and Scoles, P. E. (1979). Classification of men arrested for driving while intoxicated and treatment implications: A cluster-analytic study. _Journal of Studies on Alcohol 40:_ 222-229.

Stewart, K. and Ellingstad, V. S. (1989). Rehabilitation countermeasures for drinking drivers. In _Surgeon General's Workshop on Drunk Driving_ (pp. 234-246). Rockville, MD: U.S. Department of Health and Human Services.

Tashima, H. and Peck, R. C. (1986). _An Evaluation of the California Drunk Driving Countermeasures System. Volume III._ An Evaluation of the Specific Deterrent Effects of Alternative Sanctions for First and Repeat DUI offenders. Sacramento, CA: Department of Motor Vehicles.

Vingilis, E. (1983). Drinking drivers and alcoholics: Are they from the same population? In R. J. Wilson and R. E. Mann (Eds.), _Drinking and driving: Advances in research and prevention_ (pp. 68-95). New York: Guilford Press.

Vingilis, E., Adlaf, E., and Chung, L. (1981). The Oshawa impaired drivers programme: An evaluation of a rehabilitation programme. _Canadian Journal of Criminology 23:_ 93-102.

Voas, R. B. (1986). Evaluation of jail as a penalty for drunk driving. _Alcohol, Drugs and Driving: Abstracts and Reviews 2:_ 47-70.

Voas, R. B. and Lacey, J. H. (1989). Issues in the enforcement of impaired driving laws in the United States. In _Surgeon General's workshop on drunk driving: Background papers_ (pp. 136-156). Rockville, MD: Office of the Surgeon General, U.S. Department of Health and Human Services.

Voas, R. B. and Tippett, A. S., (1990). Evaluation of treatment and monitoring programs for drunken drivers. _Journal of Traffic Medicine 1:_ 15-26.

Walsh, D. C., Hingson, R. W., Merrigan, D. M., Levenson, S. M., Cupples, L. A., Heeren, T., Coffman, G. A., Becker, C. A., Barker, T. A., Hamilton, S. K., McGuire, T.G., and Kelly, C. A. (1991). A randomized trial of treatment options for alcohol-abusing workers. _New England Journal of Medicine 325_(11): 775-782.

Weisner, C. M. (1990). Coercion in alcohol treatment. In Institute of Medicine, (Eds.). _Broadening the base of treatment for alcohol problems_ (pp. 589-609). Washington, DC: National Academy Press.

Wells-Parker, E. (1994). Mandated treatment: Lessons from research with drinking and driving offenders. _Alcohol Health and Research World 18:_ 302-306.

Wells-Parker, E., Anderson, B. J., McMillen, D. L., and Landrum, J. W. (1989). Interactions among DUI offender characteristics and traditional intervention modalities: A long-term recidivism follow-up. _British Journal of Addiction 84:_ 381-390.

Wells-Parker, E. N., Bangert-Drowns, R., Allegrezza, J., McMillen, R., and Williams, M. (1995). Final results from a meta-analysis of remedial interventions with DUI offenders. _Addictions 9:_ 907-926.

Wells-Parker, E. N. and Cosby, P. J. (1988). Behavioral and employment consequences of driver's license suspension for drinking driving offenders. *Journal of Safety Research 19:* 5-20.

Wells-Parker, E. N., Cosby, P. J., and Landrum, J. W. (1986). A typology for drinking driving offenders: Methods of classification and policy implications. *Accident Analysis and Prevention 18:* 443-453.

Wells-Parker, E. N., Landrum, J. L., and Topping, J. (1990). Other preventive approaches: Matching the DUI offender to an effective intervention strategy. In J. Wilson and R. Mann (Eds.), *Drinking and Driving: Advances in Research and Prevention* (pp. 267-289). New York: Guilford Press.

Wieczorek, W. F. (1993). The role of treatment in reducing alcohol-related accidents involving DWI offenders. In R. R. Watson (Ed.), *Alcohol, cocaine, and accidents* (Drug and Alcohol Abuse Reviews, pp. 105-130). Totowa, NJ: Humana Press.

Wieczorek, W. F., Miller, B. A., and Nochajski, T. H. (1990). Alcohol diagnoses among DWI offenders. *Problem-Drinker Driver Project Research Note 90:* 6.

Wuth, C.H. (1987). Profile differences between DWI clients and alcoholics: Implications for treatment. *Alcoholism Treatment Quarterly 4*(3):117-121.

Chapter 9

American Psychiatric Association (1994). *Diagnostic and statistical manual of mental disorders,* Fourth edition. Washington, DC: American Psychiatric Press.

Appleton, G. M., Barkley, K. G., and Katz, J. (1986). *Creative interventions for DWI offenders.* Binghamton, NY: The Haworth Press, Inc.

Argeriou, M. and Manohar, V. (1977). Treating the problem drinking driver: Some notes on the time required to achieve impact. *British Journal of Addiction 72:* 331-338.

Argeriou, M., McCarty, D., and Blacker, E. (1985). Criminality among individuals arraigned for drinking and driving in Massachusetts. *Journal of Studies on Alcohol 46:* 525-530.

Cavaiola, A. (1984). Resistance issues in the treatment of the DWI offender. *Alcoholism Treatment Quarterly 1:* 1-6.

Cavaiola, A. A. and Wuth, C.H. (1987). Treating the family of the DWI offender. *Alcoholism Treatment Quarterly 4:* 91-103.

Century Council, The (1997). National hardcore drunk driver project. <http://www.dwidata.org>.

Donovan, D. M. and Marlatt, G. A. (1983). Personality subtypes among driving while intoxicated offenders: Relationship to drinking behavior and driving risk. *Journal of Consulting and Clinical Psychology 50*(2): 241-249.

Donovan, D. M., Marlatt, G. A., and Salzberg, P. M. (1983). Drinking behavior, personality factors and high-risk driving: A review and theoretical formulation. *Journal of Studies on Alcohol 44*(3): 395-428.

Dunbar, J. A., Penttila, A., and Pikkarainen, J. (1987). Drinking and driving: Success of random breath testing in Finland. *British Medical Journal 295:* 101-103.

Fagan, R. W. and Fagan, N. M. (1982). The impact of legal coercion on the treatment of alcoholism. *Journal of Drug Issues, Inc.* Winter: 103-114.

Fell, J. C. (1990). Drinking and driving in America: Disturbing facts—encouraging reductions. *Alcohol Health and Research World 14*(1): 18-25.

Fitzpatrick, J. L. (1988). Alcohol education programs for drunk drivers: An evaluation of programs for problem drinkers in Colorado's Fourth Judicial District. Community Development Monograph series No. 25, Colorado Springs, Colorado Center for Community Development & Design.

Fitzpatrick, J. L. (1992). Problems in the evaluation of treatment programs for drunk drivers: Goals and outcomes. *Journal of Drug Issues 22*(1): 155-167.

Foon, A. (1986). An evaluation of an educational programme for multiple drink-driver offenders. *Australian Drug and Alcohol Review 5:* 139-143.

Foon, A. (1988). The effectiveness of drinking-driving treatment programs: A critical review. *The International Journal of the Addictions 23*(2): 151-174.

Garrett, J. A. (1980). Adjustment demand: Resistance to alcoholism treatment with a DWI population. In L. Goldberg (Ed.), *Alcohol, Drugs and Traffic Safety.* Stockholm: Almquist and Wiskell International.

Holden, R. T. (1983). Rehabilitative sanctions for drunk driving: An experimental evaluation. *Journal of Research in Crime and Delinquency 10:* 55-72.

Hollister, R. G., Kemper, P., and Wooldridge, J. (1979). Lining process and impact analysis. The case of supported work. In T. D. Cook and C. S. Reichardt (Eds.), *Qualitative and Quantitative Methods in Evaluation Research* (pp. 140-158). Beverly Hills, CA: Sage Publications.

Hubbard, R. L., Valley, J., Rachel, S. G., Craddock, J., and Cavanaugh, E. R. (1984). Treatment outcome prospective study (TOPS): Client characteristics and behaviors before, during and after treatment. In F. M. Tims and J. P. Lundford (Eds.), *Drug abuse treatment evaluation: Strategies, progress, and prospects.* NIDA Research Monograph No. 51: 42-68. Rockville, MD.

Jones, R. K. and Lacey, J. H. (1998). *Evaluation of an individualized sanctioning program for DWI offenders. Final report.* Washington, DC: National Highway Traffic Safety Administration.

Jones, R. K., Wiliszowski, C. H., and Lacey, J. H. (1998). *Problems and solutions in DWI enforcement systems.* (Report No. DOT HS 808 666). Washington, DC: National Highway Traffic Safety Administration.

Lipsey, M. W. (1992). Juvenile delinquency treatment: A meta-analytic inquiry to variability of effects. In T. D. Cook (Ed.), *Meta analysis for explanation* (pp. 83-128). Beverly Hills, CA: Sage Publications.

Longabaugh, R. and Lewis R. C. (1988). Key issues in treatment outcome studies. *Alcohol Health and Research World 12*(3): 168-175.

Mann, R. E., Anglin, L., Wilkins, E. R., Vingilis, S., MacDonald, J., and Sheu, W. J., (1994). Rehabilitation for convicted drinking drivers (second offenders): Effects on mortality. *Journal of Studies on Alcohol 55:* 372-374.

Mann, R. E., Leigh, G., Vingilis, E. R., and Degenova, K. (1983). A critical review of the effectiveness of drinking-driving rehabilitation programmes. *Accident Analysis and Prevention 15*(6): 441-461.

McCarty, D. and Angeriou, M. (1988). Rearrest following residential treatment for repeat offender drunk drivers. *Journal of Studies on Alcoholism 49:* 1-6.

McCarty D. and Angeriou, M. (1988). Rearrest following residential treatment for repeat offender drunken drivers. *Journal of Studies on Alcohol 49:* 1-6.

McGuire, F. L. (1982). Treatment of the drinking driver. *Health Psychology 1:* 137-152.

McGuire, T. G., and Kelly, C. A. (1991). A randomized trial of treatment options for alcohol-abusing workers. *New England Journal of Medicine 325*(11): 775-782.

McLellan, A. T., Lubrosky, C. P., O'Brien, G. E., and Druley, K. A. (1982). Is treatment for substance abuse effective? *Journal of the American Behavioral Scientist 33:* 432-442.

Miller, B. A., Whitney, R., and Washousky, R. (1984). The decision to recommend alcoholism treatment for DWI offenders. *American Journal of Drug and Alcohol Abuse 10*(3): 447-459.

Miller, B. A. and Windle, M. (1990). Alcoholism, problem drinking, and driving while impaired. In R. J. Wilson and R. E. Mann (Eds.), *Drinking and driving: Advances in research and prevention* (pp. 68-95). New York: The Guilford Press.

Miller, W. R. and Hester, R. K. (1986). *Matching problem drinkers with optimal treatments.* In W. R. Miller and N. Heather (Eds.), *Treating addictive disorders: Processes of change* (pp.175-203). New York: Plenum Press.

Moore, D. (1989). Factors influencing treatment compliance following drunk driver intervention. Proceedings of the 11th International Conference on Alcohol, Drugs and Traffic Safety. Chicago, IL: National Safety Council.

National Commission Against Drunk Driving (1996). Chronic drunk drivers: Resources available to keep them off the road. Washington, DC: 1-37.

Nickel, W. R. (1990). Programs for the rehabilitation and treatment of drinking-driving multiple offenders in the Federal Republic of Germany. Rehabilitation and Treatment of Drinking-Driving Multiple Offenders.

Nochajski, T. H., Miller, B. A., Wieczorek, W. F., and Whitney, R. (1993). The effects of a drinker-driver treatment program: Does criminal history make a difference? *Criminal Justice and Behavior 20*(2): 174-189.

Panepinto, W. C., Garrett, J. A., Williford, W. R., and Priebe, J. A. (1982). A short-term group treatment model for problem-drinker drivers. In M. Altman and R. Crocker (Eds.), *Social Group Work and Alcoholism.* Binghamton, NY: The Haworth Press, Inc.

Panepinto, W. and Higgins, M. (1969). Keeping alcoholics in treatment. *Quarterly Journal of Alcohol Studies 38*(2): 414-419.

Perrine, M. W. (1989). Drinking patterns and problems among drunken drivers. In *High Alcohol Consumers and Traffic* (pp. 250-266). Proceedings of the International Workshop, Nov. 28-30, 1988. Paris: Institut National du Recherche sur les Transports et lent Securite.

Pikkarainen, J. and Penttila, A. (1992). Random breath testing—The Finnish experience. Widmark lecture presented at the 12th Conference on Alcohol. Drugs and Traffic Safety—T'92, Cologne, Germany, September 28-October 2.

Reis, R. E. (1983). *The traffic safety effectiveness of education programs for first offender drunk drivers* (NTIS No. OT-HS-806-558). Washington, DC: National Highway Traffic Safety Administration.

Scoles, P. and Fine, E.W. (1977). Short-term effects of an educational program for drinking drivers. *Journal of Studies on Alcohol 38:* 633-637.

Seabury, B. (1976). The contract: Uses, abuses and limitations. *Social Work 6:* 16-20.

Seigel, H. A. (1985). *Impact of a Driver Intervention Program on DWI Recidivism and Problem Drinking.* Washington, DC: Department of Transportation.

Simon, S. M. (1992). Incapacitation alternatives for repeat DWI offenders. *Alcohol, Drugs and Driving 8*(1): 51-60.

Simpson, H. M. and Mayhew, D. R. (1991). *The hard core drinking driver.* Ottawa, Ontario: The Traffic Injury Research Foundation of Canada.

Sobell, L. C. and Sobell, M. B. (1992). Timeline Follow-Back: A technique for assessing self-reported alcohol consumption. In *Measuring Alcohol Consumption: Psychosocial and Biomedical Methods* (pp. 41-72). Totowa, NJ: Humana Press.

Steer, R. A., Fine, E. W., and Scoles, P. E. (1979). Classification of men arrested for driving while intoxicated and treatment implications: A cluster-analytic study. *Journal of Studies on Alcohol 40:* 222-229.

Voas, R. B. (1996). *Chronic drunk drivers: Resources available to keep them off the road.* Conference Report. Washington, DC: NCADD.

Voas, R. B. and Tippett, A. S. (1990). Evaluation of treatment and monitoring programs for drunken drivers. *Journal of Traffic Medicine 1:* 15-26.

Walsh, D. C., Hingson, R. W., Merrigan, D. M., Levenson, S. M., Cupples, L. A., Heeren, T., Coffman, G. A., Becker, C. A., Barker, T. A., Hamilton, S. K., and Washousky, R. (1986). An alcoholic outpatient treatment program for alcoholics convicted of DWI. In D. Foley (Ed.), *Stop DWI* (pp. 77-83). Lexington, MA: DC Heath and Company.

Wechsler, H. (1999). Getting serious about eradicating binge drinking. *Chronicle of Higher Education,* November 20: B4-5.

Wells-Parker, E. (1994) Mandated treatment: Lessons from research with drinking driving offenders. *Alcohol Health and Research World, 18:* 302-306.

Wells-Parker, E., Anderson, B., McMillen, D., and Landrum, J. (1989). Interactions among DUI offenders, characteristics, and traditional intervention modalities: A long-term recidivism follow-up. *British Journal of Addiction 84:* 381-390.

Wells-Parker, E., Crosby, P. J., and Landrum, J. W. (1986). Typology for drinking driving offenders: Methods for classification and policy implications. *Accident Analysis and Prevention 18*(6): 443-453.

Wells-Parker, E., Landrum, J. W., and Topping J. S. (1990). Matching the DWI offender to an effective intervention strategy: An emerging research agenda. In R. J. Wilson and R. E. Mann (Eds.), *Drinking and Driving: Advances in Research and Prevention* (pp. 267-289). New York: Guilford Press.

Wieczorek, W. F. (1993). *The role of treatment in reducing alcohol-related accidents involving DWI offenders.* Buffalo, NY: Research Institute on Addictions.

Wieczorek, W.F., and Miller, B. A. (1992). Preliminary typology designed for treatment matching of DWI offenders. *Journal of Consulting and Clinical Psychology 60*(5): 757-765.

Wiliszowski, C. H., Murphy, P. V., Jones, R. K., and Lacey J. H. (1996). *Determine reasons for repeat drinking and driving.* (Report No. DOT HS 808 726.) Washington, DC: National Highway Traffic Safety Administration.

Chapter 10

Argeriou, M. and Marchar, V. (1977). Treating the problem drinking driver: Some notes on the time required to achieve impact. *British Journal of Addiction 72:* 331-338.

Bepko, C. and Krestan, J. (1985). *The responsibility trap: A blueprint for treating the alcoholic family.* New York: The Free Press, Macmillan, Inc.

Cavaiola, A. A. (1984). Resistance issues in the treatment of the DWI offender. *Alcoholism Treatment Quarterly 1:* 87-100.

Cavaiola, A. A. and Kane-Cavaiola, C. (1989). Basics of adolescent development for the chemical dependency counselor. In P. Henry (Ed.), *Practical Approaches in Treating Adolescent Chemical Dependency.* Binghamton, NY: The Haworth Press., Inc.

Connors, G. J. and Ersner-Hershfield, S. (1983). Treating drunk-driving recidivists: Short and long-term effects of a behavioral treatment. Paper presented at the Association for the Advancement of Behavior Therapy, June. Washington, DC.

Donovan, D. M. and Marlatt, G. A. (1982). Personality subtypes among driving-while-intoxicated offenders: Relationship to drinking behavior and driving risk. *Journal of Consulting and Clinical Psychology 50:* 241-249.

Festinger, L. (1957). *A theory of cognitive dissonance.* Stanford, CA: Stanford University Press.

Garrett, J. A. (1980). Adjustment demand: Resistance to alcoholism treatment with a DWI population. In L. Goldberg (Ed.), *Alcohol, Drugs and Traffic Safety.* Stockholm, Sweden: Almquist and Wiskell International.

Hyman, M. M. (1968a). Accident vulnerability and blood alcohol concentrations of drivers by demographic characteristics. *Quarterly Journal of Studies on Alcohol Supplement # 4:* 34-57.

Hyman, M. M. (1968b). The social characteristics of persons arrested for driving while intoxicated. *Quarterly Journal of Studies on Alcohol, Supplement #4:* 562-586.

Jackson, J. L. (1954). The adjustment of the family to the crisis of alcoholism. *Quarterly Journal of Studies on Alcohol 15:* 562-586.

Johnson, V. (1985). *I'll quit tomorrow.* Minneapolis, MN: Hazelden Publications Inc.

Larsen, E. (1985). *Stage two recovery: Life beyond addiction.* San Francisco, CA: HarperCollins.

Lennard, H. L. and Berstein, A. (1969). Clinical sociology: A new focus. *Patterns of human interaction* (pp. 22-43). San Francisco, CA: Jossey Bass.

Lidz, T., Cornelison, A., Fleck, S., and Terry, D. (1970). Marital schism and marital skew. In W. Sahakian (Ed.), *Psychopathology today: Experimentation, Theory, and research* (pp. 176-181). Chicago, IL: Peacock Publishers.

Malfetti, J. L. (1975). Re-education and rehabilitation of the drunken driver. *Journal of Drug Issues 11:* 255-269.

McGrath, R. J. (1986). An education program for collaterals of DWI offenders. *Alcoholism Treatment Quarterly 3:* 139-151.

McGrath, R. J. and Pandiani, J. A. (1987). Amount of financial rebate and collateral participation in a DWI school. *Journal of Alcohol and Drug Education 32:* 49-55.

McGuire, F. L. (1980). "Heavy" and "light" drinking drivers as separate target groups for treatment. *American Journal of Drug and Alcohol Abuse 7:* 101-107.

McGuire, F. L. (1982). Treatment of the drinking driver. *Health Psychology 1:* 137-152.

Merrill, D. G. (1983). Education and therapy programs for drunk drivers. They work! *Proceedings of the DWI Colloquium,* August, San Diego, CA.

Moskowitz, H., Walker, J., and Gomberg, C. (1979). *A Comparison of Demographic and Psychosocial Characteristics of DWI Drivers, Control Drivers and Alcoholics.* Los Angeles, CA: UCLA Alcohol Research Center of the Neuropsychiatric Institute.

Nichols, J. L., Ellingstad, U. S., and Struckman-Johnson, J. (1979). Experimental evaluation of the effectiveness of short-term education and rehabilitation programs for convicted drinking drivers. In M. Galanter (Ed.), *Currents in alcoholism*, Volume 6. New York: Grune and Stratton.

Rapaport, L. (1965). The state of crisis: Some theoretical considerations. In H. Parad (Ed.), *Crisis Intervention: Selected Readings* (pp. 22-31). New York: Family Service Association of America.

Reis, R. E. (1982). *The traffic safety effectiveness of educational counseling programs for multiple offenders.* (Contract No. DOT HS-6-01414.) Washington, DC: U.S. Department of Transportation, National Highway Traffic Safety Administration.

Sandler, I., Palmer, S., Holmen, M., and Wynkoop, R. (1975). Drinking characteristics of DWI screened as problem drinkers. *Alcohol Health and Research World* 2(2): 19-23.

Selzer, M. L. (1979). The Michigan Alcoholism Screening Test: Reflections on alcoholism screening tests. Proceedings of the Second National DWI Conference, Rochester, MN.

Selzer, M. L. and Barton, E. (1977). The drunken driver: A psychosocial study. *Drug and Alcohol Dependence 2:* 239-253.

Stanton, M. D. and Todd, T. C. (1982). *The family therapy of drug abuse and addiction.* New York: Guilford Press.

Steiner, J., (1975). *Games alcoholics play.* New York: Bantam Books.

Weeber, S. (1981). DWI repeaters and non-repeaters: A comparison. *Journal of Alcohol and Drug Education 26:* 1-9.

Woititz, J. G. (1983). *Adult children of alcoholics.* Hollywood, FL: Health Communications.

Yoder, R. D. (1975). Prearrest behavior of persons convicted of driving while intoxicated. *Journal of Studies on Alcohol 36:* 1573-1577.

Yoder, R. D. and Moore, R. A. (1973). Characteristics of convicted drunk drivers. *Quarterly Journal of Studies on Alcohol 34:* 927-936.

Chapter 11

Feeney, D. (2000). Personal communication. Monmouth County Intoxicated Driver Resource Center, Monmouth County, NJ.

Foley, D. (1997). Using victim impact panels. *Impaired Driving Update 1:* 17-32.

National Commission on Drunk Driving (1999). What the research says about treatment effectiveness and ways to apply this research. <http://www.ncadd.com/tsra/abstracts/treatment.html>.

National Highway Traffic Safety Administration. (1998). *Alcohol Traffic Safety Facts 1997.* Washington, DC: Author.

National Highway Traffic Safety Administration (1999). Individualized treatment sanctions for DWI offenders reduce recidivism. *Traffic Tech: NHTSA Technology Transfer Series, #193,* February.

Index

Page numbers followed by the letter "f" indicate figures; those followed by the letter "t" indicate tables.

273

Order Your Own Copy of
This Important Book for Your Personal Library!

ASSESSMENT AND TREATMENT OF THE DWI OFFENDER

_____in hardbound at $49.95 (ISBN: 0-7890-0870-X)

_____in softbound at $27.95 (ISBN: 0-7890-1498-X)

COST OF BOOKS_____

OUTSIDE USA/CANADA/
MEXICO: ADD 20%_____

POSTAGE & HANDLING_____
*(US: $4.00 for first book & $1.50
for each additional book)
Outside US: $5.00 for first book
& $2.00 for each additional book)*

SUBTOTAL_____

in Canada: add 7% GST_____

STATE TAX_____
*(NY, OH & MIN residents, please
add appropriate local sales tax)*

FINAL TOTAL_____
*(If paying in Canadian funds,
convert using the current
exchange rate, UNESCO
coupons welcome.)*

❏ **BILL ME LATER:** ($5 service charge will be added)
(Bill-me option is good on US/Canada/Mexico orders only;
not good to jobbers, wholesalers, or subscription agencies.)

❏ Check here if billing address is different from
shipping address and attach purchase order and
billing address information.

Signature_____

❏ **PAYMENT ENCLOSED: $**_____

❏ **PLEASE CHARGE TO MY CREDIT CARD.**

❏ Visa ❏ MasterCard ❏ AmEx ❏ Discover
❏ Diner's Club ❏ Eurocard ❏ JCB

Account # _____

Exp. Date_____

Signature_____

Prices in US dollars and subject to change without notice.

NAME_____

INSTITUTION_____

ADDRESS_____

CITY_____

STATE/ZIP_____

COUNTRY_____ COUNTY (NY residents only)_____

TEL_____ FAX_____

E-MAIL_____

May we use your e-mail address for confirmations and other types of information? ❏ Yes ❏ No
We appreciate receiving your e-mail address and fax number. Haworth would like to e-mail or fax special
discount offers to you, as a preferred customer. **We will never share, rent, or exchange your e-mail address
or fax number.** We regard such actions as an invasion of your privacy.

Order From Your Local Bookstore or Directly From
The Haworth Press, Inc.
10 Alice Street, Binghamton, New York 13904-1580 • USA
TELEPHONE: 1-800-HAWORTH (1-800-429-6784) / Outside US/Canada: (607) 722-5857
FAX: 1-800-895-0582 / Outside US/Canada: (607) 722-6362
E-mail: getinfo@haworthpressinc.com
PLEASE PHOTOCOPY THIS FORM FOR YOUR PERSONAL USE.
www.HaworthPress.com

BOF00